Romantic and Modern: Revaluations of Literary Tradition

GEORGE BORNSTEIN, Editor

Romantic and Modern

Revaluations of Literary Tradition

UNIVERSITY OF PITTSBURGH PRESS

Published by the University of Pittsburgh Press, Pittsburgh, Pa. 15260
Feffer and Simons, Inc., London
Manufactured in the United States of America

Library of Congress Cataloging in Publication Data

Main entry under title:

Romantic and modern.

Includes index.
1. American literature—20th century—History and
criticism—Addresses, essays, lectures. 2. English
literature—20th century—History and criticism—
Addresses, essays, lectures. 3. Romanticism—England—
Addresses, essays, lectures. 4. English literature—
19th century—History and criticism—Addresses, essays,
lectures. I. Bornstein, George.
PS121.R6   809'.91'4   76-6658
ISBN 0-8229-3322-5

Grateful acknowledgment is made to those who granted permission to quote material used in this book:

Excerpts from Benedetto Croce, *The Defence of Poetry*, trans. E. F. Carritt (1933); reprinted by permission of the Oxford University Press.

Lines from David Davie, *Collected Poems 1950–1970*; reprinted by permission of the Oxford University Press.

Material from Robert Duncan, *Bending the Bow* (copyright © 1965, 1968 by Robert Duncan). "The Fire, *Passages* 13" was first published in *Poetry*. Reprinted by permission of New Directions Publishing Corporation and of Jonathan Cape Ltd.

Lines from T. S. Eliot, *Poems Written in Early Youth* (copyright 1967); reprinted by permission of Farrar, Straus & Giroux, Inc. Lines from T. S. Eliot, "Sweeney Erect," *Collected Poems, 1909–1962*, and from "Little Gidding," *Four Quartets*; reprinted by permission of Harcourt Brace Jovanovich, Inc.

Excerpts from E. M. Forster, *Howards End* (copyright 1921); quoted with the kind permission of Alfred A. Knopf, Inc.

"Hum Bom" and selected lines from Allen Ginsberg, *The Fall of America* (copyright © by Allen Ginsberg) and lines from *Howl and Other Poems* (copyright © by Allen Ginsberg); reprinted by permission of City Lights Books.

Excerpts from Joseph Wood Krutch, *The Modern Temper*, are reprinted by permission of Harcourt Brace Jovanovich, Inc.; copyright, 1929, by Harcourt Brace Jovanovich, Inc.; copyright, 1957, by Joseph Wood Krutch.

Material from the book *Naked Masks: Five Plays* by Luigi Pirandello, edited by Eric Bentley, copyright 1922, 1952 by E. P. Dutton & Co., Inc., renewal, 1950, in the names of Stefano Fausto and Lietta Pirandello; reprinted by permission of the publishers, E. P. Dutton & Co., Inc., and of The Heirs of Luigi Pirandello.

Lines from Ezra Pound, *The Cantos* (copyright 1934, 1948 by Ezra Pound); reprinted by permission of New Directions Publishing Corporation and of Faber and Faber Limited.

Lines from Wallace Stevens, *The Collected Poems of Wallace Stevens* (copyright 1923, 1931, 1935, 1936, 1937, 1942, 1943, 1944, 1945, 1946, 1947, 1948, 1949, 1950, 1951, 1952, 1954 by Wallace Stevens); reprinted by permission of Alfred A. Knopf, Inc. Excerpts from Wallace Stevens, *Opus Posthumous*, ed. Samuel French Morse (copyright © 1957 by Elsie Stevens and Holly Stevens); reprinted by permission of Alfred A. Knopf, Inc. Excerpts from Wallace Stevens, *The Letters of Wallace Stevens*, ed. Holly Stevens (© copyright 1966 by Holly Stevens); reprinted by permission of Alfred A. Knopf, Inc.

Lines from William Butler Yeats, "Coole Park and Ballylee, 1931," "The Crazed Moon," "A Dialogue of Self and Soul" (copyright 1933 by Macmillan Publishing Co., Inc., renewed 1961 by Bertha Georgie Yeats) and from "The Second Coming" (copyright 1924 by Macmillan Publishing Co., Inc., renewed 1952 by Bertha Georgie Yeats) in the *Collected Poems of William Butler Yeats*; reprinted by permission of the Macmillan Publishing Co., Inc., New York, and of M. B. Yeats, Miss Anne Yeats, and The Macmillan Co. of London and Basingstoke.

To

CARLOS BAKER

distinguished scholar

skillful teacher

wise colleague

generous friend

the authors dedicate these essays

with admiration and affection

What thanks sufficient, or what recompense
Equal have I to render thee . . .
. . . who thus largely hast allay'd
The thirst I had of knowledge. . . .

Contents

GEORGE BORNSTEIN

Introduction

This book develops in new breadth a premise steadily gaining ground in contemporary Anglo-American criticism—the importance of Romanticism to Modernism. Its comprehensive revaluation of the relation between the two periods is long overdue. Such revaluation sees Modernism as post-Romantic rather than, as often has been the case earlier, anti-Romantic. The book seeks not to reduce Modern literature to mere repetition of the past, of course, but rather to identify the positive centrality of Romanticism for measuring and understanding the Modern achievement. To that end each of its thirteen original essays examines a different and important connection between Romanticism and Modernism, whether in specific writers or in broader manifestations of theme and form. They often share a mild polemicism but uniformly avoid a strident tone or the temptation to substitute one extreme position for another.

The necessity for such revaluation derives from the anti-Romantic polemics attached to the interpretation of Modern literature earlier in our century. New Humanists like Irving Babbitt, avant-garde spokesmen like T. E. Hulme, and influential poets like Ezra Pound and T. S. Eliot all seemed to be attacking Romanticism, and the chief modern Romantic—Yeats—later blamed himself for keeping silent against their onslaughts. Inspired particularly by Eliot, such authoritative later voices as the *Scrutiny* group in England and the New Critics in the United States taught a generation of readers that to defend Modernism meant to attack Romanticism. "The prevailing conception of poetry is still primarily defined for us by the achievement of the Romantic poets," lamented one prominent (and permanently valuable) critic in 1939. "The modern poetry of our time is the first to call that view seriously in question." Resultant appreciation valued mature wit, sensory precision, and impersonality in contrast to allegedly Romantic traits of naive partisanship, emotional vagueness, and egotism.

Romanticists took up the challenge quickly. Their responses occurred in two phases. First, they argued that Romanticism indeed complied with the canons of Modern criticism. Romantic poetry showed equal subtlety in its imagery, tone, and use of personae, not only in the case of Keats, to whom the Modernists had granted a special dispensation anyway, but even in that of Shelley, whom they most insistently berated. At the same time, Romanticists and others began to notice how much of Modern theory itself derived from Romantic formulations, particularly those of Coleridge in *Biographia Literaria*. Those efforts rescued Romanticism for some scholars and students, but outside their lecture rooms and specialized journals hostility most often still ruled. By the late fifties a second and more influential response began. Critics more versed in Romanticism began to develop persuasive theories applicable well beyond the traditional confines of the Romantic period. Robert Langbaum posited a poetry of experience, Frank Kermode showed the importance of the Romantic Image, and, most important of all, Northrop Frye developed a poetics based on Blake; soon critics like Harold Bloom and Geoffrey Hartman were charting new (and controversial) paths beyond a narrow formalism. By now such voices have gained a wide audience. Although anti-Romanticism still lingers, its vogue has passed.

At least two lessons seem clear. First, Modernist criticism often conflated strong, early Romanticism with its later and weaker derivatives. Early twentieth-century writers understandably attacked the debased Romanticism around them and then read their objections to its tone, conventions, and world view back onto the high Romantics. In that enterprise their more enthusiastic commentators more culpably followed. Second, in distorting Romanticism critics distorted Modernism itself. By focusing attention on a few overtly anti-Romantic developments they created a skewed view of the literature they wished to praise. Because the Romantics had been most successful at poetry, and because poets and their critics were often the chief spokesmen for Modernism, the phenomenon affected poetry most of all but extended to other genres.

Current critical climate frees this book from having to be either contrary or rigid. It needs neither to offer a single theory connecting Romanticism and Modernism, for such theories abound, nor to devise a limiting definition for each term, for we have seen the abundant bad effects of those. In any case, one could hardly expect to extract meaningful pledges of allegiance from thirteen disparate scholars. But the essays do share certain assumptions. First, they posit the importance of Romanticism to Modernism. Second, they tend to define those terms historically in relation to the chief writers of each period rather than universally in relation to, say, classic versus romantic characteristics. Sometimes they distinguish the great generation of Modernist writers earlier in the century from contemporary developments. Third, they display an advanced understanding of the subtleties of Romanticism, in contrast to the simplified distortions which prevailed until recently among nonspecialists. And finally, they share the newer and more dynamic view of literary history, which seeks less for sources or debts and more for the writer's creative transformation of his predecessors in the course of his own quest for what will suffice. While concerned chiefly with continuities, the essays often propose genuine distinctions as well.

The book opens with four essays concentrating on broad themes and forms before progressing to studies of individual writers. Stuart M. Sperry begins by proposing a definition of Romantic irony in English literature that distinguishes it from both the German and the English Metaphysical-Modern variety. To Sperry, English Romantic irony involves an openness to experience which often creates unforeseen tensions rather than a formal device for presenting foreknown truths. He traces the development of such indeterminacy in Keats, Shelley, and Byron before suggesting that it reappears in Modern novelists, like Lawrence. Walter H. Evert finds a parallel continuity between Romantic poets and Modern novelists in their conception of evil as an inevitable corruption of good rather than as a counterforce or attrition of it. Ranging widely through an array of gurus from Rousseau to Allen Ginsberg, he aligns Romantic works like Coleridge's "Christabel" and Shelley's *Cenci* with Modern ones like *The Great Gatsby* and contemporary best sellers. He emphasizes the cost of the contemporary penchant for externalizing evil at the expense of recognizing its frequently internal origins.

Michael Goldman and Richard Haven concentrate as much on form as on theme. Goldman argues that Modern drama succeeds best when it learns to treat an inherited Romantic feeling of alienation as itself an expressive device. The Romantic experience of an inadequate external counterpart—whether political or religious—to sweet internal fruition results in a radical change in the motivation of dramatic characters, who increasingly seek to conquer an inner realm for its own sake, and in the nature of the stage itself into a haunted, private place. Ibsen, Pirandello, and the early Brecht transform a Romantic dilemma into a Modern design. Richard Haven notes similar transpositions of public and private space in his discussion of lyrics by Gray, Wordsworth, and Robert Duncan. An increasing stress on the role of the observer and of the literary act itself in the creation of order often prompts a kind of circular structure, which Meyer Abrams has labeled the Greater Romantic

Lyric. Such poems begin with a determinate speaker in a localized setting, move to a kind of meditation or vision, and round on themselves to return with new insight to the original scene; Duncan's "The Fire, *Passages* 13" unexpectedly preserves the basic structure even while undermining some of its overt characteristics.

The section on individual writers fittingly emphasizes poetry, the genre in which the Romantics most excelled. The first two essays open new approaches to the two greatest Modern poets to avow a Romantic impact, Yeats and Stevens. My own essay picks up from Haven's by establishing Yeats's canon of eight Greater Romantic Lyrics and exploring his manipulation of that form. In stepping up the importance of mind over nature Yeats made vision into a summoning of images in nature's spite. He crossed the visionary autonomy of Blake and Shelley with a poetic structure developed by Coleridge, Wordsworth, and Keats to create such famous poems as "The Tower" and "The Second Coming." Yeats called himself a last Romantic, but Stevens thought of himself as a new one. A. Walton Litz examines Stevens' evolution of a new romanticism and counterpoints it with pure poetry on the one hand and the pressure of reality on the other. Faced with the need for articulating a new defense of poetry in the turbulent thirties, Stevens developed a new romantic aesthetic based on his twentieth-century understanding of imagination.

The next three essays offer surprising insights into the two Modern poets most often thought of as anti-Romantic, Pound and Eliot. Herbert N. Schneidau reminds us how much the Wordsworthian revolution against debased Neoclassic diction shares with the Poundian one against debased Romantic language. He then uses the linguistic theory of Roman Jakobson, particularly the tension between predicative and substitutive functions, to account for the recurrent fear of failure of post-Romantic poets as a confrontation of aphasia with poetic labor. Hugh Witemeyer surveys Pound's mixed reaction to Romanticism, all the more ambivalent because of his early appetite for Keats, before scrutinizing more closely his favorite writer of the early nineteenth century, Landor. Pound's Landor combined Classicism—in orderly work preserving tradition—with Romanticism—in a disordered and alienated life—to become a near projection of the modern poet's own self-image. Glenn O'Malley compares Eliot and his sometime bête noire Shelley as translators and adaptors of Dante. Eliot's interest in Dante itself suggests a romantic affinity, for in England the Romantics rehabilitated Dante after centuries of neglect (the first English translation of the *Divine Comedy* appeared only in 1802). Eliot's later praise of the Dantesque

Triumph of Life, and his adaptation of part of it in "Sweeney Erect," argue a partial recognition of his affinity with a poet whom he often attacked.

The final four essays move from poetry to other genres. James A. W. Heffernan finds in politics the most striking parallels between the Romantic period and our own time. Blake here proves central, as he does for so much contemporary art and criticism. In exploring the relation of literature to society, Heffernan contrasts Joyce Cary's use of Blake as a figure of artistic independence with Allen Ginsberg's more political use of him. The force of natural setting as a reforming agent for social relationships in the novelists Jane Austen, George Eliot, and E. M. Forster is studied by E. D. H. Johnson. He juxtaposes scenes from *Emma, Middlemarch,* and *Howards End* to show the passing of traditional, rural English life and the increasing imaginative effort necessary to come to terms with its vestiges. Joseph Blotner illuminates the romantic elements in Faulkner. From recent theories of Romanticism Blotner extracts the use of nature, strength of the past, employment of imagination, and a kind of intense experience as the most relevant. After surveying pertinent aspects of Faulkner's career, he discusses *Sartoris* as Faulkner's most romantic work. Finally, John D. Margolis appraises Joseph Wood Krutch's critical progress. After formulating an anti-Romantic Modernism in *The Modern Temper,* Krutch developed a Thoreauvian naturalism in which experience first of New England and then the Southwest enabled him to generate qualified affirmations against his earlier despair.

The thirteen essays in this book, then, bring a new breadth to current reassessment of the importance of Romanticism to Modernism. They suggest something of the variety and fecundity of connections, as well as the necessity of making distinctions. Their overall burden insists on the centrality of Romanticism without denying the creativity of Modernism. The overall thrust of revaluation carries on the enterprise of making literary history and criticism new for our time and of opening new possibilities for the future. For we have not yet seen the last Romantics.

I. Themes and Forms

STUART M. SPERRY

Toward a Definition of Romantic Irony
in English Literature

My purpose in this essay is to establish a basis for a conception of
Romantic irony in English literature of the nineteenth century.[1] The
problem is in good part theoretical and is beset on several sides by
real problems of definition, so that I must spend a little time at the
outset in making some distinctions that I hope will prove useful
and clear. The principal difficulties are liable to come from two
quite different directions. On the one hand some students of English literature, even some specialists in the period of English Romanticism, are liable to find the term unfamiliar and even puzzling.
We tend to associate irony in its conventional sense with English
literature of an earlier age, with the flourishing of satire, with the
work of Dryden and Pope and, above all, with Jonathan Swift.
Since the work of most of the great English Romantics, say Wordsworth and Keats, is ordinarily considered unnotable for, indeed
some would say positively deficient in, ironic effect, certain be-
mused readers may wonder what rare or deviant aspect of Romanticism is now, in the quest for novelty, being pushed unjustifiably
into prominence.

My use of the term is liable to inspire, however, a quite opposite
reaction from students of Romantic irony in German literature,
where the whole conception has not only been described in considerable detail in an extensive body of scholarship and criticism but
formulated in theory and practice so as to constitute what is virtually a literary genre of its own. The reaction from this quarter is
liable to be one of opposition and even indignation: "you are mis-
using or misinterpreting our conception"; or "you are misappropri-
ating a term we have defined with some exactness to describe an
eccentric perception of your own"; or even more extreme, "you
have no right to extend the notion beyond a frame of reference that
is primarily German or at least Continental."

Perhaps it would be better had I chosen some term other than
"Romantic irony." Yet I do not think this would answer for the
reason that the expression is being used today increasingly by students of British and American literature; moreover, the conception

has for long been developed by comparatists in such a way as to incorporate aspects of English Romanticism, providing a context, for example, into which Lord Byron—or at least part of him—conveniently fits.[2]

Let me make clear from the start that my purpose is not to attempt to establish a historical connection between Romantic irony in German literature and its English counterpart. Irony in German Romanticism has its roots in the soil of a development of historical and philosophic thinking that is peculiarly German. Its practitioners were in the main conscious and deliberate adherents of various theories that derive ultimately from Kantian and post-Kantian philosophy which had no British equivalent, although German ideas may have made rapid progress in England once they were introduced and popularized. In England irony is a quality of awareness that arises within the work of the younger Romantics—chiefly Byron, Shelley, and Keats—spontaneously and unconsciously and as a natural result of their attempt to work out the problems facing them through the actual creation of poetry. At this point it is only natural to ask why I pass over the first generation of Romantic writers or why, for that matter, I neglect so obvious, if eccentric, an example in the eighteenth century as Laurence Sterne. Clearly I do not intend the focus of this essay to be taken as exclusive. My reason for concentrating on the younger generation of Romantic writers is simply that, in resisting the temptation of withdrawing into a private system like Blake or into orthodoxy like Wordsworth, in maintaining approaches to the issues confronting them that were independent, flexible, and open, they raise the whole problem of ironic awareness in a higher form.[3]

The most common basic definition of irony is "saying one thing and meaning another," a device writers regularly employ in order to achieve effects that can be more dramatic or striking than simply speaking one's mind. Yet it will be clear by now that the kind of irony I am seeking to elucidate does not fit such a description just as it can not be defined as technique or device. Indeed it is precisely here that we encounter a major discrimination between Romantic irony and irony in its more familiar forms. Device necessarily implies purpose or intention. The great line of English satirists who used irony as a principal weapon—we can think of Swift as a prime example—would have been outraged at the mere suggestion that they wrote without intention, without a moral aim. For them satire was an anatomy, a deliberate holding of the mirror up to a diseased nature, not for the purpose of morbid enjoyment but in order to expose the corrupted parts for excision. If such was not invariably the case in practice, at least it was in theory. Yet the kind of irony I am seeking to characterize enjoys a life of its own. Rather than device, it is a state of mind or disposition, a kind of realization that arises, at least in the writers I shall consider, in part unconsciously.[4] If I had to describe that sense of realization in a single word, I should choose the word *indeterminacy*.

II

At this point let me break my present train of thought in order to relate it to a broader formulation, one that is admittedly simplistic. Throughout the Renaissance and Enlightenment one finds the greatest English poets writing in the longer poetic forms—such figures as Spenser, Milton, and Pope—using poetry as a way of celebrating truths and ideals that were largely traditional and received. In our own day, by contrast, we find a pervasive distrust of philosophical system among poets whose approach to verse is chiefly personal, fragmentary, and increasingly skeptical of any doctrine of received beliefs. What is particularly fascinating about the literature of English Romanticism is that it presents us with the case of writers who, faced with the beginnings of that fragmentation and skepticism we see on all sides of us today, nevertheless struggled to achieve for themselves some alternative to a world order that was collapsing around them. More specifically it was a time when major poets, faced with competing claims and counterclaims and rejecting orthodoxies they could no longer accept, nevertheless struggled to evolve, through the intent examination of their own experience, if not a philosophy of life at least a satisfactory *modus vivendi*. It was a time when poets sought to perpetuate the higher function of verse by using poetry as a means of working out, as Matthew Arnold was in a sense to urge later, the grounds for something approaching religious or philosophical commitment. In this endeavor, moreover, nothing was more crucial than the creative process, which for all the great Romantics involves much more than just the committing of thought to paper but rather a whole larger process of inner discovery in which sensation emerges into conscious realization and comes to assume the character of intellectual perception.

Hence the emergence of that kind of irresolution, the sense of indeterminacy that I have called Romantic irony, a phenomenon I want to approach more closely for a moment by way of contrast with the kind of irony we associate with Socrates.[5] In one of his letters Keats refers to Socrates and Christ as the only two "hearts" that were "completely disinterested," and I should like to think

there is a deeper bond between the poet and the Athenian than is
usually recognized. Socratic irony involves much more, of course,
than those devices we commonly associate with it: the philosopher's mischievous profession of ignorance sitting at the feet of
self-appointed authorities, or the method of interrogation by which
he leads them into a series of logical contradictions in which they
confute themselves. At a deeper level Socratic irony derives from
certain traits he in large measure shares with Keats—from a flexibil-
ity of mind and openness to experience that we associate with
Keats's word, "disinterestedness." It is hardly surprising to find
Keats, a few sentences after his admiring remarks on Socrates and
his "disinterestedness," describing himself in these terms: "I am
however young writing at random—straining at particles of light in
the midst of a great darkness—without knowing the bearing of any
one assertion of any one opinion."[6] In such words we recognize the
Keats who was preeminently the poet of "Negative Capability," the
poet who considered "Genius" as the gift for exploring the "dark
passages" (I.281) of life. For what links Keats with Socrates most
nearly is the belief that truth, if it is to have any meaning for us,
lies not in axioms or abstractions but is a vital process of discovery
that is inseparable from the dialectic of the poem or dialogue
through which it is achieved—that is to say, through the creative
process itself. Indeed we commonly feel in reading the Socratic
dialogues that their value lies more in the play and exercise of mind
than in the conclusions they reach, which are usually negative.
Even while he appears intent on "fact & reason," Socrates demonstrates throughout the ability to exist amid "uncertainties, Mysteries, doubts" (I.193–94). Yet there inevitably comes the time when
we begin to wonder whether, despite the pose of one intent on the
ultimate answers, Socrates ever really expects to arrive at definite
conclusions. At a deeper level he appears dedicated to the process
of inquiry for its own sake rather than for the solutions it may
yield. Thus there is a large measure of justification for the judgment
of Milton's Christ in the *Paradise Regained* who, in dismissing the
whole of ancient learning as "but dreams, / Conjectures, fancies,
built on nothing firm," paid a kind of backhanded tribute to Socrates as "The first and wisest of them all [who] profess'd / To know
this only, that he nothing knew"(iv.291–94). The essence of Socratic
irony seems to lie in Socrates' commitment to the process of intellectual self-inquiry combined with a skepticism concerning the ultimate conclusions it might yield.

I make these points by way of contrast with Keats because I
believe the poet, despite his words about "Negative Capability,"

was really intent on achieving through poetry something more definite, something we might be tempted to call "truth" in the absolute sense of the word. And I want to turn to Keats now in order to define more precisely what I mean by Romantic irony. One might begin with the letter of December 1817 where Keats defines "Negative Capability," that quality that "Shakespeare possessed so enormously,"

that is when man is capable of being in uncertainties, Mysteries, doubts, without any irritable reaching after fact & reason—Coleridge, for instance, would let go by a fine isolated verisimilitude caught from the Penetralium of mystery, from being incapable of remaining content with half knowledge. This pursued through Volumes would perhaps take us no further than this, that with a great poet the sense of Beauty overcomes every other consideration, or rather obliterates all consideration.   (I.193–94)

As always, when dealing with one of Keats's major formulations, one finds oneself under the necessity of starting some place, with some single strand of declaration, yet realizing that to do so is necessarily to neglect, if only for the moment, other different kinds of implication. Among so many fine ones, the phrase I want to emphasize is "the Penetralium of mystery." The conception is one Keats comes back to in his letter of May 1818 to John Hamilton Reynolds in which he compares life to "a large Mansion of Many Apartments" and in which he defines poetic genius as the power of seeing down the "dark passages" opening out from the "Chamber of Maiden Thought":

We are in a Mist, *We* are now in that state—We feel the "burden of the Mystery," To this point was Wordsworth come, as far as I can conceive when he wrote "Tintern Abbey" and it seems to me that his Genius is explorative of those dark Passages. Now if we live, and go on thinking, we too shall explore them. he is a Genius and superior [to] us, in so far as he can, more than we, make discoveries, and shed light in them.   (I.280–81)

The tone of the passage, the images of exploration and discovery, make it clear that the task, as Keats conceived it, was challenging and even invigorating. If life was a mist, a Penetralium of mystery, it was at least fascinating, rich in suggestiveness and undiscovered meanings that needed to be brought to light in a way that could make him go on to postulate a general and progressive advance of human intelligence, "a grand march of intellect."

Yet there are times when Keats is wont to be less optimistic. One can take, for example, a passage from the brooding verse epistle he sent to Reynolds in March 1818, some months after the "Negative Capability" letter:

> but my flag is not unfurl'd
> On the admiral-staff, —and to philosophise
> I dare not yet! Oh, never will the prize,
> High reason, and the lore of good and ill,
> Be my award! Things cannot to the will
> Be settled, but they tease us out of thought;
> Or is it that imagination brought
> Beyond its proper bound, yet still confin'd,
> Lost in a sort of Purgatory blind,
> Cannot refer to any standard law
> Of either earth or heaven?[7]

The question I would ask is: what is the difference between the "Penetralium of mystery" and "Purgatory blind"? As so often in Keats, there is a consistency of metaphor that links them. They both have reference to that state of irresolution in which the imagination encounters the unknown. But the two contexts are entirely different, indeed reversed. The first suggests that kind of "glorious fear" in which the charioteer looks out upon the "Shapes of delight, of mystery, and fear" that pass before him in "a dusky space" within the central vision of "Sleep and Poetry" (138–39). The second suggests the kind of occlusion and oppressiveness symbolized by the ancient sanctuary where the dreamer wakes to find himself in *The Fall of Hyperion* with its "silent massy range / Of columns north and south, ending in mist / Of nothing" (I.83–85). In the first, darkness, mist, and mystery are images full of expectation and potentiality. In the second, they suggest a blinding sense of unfathomability—a sense of indeterminacy. Throughout Keats's poetry, as in the last stanza of the "Ode to Psyche," one can find places where the two contexts are juxtaposed and even in some sense debated. However it can be said that the second, darker recognition is the one that grows and deepens as his career proceeds.

Even more significant than the awareness of indeterminacy, perhaps, is the manner in which it arises—the way, as I have attempted to show, in which a governing metaphor will recur in a way that totally alters its original meaning. Let me take another example. No metaphor of Keats is better known than his comparison of the truth of imagination to Adam's dream in his letter of November 1817 to Benjamin Bailey. "I am certain of nothing but of the holiness of the Heart's affections and the truth of Imagination," he declared. "What the imagination seizes as Beauty must be truth—

whether it existed before or not—for I have the same Idea of all our Passions as of Love they are all in their sublime, creative of essential Beauty. . . . The Imagination may be compared to Adam's dream—he awoke and found it truth" (I.184–85). With this passage one might compare some sentences Keats wrote to his friend Charles Brown in one of the last of his surviving letters, written after he had left England on the journey to his death in Rome. "The thought of leaving Miss Brawne is beyond every thing horrible— the sense of darkness coming over me—I eternally see her figure eternally vanishing. Some of the phrases she was in the habit of using during my last nursing at Wentworth place ring in my ears— Is there another Life? Shall I awake and find all this a dream? There must be we cannot be created for this sort of suffering" (II.345–46). One is struck again by the haunting continuity of metaphor, the figure of dream and awakening into reality that is so characteristic of Keats. It is just that its terms, its entire context, are so strikingly and unpredictably altered. The vision of human life and its "spiritual repetition" has narrowed to the image of a beloved figure eternally vanishing. The conception of the "Imagination and its empyreal reflection" has become the horror of what Keats called "my posthumous existence." Surely there is an irony here but, although it has its roots in Keats's life and thought, it is not primarily an aesthetic one. It is too unforeseen, too inscrutable, too—in its origins at least—unconscious.

"A Man's life of any worth is a continual allegory," Keats wrote. "Lord Byron cuts a figure—but he is not figurative—Shakspeare led a life of Allegory; his works are the comments on it" (II.67). Allegory as a conception is something we are accustomed to dealing with in works of art—in the *Faerie Queene*, for example, where the strands of allegorical significance, however rich or complex, are orderly and determined. Yet it seems necessary to consider the broader extension Keats's phrase—"a *life* of Allegory"—invites and to go on, further, to attempt to read his life, "like the scriptures," allegorically. And here, at the risk of being wrong, I must confess that I do not believe his career approximates allegory, taken in the higher sense he intended. For if we begin, as his statement suggests, from his works, we do not find, despite the prominence one is tempted to give to "To Autumn," the completeness of patterning allegory implies. We can begin with the allegory of *Endymion*, a poem where the poet intervenes rather awkwardly near the end to advise the reader that the "truth" that is emerging is not the one he had originally intended and to warn him that he is going to have to end the work artificially and in a way he really disapproves. One can then go on to what most critics today consider his finest verse, the great odes, a poetry of symbolic debate in which alternative responses to the dilemma of human mortality are not resolved but juxtaposed and turned over in the mind. And then one can move forward, or backward, to the larger effect of *Hyperion* and to the kind of poetry that, as I conceive it, Keats's Arnoldian conscience was continually urging him to write—a poetry struggling for self-knowledge, authority, and deliberate statement. What strikes one most about the two versions of the work—the epic and the vision—is not their incompleteness or the differences between them, remarkable as those are, but rather how radically each version changed during the time Keats worked upon them.

The problem is crystallized in the second version, *The Fall of Hyperion*, for it is here that Keats was seeking to compose an allegory, a redemptive allegory, of the poetic conscience, of the poetic soul. The evidence for this assertion lies in his choice and treatment, as the scaffold of his vision, of one of the great Romantic myths: the Christian story of man's fall and ultimate redemption. Within the sacramental logic of the new induction to the poem, the poet-dreamer sins by tasting the forbidden fruit, the draught of transparent juice, the "refuse of a meal / By angel tasted or our Mother Eve" (1.30–31).[8] Nevertheless he is restored to health and sanctity, unlike the mere dreamers who rot before Moneta's altar, by vicariously accepting her vision of human suffering and the immense pain it imposes. The logic of the progression that leads the dreamer from the fragrant garden to the awesome temple to the struggle to ascend Moneta's altar begins as far back as Keats's first visionary poem, "Sleep and Poetry." However, the passage of self-accusing, self-flagellating lines which Woodhouse recorded "Keats seems to have intended to erase"[9] shows how susceptible the redemptive thrust of the argument was to the pressure of actual misgivings. Above all, it is the vision of Moneta as she parts her veils, the vision the dreamer has struggled so arduously to achieve and that holds the key to his rehabilitation, that gives us pause:

> Then saw I a wan face,
> Not pined by human sorrows, but bright-blanch'd
> By an immortal sickness which kills not;
> It works a constant change, which happy death
> Can put no end to; deathwards progressing
> To no death was that visage; it had pass'd
> The lily and the snow; and beyond these
> I must not think now, though I saw that face.
> But for her eyes I should have fled away.

> They held me back with a benignant light,
> Soft mitigated by divinest lids
> Half closed, and visionless entire they seem'd
> Of all external things—they saw me not,
> But, in blank splendour, beam'd like the mild moon,
> Who comforts those she sees not, who knows not
> What eyes are upward cast.   (1.256–71)

One critic, D. G. James, has seen behind this vision the agonized features of the suffering Christ;[10] and such a reading supports the redemptive force of Keats's allegory. Yet returning to the central passage, I do not think it ultimately sustains such an interpretation. The passage, on the contrary, seems curiously suspended between terror and benignity, concern and indifference, serenity and despair. Nor can one escape the paradox that the poet's physician in his "sickness not ignoble" (1.184) is herself sick, sick not to death but fated to a process of eternal wasting that exceeds his very power to imagine it. As redemptress, Moneta is nevertheless involved in and fated to endure the very processes she would transcend. Nor is it long before the dreamer has lost his height of vision in the dreadful vale—a life-in-death that is the ironic inversion of Keats's earlier metaphor of life as the "vale of Soul-making" (II.102):

> And every day by day methought I grew
> More gaunt and ghostly. Oftentimes I pray'd
> Intense, that death would take me from the vale
> And all its burthens—Gasping with despair
> Of change, hour after hour I curs'd myself.   (1.395–99)

Those lines reflect the devastating course of Tom's illness during the time Keats worked on his epic, the same process the poet himself would undergo in his final weeks in Rome. More than a poem he was unable to finish, what we have in *Hyperion* is a work whose conceptual grounds underwent a total alteration as it proceeded through a deepening of human awareness. It distils that kind of indeterminacy that I have been attempting to define as peculiarly Romantic.

The problem, if we choose to conceive of it in those terms, is one that is inseparable from Keats's chief attractions as a poet—his responsiveness and openness to life in all its varied manifestations. The question is: To what degree is this kind of honesty to experience, this susceptibility to varying impressions, compatible with the kind of poetry that he wanted ultimately to write? If, like the greatest of his poetic contemporaries, he dispensed not with the

myths and poetic forms he inherited from the past but rather with
the established beliefs and orthodoxies they had served, it became
necessary for him to intuit some meaningful vision of his own. This
he sought to accomplish by making such intuition a vital part of the
process of poetic composition itself—by making the poetic process
more fully inventive and determining than it had ever been for
Dryden, or Pope, or Johnson. His career, it seems to me, illustrates
if not the failure, at least the difficulties of such a task. For it demonstrates how the insight for which he struggled was never secure
from the pervasive ironies of human experience.

III

I must pass on to Shelley, for, as I have indicated, I want to place
both him and Byron within the formulation I have been seeking to
make. And it would seem at first glance that I should be far less
happy about dealing with Shelley than with Keats. For if the
younger poet's proper province was sensation—sensation continually extending itself through association, toward speculation, a kind
of "shadowy thought"—Shelley was an intellectual poet of the most
strenuous kind. Not only was he a voracious reader of philosophy
but he possessed the kind of analytical temperament that Keats
instinctively distrusted. Shelley displayed an intellectual brilliance
that could dazzle and intimidate (which is not to say that his poetic
talent was necessarily the greater); and reading between the lines in
those letters where they refer to each other, one can see that Keats
was always emulous but also slightly afraid of his older rival,
Hunt's favorite protégé, from whom he needed to keep, as he put
it, "my own unfettered scope" (I.170). If these distinctions were not
sufficiently pronounced, modern Shelley scholarship has emphasized both the systematic quality of his mind and the relative cohe-
siveness of his ideas—what has come to be called "the intellectual
philosophy." Not only did this philosophy, this system of assumptions and beliefs, emerge relatively early in Shelley's career, but it
remained more or less constant and unchanged to the end.[11] On the
surface of it, Shelley would hardly seem to promise well as an
instance of the kind of indeterminacy I have been discussing.

Such, curiously, is not the case. Indeed, in one way or another,
one finds all Shelley's major critics habitually confronting the kind
of irresolution I have been describing. Part of the explanation is
that "the intellectual philosophy," as we find it elaborated, is so
extraordinarily encompassing. Within it Shelley sought to provide
room for an idealism, partly Neoplatonic, partly Berkeleian, of the
most radical kind. At the same time he was a rationalist and an

empiricist who admired and endorsed the skeptical method of David Hume. The result is that "the intellectual philosophy" enjoys a unity that is more conceptual than practical. What it affords is a justification for perceiving a given fact or situation simultaneously from several different points of view. Thus the poet is one whose duty it is to depict the most "beautiful idealisms of moral excellence,"[12] to imagine the perfection of human nature and society carried to its fullest realization, even while, from another standpoint, he can never forget the "sad reality,"[13] the actual fact of man's self-denial or betrayal and the unlikelihood of any change in the status quo. Correspondingly Shelley's is a poetry where perspective is all-important and where the most dramatic shifts in attitude or tone—witness *Adonais*—can take place with stunning swiftness.

This bifurcated vision can be seen in the first important poem of his maturity, his *Alastor*. The poem has always been a puzzle for critics, for in the preface and the poem itself Shelley seems both to praise and condemn his hero. One must take note here of Earl Wasserman's ingenious method for resolving the dilemma which he develops through close study of the poem's focus of narration. Shelley's hero, the well-raised and nobly minded poet, is fired to the pursuit of his visionary ideal which inexorably drives him beyond the limits of the mortal world to his lonely and solipsistic death in an eerie realm of shadows. Wasserman points out that this account, however, is in greater part related not by Shelley himself but by Shelley's narrator, a commentator roughly equivalent to the character of the Wanderer in Wordsworth's *Excursion*. In pitying the visionary-poet and his plight, the narrator is limited by his own allegiance to nature conceived as a beneficent and transcendent power. (Shelley broke decisively with Wordsworth's view of nature: for him nature *always* betrayed the heart that trusted her.) Thus the poem is a kind of device, for which the model is Shelley's skeptical dialogue, *A Refutation of Deism*, which plays one kind or view of poetry off against another, displaying the shortcomings of each, and which effectually removes Shelley himself from the poem as a kind of disinterested spectator. Indeed, by a stroke that may seem to some overingenious, Wasserman goes so far as to argue that the prose preface to the poem, with its contradictory dialectics, should be imagined as written not by Shelley himself as author but by Shelley in the character of his narrator, bound by his faith in natural piety.[14] Poised indeterminately between two views of poetry or of nature, the poem, in one sense at least, could hardly be more ironical. However, it is necessary to point out an essential distinction: to observe that *Alastor*, or at least this view of it, does not illustrate the kind of irony I have been up to now discussing. For the kind or kinds of irony it generates are ones against which Shelley himself, in Wasserman's view, is thoroughly protected, indeed immunized. The poem, as we have seen, is a device, and the ironies with which it plays are not unconscious or unforeseen but deliberate and intended. The ambivalences are all built-in, self-contained. It distils an irony that has been mastered.[15]

In order to deal with the apparent contradiction in my argument, it is necessary to pose some questions of broader relevance to Shelley scholarship, questions that, if they have already been partly raised, have not been adequately pursued. I hope it is not ungenerous of me to state that, reading through much recent criticism of Shelley like Wasserman's, admiring as one must the closeness of its reasoning, one is nevertheless struck by its abstract, almost antiseptic quality. It is not just that the poetry is taken up in isolation from the life of the poet, from the deeper logic of his career both in itself and in relation to the history of his times, although that fact is continuously disconcerting. It is further that in reducing the verse to a structure of ideas, criticism has gone far toward depriving it of all emotional reality. In recent years the power and urgency of Shelley's appeal have been affirmed by critical declaration rather than by revelation; and it is time to demand more intently whether the failure lies with the critics or with Shelley himself. The current difficulty of engaging Shelley on the level of the emotions has left a number of questions that are not without practical ramifications. Was *Alastor* written, as Wasserman's discussion would imply, as a brilliant intellectual exercise, a poetic *reductio ad absurdum?* Or was the experience of composition, whether or not we use such terms as "purgatorial" or "cathartic," itself decisive and informing? For the way we answer such questions is bound to determine the kind of irony we visualize the poem as distilling. If there are those who argue that I am introducing into my consideration of irony criteria that are troublingly subjective, I can only plead guilty to the charge. Much as we should like to think otherwise, the problem of irony and the questions it raises cannot be neatly confined to consideration of a printed text: they involve issues of biographical interpretation; they overlap broadly with life.[16]

In his single reference to Shelley in his admirable *Compass of Irony*, D. C. Muecke quotes a section from the famous comparison of the mind in creation to a fading coal in *The Defence of Poetry* and goes on to comment: "There is obviously matter for irony in the idea that what is permanent, the created work, is necessarily less authentic or valuable than the transitory moments of creation. Shelley, however, seems rather more gratified than otherwise with this state of affairs. His sense of the ironic, fitful at best, did not reveal to him the potential irony in this predicament the poets were in. More alert were his contemporaries in Germany."[17] It is only relatively recently that we have begun to sense that something is radically wrong with such a judgment. Even so, however, we are not sure exactly what. If Shelley *did* possess a sense of irony, was it established from the outset or did it alter and deepen? Did it nourish or deplete his creative energies? Were its manifestations (note Muecke's word, "gratified") predominantly comic or tragic? Again, if Shelley was not as far behind his German contemporaries as Muecke's comment presumes, in what ways did his perception of the problem differ from theirs? By what set of criteria can they be confidently grouped as exponents of "Romantic irony" in such a way as to exclude him; and presuming this possible, is there not justice and value in a broader definition?

I have already stated my conviction that these issues cannot be settled on stylistic grounds alone but involve us in the whole fabric of Shelley's life, where we labor under notable disadvantages. The mere fact that we have at least three modern lives of Keats—works that closely interrelate the man and poet—while we are still largely dependent for our knowledge of Shelley on the pioneering but essentially Victorian interpretation of Newman Ivey White has been of great significance.[18] Looking back into the nineteenth century one can detect a radical uncertainty as to how to interpret the tone, not just of particular works of Shelley, but of his whole career. One can perceive it in Arnold's indecision in choosing between "mad Shelley," the Shelley who was "not entirely sane," who was "ridiculous and odious," and his better angel, the Shelley who was "beautiful and lovable." In the closing pages of his rehabilitating essay Arnold brings us round to a kinder view: "And so we have come back again, at last, to our original Shelley—to the Shelley of the lovely and well-known picture, to the Shelley with 'flushed, feminine, artless face,' the Shelley 'blushing like a girl,' of Trelawny." Modern criticism has rejected Arnold's portrait of the "beautiful and ineffectual angel."[19] However it has too often substituted in its stead Shelley as his own creation, his hermaphrodite, a perfect, sexless creature compounded of violent contraries sailing placidly between the human world and the divine; and there is just enough truth in the resemblance, since the hermaphrodite in *The Witch of Atlas* is in part a lovely bit of self-parody, to make the likeness dangerous. In reducing Shelley to an intellectual abstraction, a philosophical Ariel blithely resolving earthly insolubilities through the metaphysical alchemy of his verse, modern criticism has only furthered Arnold's dehumanizing tendencies. In ignoring or evading the tone of the life, it has left unanswered major questions about the poetry.

Ultimately Shelley the man and his career transcend and condition his poetry. Like some of the students who have come in recent years to admire him, he led a disordered life in a disordered world and his dissatisfaction with both is reflected in his poetry. Although he may at times have sought it, he never found a refuge from life and its concerns in the abstractions of verse. That fact is reflected merely in his rapid alternation between the esoteric and the exoteric strain,[20] between the poetry he wrote and frequently published himself for that small coterie of admirers by whom he could depend on being appreciated and understood and the public verse he addressed in moments of outrage at human injustice to a populace he could never bring himself to admit had gone out of hearing. With neither kind of poetry was he altogether happy; by neither conception of the poet was he satisfied. Indeed there is at work in his career a psychological principle of compensation which drives him as fiercely to one extreme as he has extended himself in the other. Thus he breaks off his work between the third and final acts of *Prometheus Unbound,* a play that distils a vision of millennial regeneration more grandiose than any other poet has written, to compose *The Cenci,* a work that describes in terrifying step-by-step detail the inexorable corrupting power of evil. The necessity of raising up a new Adam in *Prometheus* seems to inspire by way of recoil the compulsion to portray the moral debasement of Beatrice, a degradation that is only the more frightening for the reason that she herself is unaware of the way her father, Count Cenci, has triumphed over her in the end. Shelley's groping toward "the burden of the Mystery" was admittedly more systematic and deliberate than Keats's; but his divided view of the human situation, his insight into its pervasive irony, did not provide him with the resources for coping with it, for making it any less oppressive. Although the perception infuses his verse with a schizophrenic, at times monotonous, power—its characteristically high pitch—it did not give him the stability he needed. It did not permit him to become the kind of poet he wanted to be. It did not make him happy. These truths, or opinions, are not fully revealed in any single work he composed. They arise from a sense of his career.

There are two later works that reveal Shelley returning to the fundamental problem of *Alastor* with renewed involvement and emotional intensity. The one is comedy tinged with bitterness, the other tragedy permeated by comedy in the Dantean sense: *The Witch of Atlas* and *The Triumph of Life*.[21] In his dedication to the *Witch*, Shelley, while slightly reproachful of his wife, playfully entreats her not to condemn his latest verses "because they tell no story, false or true," to permit him the indulgence of one more "visionary rhyme." Then presumably having received his permission, his release from the common-sense world which the dedication sets off, he departs with his witch and her hermaphroditical companion on a voyage into the realm of pure indeterminacy, a moon voyage in which the ordinary gravitational laws are suspended. Thus the normal distinctions between truth and error, reality and illusion, life and death simply no longer apply. In a sort of allegory of art as pure play, the Witch performs her pranks, in Douglas Bush's phrase, like "Asia on a holiday."[22] The point is, however, that Shelley never forgets that it is a holiday and only that. In a work of many subtle shifts in tone, the sportiveness becomes transformed in the poem's conclusion which, as Harold Bloom has said, is haunted by "a unique sadness":[23]

> These were the pranks she played among the cities
>   Of mortal men, and what she did to Sprites
> And Gods, entangling them in her sweet ditties
>   To do her will, and show their subtle sleights,
> I will declare another time; for it is
>   A tale more fit for the weird winter nights
> Than for these garish summer days, when we
> Scarcely believe much more than we can see.   (665–72)

The offhandedness of "I will declare another time" (a little like Keats's "It was no dream; or say a dream it was" [*Lamia* 1.126]) shades rapidly into undisguised bitterness as the garish summer light, the old oppressive sense of things, leaks in beneath the poem's edges.

Shelley returns to that garish light in *The Triumph of Life* for his principal image—that "cold glare intenser than the noon / But icy cold" (77–78)[24] that heralds the onrushing chariot that dominates his vision. *The Triumph of Life*: no title of Shelley's invention is more obviously yet compellingly ironic. For there is no way of escaping the meaningless and desolating pageant the poem twice unfolds, first before the dreamer and then again in Rousseau's narration. There may be those "sacred few" (128) who after their first brief encounter "Fled back like eagles to their native noon" (131), but Shelley knows he is not and never could be one of them. He

knows only the world's corrosive, staining power and "the mutiny
within" (213), the mutiny of the human heart. One may be re-
minded of the later Yeats and his boast in the face of this monotonous disfiguration: "I am content to live it all again / And yet
again"—the

> toil of growing up;
> The ignominy of boyhood; the distress
> Of boyhood changing into man,[25]

and all the rest of it. But Yeats had learned well from, in a sense
gone beyond, his master. For the irony, the sense of probing irresolution that vibrates through Shelley's poem, is contained and polar-
ized by the antinomies of Yeats's system. Yeats's vision, by which I
mean both the system and what it becomes in his poetry, permitted
that kind of transcendence, ultimately acceptance, that is blessed.

But for Shelley there was no such resolution, no escape. I have
already argued for the particular quality of irony that derives from
the inconclusiveness of Keats's whole *Hyperion* effort, and more
specially from *The Fall* and its effect of cul-de-sac. Much the same
quality permeates Shelley's *Triumph*. Merely in form and style the
similarities between the two great fragments are almost preternatu-
rally striking, so that one is led to imagine again, even after Keats's
death, some mysterious resonance between the two careers. Both
fragments are visions, dreams within dreams. In each a vision is
inspired by a mysterious draught—Keats's "cool vessel of transparent juice" (1.42) and Shelley's "crystal glass / Mantling with bright
Nepenthe" (358–59). In each the draught leads to a transformation
of awareness corresponding to the change from innocence to experience. In each the dreamer is partly conducted by a guide, Keats's
Mnemosyne-Moneta, Shelley's Rousseau, up to a confrontation of
the ultimate questions. And in each the questions go unanswered.
Keats's indecision is revealed as much as anywhere in Moneta's
unsettling interrogation of the dreamer in the passage of disputed
lines. Shelley's fragment breaks off leaving us to ponder the ultimate question, "Then, what is Life?" (544). There are those, of
course, who will argue for a fundamental difference: that Keats's
failure was a failure of conception, while Shelley's poem was interrupted by the tragedy that overtook him in the Gulf of Spezia. If,
nevertheless, we read a poet's life, as Keats would urge us, allegorically, it is possible to feel that Shelley had raised questions that
could find no answer short of death, to sense an admittedly unprov-
able connection between the final sheets of the manuscript of the

poem, trailing off into sketches of sails, and his watery end.[26] Harold Bloom has written of the poet's final phase: "The theme of life's triumph over everything imaginative that seeks to redeem life had been a long time in coming to Shelley's poetry, but when it did come it came as devastation."[27] The vision of life as an irresolvable anomaly is written large in Shelley's *Triumph*, just as it dominates the sorrow of his final months.

IV

In most respects Byron fits more obviously within the context of Romantic irony. For one thing, he has often been granted a place by comparatists whose formulation of Romantic irony as a theory has commonly excluded Keats and Shelley. Within the context we have been developing, Byron comes as the exception that proves the rule. One way of seeing this is by returning to Morse Peckham's classic essay, "Toward a Theory of Romanticism."[28] It will be recalled that, well into his formulation, Peckham raises the question, "What about Byron?" Here he is impelled to introduce two new terms and to distinguish between "Positive" and "Negative" Romanticism, for the former, he notes, by itself "cannot explain Byron" (p. 15). "Negative Romanticism, " he goes on to explain, "is the expression of the attitudes, the feelings, and the ideas of a man who has left static mechanism but has not yet arrived at a reintegration of his thought and art in terms of dynamic organicism" (p. 16). Negative Romanticism, in other words, is the condition of being cut loose from the old certainties, the old orthodoxies, without the attainment of the new insights necessary for progressing on to an organic reintegration—the state of Carlyle's "Everlasting No" before the attainment of "The Everlasting Yea." "Negative Romanticism," Peckham goes on to write, "causes isolation and despair because it offers no cosmic explanations, while Positive Romanticism offers cosmic explanations which are not shared by the society of which one is a part" (p. 23).

Like many others before me, I have found Peckham's whole way of thinking stimulating. Yet considering his theory in the light of my own ideas about Romantic irony, I should want to suggest changes. Indeed, I should want to reverse his positive and negative poles. Using his own phrasing, I should want to reformulate his position (at least in the case of the poets we are considering) thus: Positive Romanticism causes isolation and despair, because it offers cosmic explanations that are never satisfactory or final, that are never secure from the infiltrating ironies of human experience. Negative Romanticism brings, if not happiness, at least release, because it springs from just such a realization, because it derives from an understanding of the hopelessness of using poetry either as a means of discovering or celebrating some fully harmonizing, reintegrating view of existence. It may seem perverse to make Byron, traditionally the chief exponent of the darker aspects of Romanticism, into a representative of its positive side. But is not the deeper problem that the terms, "Positive" and "Negative," as Peckham employs them, commit one to the possibility of psychological or historical anachronism? To put it briefly, is it correct to view Byron at the time of his death as occupying, as Peckham sees him, some halfway house on the way toward a new organic reintegration of experience, as occupying a position that is similar to Wordsworth after the rejection of Godwin, or the Ancient Mariner alone on the wide, wide sea, or Teufelsdröckh wandering through the Centre of Indifference? Is it not true, rather, that we see reflected in *Don Juan* a poet for whom the Wordsworthian reintegration is no longer either desirable or possible, a poet who in a sense has gone beyond Wordsworth by transcending the kind of need for certainty, or at least security, the older poet's case so manifests? Is it not true that "Positive" and "Negative" have value relative to each other, depending on which we make the transitional term?

What is at issue, once again, is the logic of a poetic career. However, I would argue that, partly as a result of time, I have on my side a more modern view of Byron and his development than did Peckham. It is possible to see, amid the windy turbulence of the poetry of Byron's middle years, a certain kind of soul-searching—in Blake's phrase, "LORD BYRON in the wilderness."[29] In the third canto of *Childe Harold*, for example, one can see the poet, partly with the encouragement of Shelley, seeking to assuage his grief and remorse by looking on nature through Wordsworth's eyes, though it is hard to separate out whatever may be serious from the poet's habitual posturing. However, it is Byron's greatest drama, his *Manfred*, that exemplifies the crucial catharsis that made *Don Juan* possible. For the play takes up the process of negation and, instead of abandoning it, follows it through to its logical conclusion. Briefly, one sees Manfred successively confronting and rejecting the Chamois Hunter, the Witch of the Alps, Arimanes, and the Abbot of St. Maurice—the representatives of democratic humanitarianism, natural transcendentalism, Manichaean fatalism, and orthodox Christianity. Having one by one rejected these symbols of established faiths, the hero goes on, in the final act, to defy the grim Mephistophelian apparition who arises to claim him as his own and who represents, if I am not mistaken, the figure of the Byronic hero himself—the persona on whom the poet compulsively relied but who was in danger, as Byron surely if only unconsciously realized, of engrossing his creator.[30] In the end Manfred dies; but the death is a symbolic one that permits Byron to go on to write *Don Juan.*

No major work of the nineteenth century better illustrates Romantic irony—that quality of indeterminacy—than *Don Juan.* It is, to begin with, in the phrase of one critic "calculatedly formless."[31] Or, to look at it from the opposite point of view, it is a brilliantly anachronistic fusion of a variety of forms, epic and novel, verse satire and romance, lyric drama and epistle. It is "in every sense inconclusive."[32] Its proportions are infinitely elastic. Byron took it up and put it down with equal ease, and it is hard, despite his temptation to finish his hero off in hell or its equivalent, an unhappy marriage, to imagine for the poem any termination. It could go on endlessly. Moreover the work illustrates the attribute that Lady Blessington, among others, saw as an ingrained part of the poet's nature, his "mobility."[33] "I have heard him assert opinions one day, and maintain the most opposite, with equal warmth, the day after, " she wrote; "this arises not so much from insincerity, as from being wholly governed by the feeling of the moment: he has no fixed principle of conduct or of thought." "Now, if I know myself," she goes on to quote him, in a statement that is the counterpart of Keats's declaration that the poet "has no Identity" (I.387), "I should say, that I have no character at all."[34] In *Don Juan,* Byron devised the ideal means for indulging his mobility of character, a work that permitted him to be, as he put it, "a little quietly facetious upon every thing."[35] Parts of the poem, it is true, can be read as satire upon contemporary abuses. Throughout, however, Byron plays one mood or attitude off against another. What we have is a work in which each position, philosophic or emotional, ironizes every other. What emerges as its final value is the spirit of mobility or irony itself, seen as a governing principle of life. As Byron wrote to Douglas Kinnaird in a passage that seems best to express the evaluation he placed on it: "confess, confess—you dog . . . is it not *life, is it not the thing?*"[36]

Pausing to look back at the distance we have come with the concept of Romantic irony, developed, as it has been, with relation to three such different poets, one can readily see a need for further discriminations. One major distinction to be drawn between, say, Keats and Byron is the degree to which such irony is deliberate or self-conscious. As I have argued, the kind of irony that manifests itself in Keats arises spontaneously and unconsciously, largely through the experience of change or contradiction, and rarely if ever

(*Lamia* may be an exception) becomes an intentional principle of structure or meaning. At the risk of multiplying distinctions, I am tempted to refer to it as proto-Romantic irony.[37] In Byron, on the other hand, and more particularly in *Don Juan*, we encounter an irony that is largely conscious and deliberate and that consequently is much closer to the theory or theories of Romantic irony as they have been traditionally formulated. Between these two extremes fall sections of Byron's earlier work and much of Shelley's, about which there exist, as we have partly seen, questions of intention that are, as I have argued, not merely of hypothetical interest but that remain ultimately crucial to interpretation.

V

By way of concluding an essay that has been, of necessity, largely theoretic, let me add a final hypothesis by proposing that during the Victorian period in England Romantic irony goes underground to reemerge very powerfully in this century in the novel. In saying that such irony went underground, I do not mean to imply, of course, that it disappeared from Victorian awareness. Indeed nothing accounts so much for Byron's decline, his eclipse by Wordsworth early in the Victorian period, than the realization of many writers and thinkers of the particular dangers he presented. Carlyle's famous directive, "Close thy *Byron*: open thy *Goethe*,"[38] summed up the conviction that Byron had eloquently expressed the disillusionment of the post-Enlightenment world but that he lacked affirmative value, that he was a poet without vision, without constructive thought. Arnold, similarly, celebrated the poet's ability to make men feel, but found it secondary to "Wordsworth's healing power."[39] Arnold's adaptation of Goethe's comment, "The moment he reflects, he is a child,"[40] as a final judgment on the poet must be taken, after a point, to mean principally that Byron did not think in ways Arnold approved. As for the Victorian poets who were approved (including, with reservations, Arnold himself), they were, as E. D. H. Johnson has shown,[41] largely committed to the perpetuation of an affirmative public vision which permitted private doubts and misgivings to emerge only in curiously refracted ways.

In England Romantic irony reemerges very powerfully in this century, as I have said, within the novel. By way of example, there is space only to examine some relatively neglected aspects of the ending of D. H. Lawrence's greatest novel, *Women in Love*. It will be recalled that in the closing chapters the two pairs of lovers, Gudrun and Gerald, Ursula and Birkin, make their escape from England to a resort high in the Alps where Gudrun momentarily begins to feel a new sense of elation and release. "But even as she lay in fictitious transport," Lawrence tells us, "bathed in the strange, false sunshine of hope in life, something seemed to snap in her, and a terrible cynicism began to gain upon her, blowing in like a wind. Everything turned to irony with her: the last flavour of everything was ironical. When she felt her pang of undeniable reality, this was when she knew the hard irony of hopes and ideas."[42] It is at this point that Gudrun begins to exchange Gerald as her lover for Herr Loerke, one of Lawrence's most fascinating creations, a gnomelike creature, "a little obscene monster of the darkness," living "like a rat in the river of corruption, just where it falls over into the bottomless pit," a "gnawing little negation, gnawing at the roots of life" (pp. 418–19). It is Loerke who now takes over from Gerald, supplying her with all "the subtle thrills of extreme sensation in reduction . . . , the obscene religious mystery of ultimate reduction . . . disintegrating the vital organic body of life" (pp. 442–43). As the novel puts it very simply, "There was no going beyond him" (p. 418). One recalls, too, their diversions, how they "played with the past, and with the great figures of the past, a sort of little game of chess, or marionettes, all to please themselves. They had all the great men for their marionettes, and they two were the God of the show, working it all" (p. 444). One recalls their favorite mode of communication, talking, like giddy comparatists, "in a mixture of languages."

The ground-work was French, in either case. But he ended most of his sentences in a stumble of English and a conclusion of German, she skilfully wove herself to her end in whatever phrase came to her. She took a peculiar delight in this conversation. It was full of odd, fantastic expression, of double meanings, of evasions, of suggestive vagueness. It was a real physical pleasure to her to make this thread of conversation out of the different-coloured strands of three languages. (P. 445)

Is it not significant amid these games, this "sentimental, childish delight in the achieved perfections of the past," that Lawrence tells us that "particularly they liked the late eighteenth century, the period of Goethe and of Shelley, and Mozart" (p. 444)?

For the ending of Lawrence's novel distils, in its fullest manifestation, an awareness of irony that had for long been growing latently and in various degrees of consciousness among the poets I have earlier discussed. Only in Lawrence the whole process has achieved a radical degree of consciousness and moral awareness. The cold wind that blows through Gudrun's soul is the beginning of Law-

rence's terrifying image of a world "Snowed Up" and frozen, a world
that has been entirely ironized. One need only turn to a passage that
describes Gudrun near the end of the novel to see the way in which
Lawrence's major image of the snow takes on the peculiar characteristics of that kind of indeterminacy I have earlier described.

In the afternoon she had to go out with Loerke. Her tomorrow was perfectly
vague before her. This was what gave her pleasure. She might be going to
England with Gerald, she might be going to Dresden with Loerke, she
might be going to Munich, to a girl-friend she had there. Anything might
come to pass on the morrow. And to-day was the white, snowy iridescent
threshold of all possibility. All possibility—that was the charm to her, the
lovely, iridescent, indefinite charm—pure illusion. All possibility—because
death was inevitable, and *nothing* was possible but death.   (P. 459)

"Pure illusion. All possibility—because death was inevitable, and
nothing was possible but death": the concluding sentences, vibrant
with paradox, strike us today as banal, even trite. Yet, within the
context of Lawrence's fiction, they possess a genuine power, just as
his perception of ultimate indeterminacy lies at the heart of his
view of the paralyzing neurosis of modern civilization. If the kind
of paradox he depicts seems so familiar, such a part of our everyday
awareness, it is because it has come into full consciousness through
time. Needless to say, Lawrence's insight stems from a multitude of
sources, just as his novel, beginning as a criticism of English society, culminates in an indictment of the whole of European culture.
In representing irony above all as a mood, a mood of ultimately
engulfing enervation and estrangement, however, he was developing a perception that has its roots, or at least a major part of them,
in the poets of the Romantic period.

NOTES

1. This essay was originally delivered in an earlier form as a lecture sponsored by
the Department of English at the University of Wisconsin on 11 February 1974.

2. See, for example, Irving Babbitt's chapter on Romantic irony in his influential
Rousseau and Romanticism (Boston: Houghton Mifflin, 1919) and Morton L. Gure-
witch's unpublished Columbia University Ph.D. dissertation, "European Romantic
Irony," University Microfilms, 17 (Ann Arbor, 1957). By far my greatest debt is to D.
C. Muecke's learned and urbane *The Compass of Irony* (London: Methuen, 1969)
which discusses Romantic irony illuminatingly within a broadly comparatist framework. "Romantic Irony," he writes, "is a fusion of Romanticism and irony, in which
what is Romantic cannot be understood without a new concept of irony and what is
ironic cannot be understood without a much deeper and more complex understand-

ing of Romanticism" (p. 181). Muecke derives Romantic irony from an awareness of, but more narrowly as a self-conscious reaction to, the existence of "General Irony"— the sense that life itself is fundamentally paradoxical or contradictory (see note 4 below). Hence, while he begins from a broader definition of Romantic irony, he falls back, quite naturally, perhaps, as his discussion proceeds, on a more traditional and Germanic formulation. Thus he writes that "in England, excepting always the Germanists, Romantic Irony is almost unknown" (p. 184); and again, "behind the theory of Romantic Irony is the subjective idealism of Fichte" (p. 191). It is a contention of this essay that in England Romantic irony enjoys its own peculiar kind of evolution, one that, especially in its genesis, must be studied on its own terms, but which, none the less, possesses essential affinities with the broader definition that Muecke and others have encouraged.

3. It seems to me that "Resolution and Independence" exhibits the kind of irony this essay seeks to define. Most of Wordsworth's late verse, however, does not.

4. At this point one runs into the objections of colleagues who argue that irony must be conscious and intentional (and therefore a device), that the term loses all meaning when applied vaguely to any reaction to human experience. In rebuttal, I draw support from Muecke's distinction between "specific" or "corrective" irony and "General Irony"—"'life itself or any general aspect of life seen as fundamentally and inescapably an ironic state of affairs"—which "characterizes (though it is not confined to) the modern period and more particularly the last two hundred years" (pp. 120, 123). The distinction is echoed and reinforced by Wayne Booth in his insistence on the crucial discrimination between "stable" and "unstable" irony throughout his recent *Rhetoric of Irony* (Chicago: University of Chicago Press, 1974). While the two kinds can and need to be distinguished, however, it is in practice often difficult to do so, especially in the Romantic period when poets relied more than ever before on the processes of composition for the groundwork of ideology. All irony involves us inescapably with life but never more than in the literature of Romanticism, where fundamental ironies arise not through the juxtaposing of positions already foreseen but through an earnest encounter with the unexpected. Hence in my assertion above that Romantic irony is a realization that "arises . . . in part unconsciously," the phrase "in part" is not a mere escape hatch, for I am seeking to discriminate precisely that point at which states of realization that are only latent or subliminal pass over into conscious recognition, often during the process of composition itself. Hence, too, my later and somewhat awkward distinction between a latent or "proto-Romantic" irony and a Romantic irony that is more conscious of itself. The point is that between the historical prevalence of specific or corrective irony and the whole line of development that leads up to the all-pervading ironies of Beckett and Genet, a development, in Kierkegaard's phrase, toward "absolute infinite negativity" and which that philosopher, from his standpoint in Hegel, foresaw in *The Concept of Irony* (1841) with a loathing close to physical nausea, there are innumerable gradations. It is a historical evolution of consciousness in which the literature of English Romanticism deserves to be studied as a major turning point.

5. Wayne Booth has observed (p. 269) that "the ironic Socrates" of Plato is "perhaps the best schoolmaster for reading supreme ironies," and he ends his final chapter on "Infinite Instabilities" with a consideration of Socrates.

6. *The Letters of John Keats, 1814–1821,* ed. Hyder Edward Rollins (Cambridge, Mass.: Harvard University Press, 1958), II, 80. References by volume and page number to this edition are hereafter included in the text.

7. "Epistle to John Hamilton Reynolds," lines 72–82. Quotations from Keats's

poetry are from *John Keats: Selected Poems and Letters,* ed. Douglas Bush (Boston: Houghton Mifflin, 1959), hereafter cited in the text.

8. It is, perhaps, a moot point to what degree the dreamer's drinking the draught represents, as Brian Wicker has argued ("The Disputed Lines in *The Fall of Hyperion,*" *Essays in Criticism,* 7 [1957], 39), a sacramental and therefore necessary communion with the past and to what degree it constitutes, as I have argued (*Keats the Poet* [Princeton: Princeton University Press, 1973], pp. 314–16, 318–21), an act of transgression analogous to original sin. Different though they may be in emphasis, the two readings do not seem to me in the end mutually exclusive. It is notable that the most recent study of the two *Hyperions,* Geoffrey Hartman's "Spectral Symbolism and the Authorial Self: An Approach to Keats's *Hyperion,*" *Essays in Criticism,* 24 (1974), 1–19, sees the whole venture proceeding out of the theme of trespass and profanation.

9. See Bush's note to 1.187–210.

10. *The Romantic Comedy* (London: Oxford University Press, 1948), p. 150.

11. These general conclusions have been reinforced by the most formidable of recent students of Shelley's thought, the late Earl Wasserman, in his *Shelley: A Critical Reading* (Baltimore: Johns Hopkins University Press, 1971).

12. Preface to *Prometheus Unbound,* in *The Complete Poetical Works of Percy Bysshe Shelley,* ed. Thomas Hutchinson (London: Oxford University Press, 1945), p. 207. Quotations from Shelley's poetry are from this edition and are cited in the text.

13. Dedication to *The Cenci,* Hutchinson, p. 275.

14. See Wasserman's discussion of *Alastor* at the opening of *Shelley: A Critical Reading,* pp. 3–46.

15. This kind of irony is, indeed, closer to the conception developed within the various apothegms of Friedrich Schlegel which visualizes the artist as both involved in and withdrawn from his creation, aware of the contradictions of his vision but transcending them.

16. As Booth has written: "In reading any irony worth bothering about, we read life itself, and we work on our relations to others as they deal with it. We read character and value, we refer to our deepest convictions" (pp. 43–44). Much of his book is concerned to demonstrate the real complexity of judgments about irony—its presence or absence, its quality, its limits—that we ordinarily overlook or take for granted.

17. Muecke, p. 171.

18. This essay was completed before the appearance of Richard Holmes's *Shelley: The Pursuit* (London: Weidenfeld and Nicolson, 1974).

19. Matthew Arnold, "Shelley," *Essays in Criticism, Second Series* (London: Macmillan, 1902), pp. 213, 249–52.

20. The distinction is emphasized throughout Carlos Baker's invaluable *Shelley's Major Poetry: The Fabric of a Vision* (Princeton: Princeton University Press, 1948).

21. It is notable that Wasserman discusses neither work in his *Shelley: A Critical Reading.* The question comes to mind: If Shelley's grasp of the situation of the *Alastor* poet was as complete and self-assured as Wasserman's exegesis of the poem implies, why did Shelley keep returning to it in his later verse?

22. *Mythology and The Romantic Tradition in English Poetry,* rev. ed. (Cambridge, Mass: Harvard University Press, 1969), pp. 139–40.

23. *Shelley's Mythmaking* (New Haven: Yale University Press, 1959), p. 204.

24. For *The Triumph* textual citations are to the edition of Donald H. Reiman in

Shelley's "The Triumph of Life": A Critical Study (Urbana, Illinois: University of Illinois Press, 1965).

25. "A Dialogue of Self and Soul," *The Variorum Edition of the Poems of W. B. Yeats,* ed. Peter Allt and Russell K. Alspach (New York: Macmillan, 1965), pp. 478–79.

26. See the last chapter of James Rieger's *The Mutiny Within: The Heresies of Percy Bysshe Shelley* (New York: George Braziller, 1967) which, partly through a study of the accounts of the foundering of the *Don Juan,* pushes the case as far as it will go.

27. *The Visionary Company* (New York: Doubleday, 1961), p. 343.

28. *PMLA,* 66 (1951); rpt. in *The Triumph of Romanticism* (Columbia, S.C.: University of South Carolina Press, 1970). Page references to the latter edition are included in the text. I think it fair to take issue with Peckham's essay of 1950 even though his early views of Romanticism have undergone changes. His later essay, "Toward a Theory of Romanticism: II. Reconsiderations" (1960), does not significantly modify his view of Byron. Peckham republished both essays in his 1970 collection and in his preface invited readers, in the spirit of Socrates, to argue against him wherever they found it useful.

29. Dedication to "The Ghost of Abel."

30. See my essay, "Byron and the Meaning of 'Manfred,' " *Criticism,* 16 (1974), 189–202.

31. Brian Wilkie, *Romantic Poets and Epic Tradition* (Madison, Wis.: University of Wisconsin Press, 1965), p. 189.

32. Wilkie, p. 211.

33. Byron appears to have adopted the word, which he uses in *Don Juan* (16.97), from Madame de Staël. See his remarks on the term, which he defines in his note to the poem as "an excessive susceptibility of immediate impressions—at the same time without *losing* the past, . . . a most painful and unhappy attribute" (Byron's italics). See also George M. Ridenour's discussion in *The Style of Don Juan* (New Haven: Yale University Press, 1960), pp. 162–66.

34. *Lady Blessington's Conversations of Lord Byron,* ed. Ernest J. Lovell, Jr. (Princeton: Princeton University Press, 1969), pp. 195, 220.

35. *The Works of Lord Byron: Letters and Journals,* ed. Rowland E. Prothero (London: John Murray, 1898–1901), IV, 260.

36. Letter of 26 October 1819 to Douglas Kinnaird as quoted by Leslie Marchand, with corrections and omissions supplied, in *Byron* (New York: Alfred A. Knopf, 1957), II, 823–24 (Byron's italics).

37. One problem is that Muecke has appropriated the term to describe that deliberate disruption of artistic illusion (through authorial intrusion, intentional anachronism, and other Shandeyisms) so dear to the hearts of Germanists and which some of them are wont to take as Romantic irony itself. Once again one admires the aptness of Muecke's reasoning and his concern to discriminate between various states of consciousness, even while one seeks a broader application of his terms. "The term 'proto-Romantic Irony,' " he writes, "is intended also to suggest an historical development. The so-called destruction of artistic illusion or the entrance of an author into his work even when it is done ironically is only a step in the direction of Romantic Irony, but the artistic attitude and awareness that makes such a step possible is also a prerequisite of Romantic Irony" (pp. 164–65). There is little in Muecke to suggest that such a definition might include the effect and subsequent realization created by Keats's awkward, unwilling intervention near the end of the last book of *Endymion* (4.770 ff.) to confess that his poem is working out in a way quite different from any he had foreseen.

38. *Sartor Resartus.* See *Byron: The Critical Heritage,* ed. Andrew Rutherford (London: Routledge & Kegan Paul, 1970), p. 294.

39. "Memorial Verses," Rutherford, p. 441.

40. Essay on Byron reprinted in *Essays in Criticism: Second Series,* Rutherford, p. 452.

41. *The Alien Vision of Victorian Poetry* (Princeton: Princeton University Press, 1952).

42. D. H. Lawrence, *Women in Love* (New York: Viking Press, Viking Compass ed., 1960), p. 408. Page references are hereafter included within the text.

WALTER H. EVERT

Coadjutors of Oppression:
A Romantic and Modern Theory of Evil

I wish to discuss the effects on literature of a general theory of evil
that seems to me peculiarly a constituent of the modern mind. Indeed, one might more properly speak of the modern *consciousness,*
as the notion is not so much an idea held *in* the mind as it is a
postulate of thought or a structural component of our modern moral
despair. Briefly stated, it would go something like this: The nature
of absolute evil is not the opposition of a counterforce to good
which strives to overcome the good in equal combat, nor is it the
attrition of the good through nature's decay or the infirmity of human will, and least of all is it the result of a primordial catastrophe
that drove the gods into the sky and left man with his faculties
impaired or incomplete. The nature of absolute evil is the insidious
and inevitable corruption of good *into* evil, a corruption that is
successful precisely in proportion to the real purity of the good. We
shall consider subdivisions and modifications presently, but this is
the essence.

It may be presumptuous to call this a "theory" of evil, as I am not
aware of anyone's having given it theoretical definition. The nearest
that one can come is perhaps the Hegelian dialectic, which is essentially concerned with process rather than value, or with process *as*
value, and the application of it by Marx and Engels to an economic
system that they thought had been mistaken for a good or was an
actual good only to the entrepreneurial class, and therefore was not
a true human good at all. Lacking theoretical formulation, we might
best verify the existence of the idea by listening to the *discordia
concors* of some curiously blended modern voices.

Psychology, whose righteous task it is to free man to grow in wisdom and
sacred pleasure, has increasingly sought instead to subdue him to efficient
social routines. To implement the goals of the state it serves through control
of the apparatus of conditioning, psychology has become more and more a
science of social control . . . to curb man's impulse toward freedom and
pleasure.   (Timothy Leary)[1]

The injustice and violence of men in a state of society, produced the demand for government. . . . Government was intended to suppress injustice, but it offers new occasions and temptations for the commission of it. By concentrating the force of the community, it gives occasion to wild projects of calamity, to oppression, despotism, war, and conquest. By perpetuating and aggravating the inequality of property, it fosters many injurious passions, and excites men to the practice of robbery and fraud. Government was intended to suppress injustice, but its effect has been to embody and perpetuate it.   (William Godwin)[2]

I have felt the godlike power man derives from his machines. . . . But I have seen the science I worshiped and the aircraft I loved destroying the civilization I expected them to serve.   (Charles A. Lindbergh)[3]

Detached from the rest of life, the scientific ego becomes automatic; and automatons cannot give provident directions to other automatons. This perhaps explains why, though one part of our culture, that dominated by science and technics, has reached the highest point ever . . . the rest of our existence is falling into planless confusion, directed toward life-negating and irrational goals. . . . [Science is] so committed to answering only [a] limited range of questions . . . that it lacks the saving intelligence to turn off its own compulsive mechanism, even though it is pushing science as well as civilization to its own doom.   (Lewis Mumford)[4]

The study of human nature suggests this awful truth, that . . . sin and crime are apt to start from their very opposite qualities.
                                                    (William Wordsworth)[5]

Because it is not directly to the point, I have not included in this chorus the remark of Allen Ginsberg, who clearly felt the same anxiety when, asked a few years ago on a television talk show how he would correct the world's evils, unhesitatingly replied, "Put all the metal back underground." This is of course the radical pastoral solution, that primitivist bias that sees all human artificers as having mistaken the good, and, in their artifices, having warped man away from his natural identity. Though its ghostly parents are in Hesiod and Genesis and the whole pastoral tradition in the arts, the bellwether for modern history is probably Shaftesbury, of whom nothing is more characteristic than the invariable synonymy in his writings of the words "vicious," "corrupt," and "unnatural."

The most influential writer in this vein, if not the best understood, was of course Jean-Jacques Rousseau. As it happens, he was also the earliest in the modern era of whom I am aware who made a specific commentary on the moral idea we are considering. For the record's sake, let us recall that in 1750 Rousseau won the prize offered by the Academy of Dijon for an essay on the question: *Si le rétablissement des Sciences et des Arts a contribué à épurer les moeurs*. Whether as the result of an "illumination" under a tree in Vincennes, as Rousseau later claimed, or at the suggestion of Diderot, whom he was on the way to visit when he read the announcement of the prize contest, and on whose behalf credit was later claimed, Rousseau chose to argue the negative side of the question. His position did not rest simply in the denial that the arts and sciences had improved morals[6] but affirmed that both personal and public morality degenerated in proportion as the arts and sciences flourished, and that this truth not only was demonstrable in the current state of Europe but could be validated historically by analysis of every great civilization that had fallen into ruin. To a modern reader who does not approach it reverently the essay is a masterpiece of *post hoc ergo propter hoc* argument, liberally salted with flattery of the judges as uniquely immune to the occupational risks of their trades. While polemicists, from that day to this, have often given Rousseau less than his moral due, one must say that, as argument, the essay would convince a strict logician of nothing but that Rousseau was not a strict logician. One must infer that it won the prize chiefly for its novelty and audacity in challenging the greatest of civilization's supposed goods as in fact the sources of its evils. As I have not been trained in the philosophic disciplines, however, and may be giving offense to those who have been, let us simply note that the first major work of one of the most influential ethical writers of his time enunciated, on the broadest possible scale, the evil-out-of-good hypothesis.

Any attempt to trace Rousseau's direct influence on the English Romantic writers is a vexation of spirit. It comes to mind, of course, that Shelley uses him ambiguously (to the extent that an unfinished poem is necessarily indeterminate) in *The Triumph of Life,* and Blake excoriates him in the unlikely company of Voltaire and, in *Jerusalem,* of the rationalists of every stripe. In recent scholarly writing about the English Romantics (since about, say, World War II), however, it is rare to find Rousseau treated at more than occasional footnote length. Even Irving Babbitt, of an earlier and more influence-oriented time, tended to find affinities, rather than direct lines of force, between Rousseau and his creative successors in England. One might fall back, without apology, on *Zeitgeist,* or on Coleridge's dictum that there are such things as fountains in the world, though there are more tangible possibilities. William Godwin, for example, acknowledged his intellectual indebtedness to Rousseau in the preface to *Political Justice,* and there is no major

English poet, from Blake to Byron, who did not know Godwin or his works. We have already seen Godwin's use of the evil-out-of-good idea as applied to the tendency of government to misdirect the massed moral force of the community which is vested in it, and this orientation appears not only throughout *Political Justice*, but explicitly in *Caleb Williams:* "Wealth and despotism easily know how to engage those laws as the coadjutors of their oppression which were perhaps at first intended [witless and miserable precaution!] for the safeguards of the poor."[7] Godwin's emphasis in his comments on government falls on the propensity of evil people to abuse a good, and this is the most common fictional form of the dilemma: evil is a parasite that converts the good to its own substance through a process of what one might (revoltingly) call social digestion. The anomaly is seen more "purely" in the novel's larger narrative structure, chiefly involving Falkland and Williams, both of whom bring about their own downfalls, as do several minor characters, and commit self-confessed evil deeds precisely because of their unwavering commitments to the highest moral principles that either can conceive. That these may be in turn mere rationalizations of pride, aggressiveness, and a sense of social vulnerability is a possibility that Godwin frequently tantalizes us with, but the ambiguities of the novel's final confrontation scene provide no answers and even suggest that Godwin was himself adrift. However that may be, his work is permeated with that sense of self-generating erosion that found its first denunciation in Rousseau's attack on the highest achievements of human intellect.[8]

No certain line of transmission being ascertainable, either directly from Rousseau or through disciples in England, let us simply recognize that we are dealing with a wretched idea whose time had come and then look at some of the ways it found literary expression. We have heard Wordsworth speak (above) of the tendency of evil to originate in its opposite, though the play supposed to embody that insight is more in the *Othello* vein, showing the evil that good men are tempted to by misinformation. More to the immediate point, in Wordsworth's major poetry, is the story of *Michael*. Two criticisms of the poem that one frequently hears are that Michael seems more concerned with his property than with his progeny and that the rapid disintegration of Luke's moral character in the city, after his nurture into young manhood in ideal Wordsworthian conditions, unwittingly reveals how tenuous even in the poet's mind were the principles upon which he had built his epistemology. Such ad hominem criticism misses Wordsworth's own center. For the first, the relationship between the transmission of love and of property, as that is to be understood for the reading of Michael's (not Wordsworth's) character, is given in lines 361–82. From generation to generation the property is improved and increasingly secured, not for the sole sake of gain but as an embodiment of love. In each generation the love and the land pass *from* those who had them to give, *through* the currently vital possessors, *to* those who are to receive them as the gift of no merit but the love principle alone. Break the chain at any point and both love and land lose their meaning. Rightly or wrongly, and the old shepherd himself has doubts, love is the investment of our lives in one another, and we must take the risks that go with it. A proper answer to the second objection, concerning the poet's tacit acknowledgment of sandy foundations under his philosophy, would be allied to the first in that it simply isn't what the poem is about. The poem is not *about* a system of natural education, it *is* a tragedy in which the pastoral world is brought to the level of high seriousness that one finds in, say, *King Lear*. And the tragedy is not Luke's but Michael's, the son being a necessary narrative adjunct of the father. If it is not contemptible at any human or philosophical level for Cordelia to be merely an instrumentality in the old king's catastrophe, then neither is it a failure of Wordsworth's philosophy or humanity for Luke to play that role in the old shepherd's tragedy. And the tragedy has its roots in the lines mentioned above which express the highest synthesis of experiential value that Michael (and not necessarily Wordsworth) could conceive. Had Michael been less good, aspired to less for those he loved, he could have lived out his life in comfortable retirement. What the poem is *about* (among other things) is the last, worst irony of human life, that we inherit evil only to the measure of goodness in our aspirations.

One thinks spontaneously here of Keats, of the great "Ode on Melancholy," the derivative but, well, Keatsian "Fill for me a brimming bowl," and so much else that treats of comparable anomalies. In my heart of hearts, however, I would rather tell a truth than make a case; and Keats seems to me so much a poet of reconciliation and acceptance, so much more committed to the realities of process than to the security of norms, that I must make him an honorable exception to this pessimistic company.

The pervasiveness of any idea is of course often shown best at levels other than the highest. If we move from the sublime of poetry to the sensationalism of the Gothic novel, we may find perhaps the clearest treatment of the evil-out-of-good theme, as we find the most extreme of all tendencies, in M. G. Lewis's *Monk*. By "clearest" I mean that perception of evil as *necessarily* growing out of good. But there are two relevant levels of vulnerability in the novel, one having to do with the initial fall and the other with its consequences. To take the latter first, one might observe that, while the increasingly horrible crimes that Ambrosio commits are fueled by the familiar passions and appetites insufficiently governed, there is more than a hint that his insatiability in depravity is a function of his earlier abstinence. Had he dealt in the small change of debauchery, as ordinary men do, he would not have been so susceptible to the novelty of his temptations and the accumulated power of his dammed-up passions. But this is, as it were, the Newtonian dimension, having to do with the measure of psychic masses and forces. The fall itself is purely qualitative, effected through Ambrosio's piety and humanity and the visible symbol of their mediatrix. His compassion for the youthful novice Rosario and his abstract love of the principles represented by the Blessed Virgin create a momentum toward his fall that is irresistible when Rosario proves in fact to be a woman, and the mirror image of the Virgin's portrait that Ambrosio venerates in his cell. The human weakness of loving the good too much in its human form was predicated (as an impossibility for himself) by Ambrosio at an earlier time, and was predicted for him by Agnes when Ambrosio exposed *her* weakness to human temptation. But the anterior weakness, of which the sexual fall is perhaps only emblematic, is the sin of pride. We have seen the private Ambrosio taking satisfaction in his virtuous superiority to other men. This of course makes him vulnerable to the flattery of "Rosario" and destines him for that fall before which pride goeth. And how could it be humanly otherwise, short of an unconsciousness of his own virtue wholly inconsistent with the intellectual qualities that make him so effective a preacher and teacher? As canny old Ben Franklin said, pride is the hardest vice to root out of the heart because, supposing it to be possible, we should then no doubt be proud of our hard-won humility. The credibility of the novel depends, then, to the extent that we are willing to accept the grotesque as a possible paradigm of reality, upon our ability to see the peril, and the almost inevitable defeat, in reaching beyond the normal bar to human perfectibility. If *Measure for Measure* comes to mind (and I certainly don't wish to make any absurd comparisons, even with a textually flawed play), one might observe that Shakespeare works within the security of a generally acknowledged theology, while Lewis dares hand-to-hand combat with the devil we know in our fantasies and fingers-ends. He seems to have lost, for the most part, but his risk is revelatory.

Mary Shelley's *Frankenstein* takes a harder look at some of the same problems. Again, we have aspiration toward the highest good as the motivation of both Dr. Frankenstein and Walton, his alter ego in the framing story. They differ from Lewis's monk in that the good they mean to do is not conceived as an extension of personal perfection but rather as a hoped-for consequence of submitting themselves to such hazards as exploration of the unknown may require. Where Ambrosio moves confidently into the farthest reaches of what he thinks he knows, only to discover that he does not know enough, Walton and Frankenstein risk their lives (and, we are to understand, their souls) in extending for the common good the limits of the known. Frankenstein discovers that he knows too much, but the novel takes no simplistic view of the retribution that is visited upon those who usurp divine prerogatives. Frankenstein's problem is like that of science in general, as characterized, above, by Lewis Mumford. He demonstrably knows everything there is to know in his field of scientific inquiry, but he does not know how to predict or control the consequences of his success; the good he seeks becomes evil in the execution because, as Mumford says in our contemporary context, he asks questions within too limited a range. At a higher level, however, his failure is not of knowledge but of humanity. We are given every reason to believe that the monster has naturally amiable social instincts that are warped toward violence by the treatment he receives. And that treatment begins in his first moment of life when he is rejected by his creator only because he has not been fashioned as more beautiful by that creator. The climactic event is of course Frankenstein's refusal to create a mate-companion for the monster, ignoring in the name of human good a human need for the fellowship of kind that is thematically introduced into the novel in its opening pages and played upon throughout. In these and other failures of sympathy Dr. Frankenstein is shown to be, for all his brilliance, less than fully human, and therefore himself a monster or an automaton. Although there are many other strands in the novel, the verdict on this one would have to be that the good is not so much turned to evil as it is insufficiently good in the first place. Had it been otherwise, the monster's natural goodness would have remained uncorrupted. The normative foil to Frankenstein in this mode is Walton, who gives up his own quest so as not to endanger the lives of his crew. Though he calls this decision cowardly, he clearly feels that the greatest good of the greatest number in an unknowable posterity cannot justify the sacrifice of his living companions. In this he substitutes a proximate and tangible good for an ideal conception of the good, the failure of his vision becoming the triumph of his humanity.

   The dilemma is probably seen in its most Romantic form in the Byronic hero. While not wishing to claim philosophic subtlety for a poet who did not claim it for himself, I would yet suggest, despite the unsystematic character of his thought and the arrogance of his personal style (both of which have worked against him in the critical academy), that Byron does represent the Romantic, and human, anomaly in something like its quintessential form. The persona of *Childe Harold's* third canto, or, more strictly, the narrative voice, since it is often unclear whether Byron, Harold, or a disembodied wisdom is the momentary proprietor of the feelings expressed, is alienated from his kind because of a personally felt mental and moral superiority to the human mass. We tolerate this solipsistic prig because he often moves us, willy-nilly, but we also find him periodically jejune or petulant.

   It is another matter, I think, when we come to *Manfred,* that most Shelleyan drama of spirit voices, anthropomorphized cosmic forces, and the epipsyche disastrously found, and that most Byronic drama of self-beatifying catastrophe resulting from greater gifts and higher aspirations than are common among us.[9] Quite apart from our preconceptions about the Byronic hero and Byronic self-dramatization, if we are to enter into the play's world we must accept Manfred's powers at their demonstrated level of reality. He *is* superior to us in knowledge and in the means to act upon it, and superiority is a mode of difference. Such a person will aspire to fulfillments that cannot be conceived by our more limited imaginations and will be constrained far less than we by prudential timidities. It may well be true, as Sperry says, that the writing of the play was for Byron a form of self-confrontation—every work of art must grow out of the artist's inner experience in some way.[10] But to have meaning for *us* it must have some more general human application, must be related in some way to the lives *we* live and not simply to the one that *he* lived. Given that we cannot call spirits from the vasty deep, each of us, with one misfortunate exception, is inevitably superior to, and therefore is in that way different from, *someone* and probably many others. But we also share the common limitations of earthboundness, mortality, and social interdependence. The questions raised for us by Byron's play, however he himself resolved them, have to do with such things as the permissible limits of individual autonomy and the penalties one will almost surely pay, as well as those one ought not be asked to pay, for being different. The play itself seems to demand the highest degree of individual liberty as its ultimate good, at least for those who feel within themselves the ability and desire to be different. And yet the play is a tragedy

whose hero, in the execution of that good, lives in perpetual torment over the knowledge that in his self-assertion he has killed the
thing he loved. Desiring the greatest good, to act with godlike freedom, he ends up lost to the world, his extraordinary powers use-
less, imprisoned within himself through his inescapable self-consciousness. Given the ultimate sterility of that perception, indeed
"'tis not so difficult to die."

I have so far introduced examples of our theme as treated by
several authors in various genres, not for the sake of explicating
complex works in terms of one reductive formula but rather to indicate through selected examples the pervasiveness of the idea in the
collective artistic consciousness of the time. I should like to give
somewhat more extended attention, however, to two works that
have eluded critical consensus and in which I think it possible that
this theory of evil played a controlling role, Coleridge's "Christabel" and Shelley's *Cenci*.

"Christabel" may have been headed in any of the two-and-
twenty directions conjectured for it by its critics; it is virtually impossible to "prove" from the poem's evidence that any direction of
inquiry is mistaken. Unfinished poems that deal with undefined
supernatural forces do not lend themselves to definitive statement,
and it is with the humility enforced by that fact that I make my own
tentative bid. I begin with a single observation: While we have
seen in other works the mistaken identification of a good, or the
identification of an ideal good that could not be domesticated to the
world of our mortality, the good is concrete and actual in "Christabel." The title character herself is good and acts upon her good
impulses. Her father is restored to a magnanimity that he has not
felt for many years. The castle has been blessed, and the good angel
who is Christabel's departed mother gives her daughter spiritual
protection. And yet, at the point where the poem now ends, Christabel has been visibly tainted by some evil, and the mutual love of
parent and child have been turned into a recriminatory bitterness
that is on its way to becoming hatred. How could that possibly
have come about?

The only real evidence we have to work with is the text of the
poem itself. We know one thing, that in the person of Geraldine a
corrupting evil has been introduced into this peaceful setting. Many
attempts have been made to identify the specific kind of evil that
she represents, but, as nothing can be proved that does not depend
upon the speculative frame of reference, I accept the possibility that
Coleridge left her undefined because he was not dealing with les-
bian seduction or the Doctrine of Atonement or any other specific

allegory but meant us to look directly at the problem of evil as a profound dilemma of human experience.[11] And there is one other thing that we know from the poem: Geraldine's power to sow corruption and hatred depends entirely upon the propensities to goodness in her victims. She systematically uses their virtue to accomplish her ends.

This is done in four stages, during the first three of which Geraldine seems powerless to act without Christabel's aid. The first incident is of course Christabel's midnight discovery of the strange and beautiful lady. She is frightened, but, instead of fleeing to save herself, she calls upon the Virgin for protection and stays to discover who the unfortunate lady may be. The very first thing Geraldine says to her is that she is almost too weary even to speak (and so to do anything more strenuous), and she begs Christabel, "Stretch forth thy hand" (75).[12] Without interruption she goes on to tell the story of her kidnapping and concludes with the same request, "Stretch forth thy hand (thus ended she), / And help a wretched maid to flee" (102–03). And immediately, "Then Christabel stretched forth her hand" (104). The poet's unusual emphasis in beginning and ending Geraldine's first speech with the same request, and in beginning a new verse paragraph with Christabel's compliance, must imply one of two things: either Geraldine is powerless to act without assistance, or she feigns weakness because whatever it is that she has set herself to do cannot be accomplished without Christabel's willing cooperation. In either case her purpose would be frustrated if Christabel, in a greater concern for her own safety, were to run away, or if she were not compassionate enough to respond immediately and directly to the unhappy tale she is told.

The second stage has been much noticed and explained. It is the description (129–34) of Geraldine's sinking, "belike" through pain, before the gate of the castle and being carried, with great difficulty, by Christabel across the threshold, after which Geraldine's pain and weariness seem immediately to leave her. It is universally understood that the gate has been blessed and that an impure spirit of any kind would be unable to pass through without the help of a pure one. Such an explanation of the passage is of course its own commentary: the evil that Geraldine represents could not enter the scene of Christabel's life if Christabel were less purely good than she demonstrably is.

The third stage consists of the episode (184–225) in which, after Geraldine sinks to the floor of Christabel's chamber "in wretched plight," Christabel offers her a draught of "wine of virtuous powers"; her drinking of it is then interrupted by the protective appearance to Geraldine of the guardian angel mother. The ensuing combat of wills is won by Geraldine at the apparent cost of her last remaining strength. She is revived again by the solicitous Christabel and is restored to vigor by the wine of miraculous powers. Ironically, the wine that brings about the effect was lovingly made by Christabel's mother for her daughter's help in time of need, but the unselfish heart of the daughter does not hesitate to offer the irreplaceable cordial to a stranger whose condition requires it. One might conjecture that the first sips of the wine made by the mother are what give Geraldine the strength to resist the spirit-mother's protective attempt. In any case, the one thing that is unambiguously clear is that, at every crisis of Geraldine's weakness, it is the generosity, prudential thoughtfulness, or physical effort of Christabel that makes possible Geraldine's penetration to the vulnerable center of the stronghold.

The fourth stage is more complex and is something of a culmination—perhaps as far as the poem could have gone in a straight line of development. On the following day the Baron hears Geraldine's story and recognizes her purported father as the friend of his youth whom he has, however, for trivial reasons, long held in enmity. He is so moved by Geraldine's story that, despite his long hatred of her father, he vows to do justice upon the villains who have harmed her. At this, Christabel, who has received some taint of serpent-hood from Geraldine's nocturnal touch, draws in her breath with a hissing sound (459) but resumes her normal saintly expression by the time her startled father is able to whirl around and see her face. Christabel clearly knows that her father is being taken in by an evil force but is unable to help him by expressing it directly. Carried away by the magnanimity swelling in his heart, the Baron then goes all the way, vowing not only to avenge Geraldine's wrong but to see her safely returned to her father's care and, most significantly, to give up his foolish pride, apologize for the "words of fierce disdain" with which he had alienated his old companion, and seek a reconciliation. Christabel, still entranced and unable to express fully the evil she sees at work, does then manage at least to give her father some warning: "By my mother's soul do I entreat / That thou this woman send away!" (616–17). The Baron, feeling humiliated and dishonored by her contravention of his hospitable gestures, turns upon her in a seething rage. And that is where the action stops. What has happened is that, through the power of her goodness, Christabel has brought an unintended evil into their midst. Herself somewhat tainted and weakened by this evil, she has nevertheless the remaining goodness and strength of will partially to overcome the evil spell upon herself so as to try to warn her father. He, on the other hand, has been brought by Geraldine's story to a magnanimity and condition of original goodness that he has not enjoyed for many years; and it is the power and purity of those feelings that lead him (since he cannot possibly know better) to misunderstand his daughter's words and to hate her with the passion of his own newfound purity. A lesser condition or intention of goodness on the part of either *could not* have brought them to this condition. I therefore consider it possible, especially given Coleridge's emphases in the poem, that it was precisely this exposition of evil that the poem was intended to explore.

Of course, it may not have been. If we can believe Coleridge at all, however, we do have his claim that the poem was not to be merely a verse romance but rather was to be the working out of an idea so "extremely subtle and difficult" that he finally had to abandon the poem because his powers were not up to the level of his conception.[13] While he hinted in various places at several possible ideas inspiriting the poem, he never specifically defined the one that he said lay at the heart of it. What he did strongly imply in the plot outline given to Dr. Gillman, however, was that the narrative emphasis would fall on the increasing alienation between father and daughter.[14] Geraldine was for a time to change her form into that of Christabel's absent fiancé, with Christabel not understanding why she felt so strongly repelled by one whom she had wholly loved. And, in Gillman's words, "this coldness is very painful to the Baron, who has no more conception than herself of the supernatural transformation." Eventually, however, the true knight appears on the scene, Geraldine disappears, and there "follows a reconciliation and explanation between the father and daughter." The story has dealt with a conflict between father and child, which has been made possible by the best instincts in the nature of each, and is narratively resolved in their reconciliation. The moral problem has been with the corruption of natural feelings by a purity so sensitive that, in the case of Christabel, she intuits an evil in what she should by all outward marks love and yield herself to. This baffles and angers a father whose love for his daughter perceives that her normal and natural feelings seem to have become corrupted—that is, the springs of love seem to him to have become tainted. Because the father cannot know that the constraint is imposed by a purity of nature that cannot join itself with anything in the least impure, the initial conflict between father and daughter is exacerbated. I said earlier that perhaps Coleridge abandoned the poem because, at the point at which its printed version ends (though Coleridge claimed to have written much more), it had gone as far as it could go in a straight line of development. What I mean by that is simply that the effect had been fully accomplished, narratively and morally, with the initial alienation of parent and child in the version we have. Gillman's outline adds repetitively but not substantively to the culmination that had already been reached, and Coleridge lacked either the invention or the will to elaborate further the "extremely subtle and difficult" idea of which he had successfully and perhaps prematurely completed the expression in the fragment that he did pass on to us.

Another who employed this concept of evil, sometimes quite explicitly, was Shelley. One of the more open examples is the scene in *Prometheus Unbound* in which the Furies, unable to overcome Prometheus' will by means of physical pain, torment him with a vision of the future which demonstrates the transitoriness of any victory that his stubbornness might seem to give him over Jupiter. If he thinks that his suffering may be somehow redemptive of mankind and purgative of evil in human affairs, let him see how the message of love, brought by that Christ yet to come, will be used as a pretext for future wars and oppressions; how the French Revolution (presumably), in the name of Truth and Freedom, leads to fratricide and new tyranny (1.540–77),[15] and how throughout human history to come "all best things are thus confused to ill" (1.628). This is of course not an ultimate vision but a view of history used tactically by the Furies to create despair in their victim's heart. They are also self-corrupting and thereby limited in the scope of vision possible to them, like Blake's angel who sees a fiery inferno in a pastoral meadow because his theology has taught him to see with, instead of through, the eye. And so, though Shelley here uses the concept, it is seen as an error in cosmic vision, and his poem finally exists in order to affirm the infinitely greater contrary.

I do think, however, that, aided by its finite dimensions in history and the conventional expectations of tragic form, *The Cenci* is, and is meant to be, a virtually definitive treatment of the evil-out-of-good hypothesis.[16] The tragic catastrophe of the play, as I see it, is not the execution of Beatrice but the total overthrow of her moral nature and her inability even to understand what has been done to her, or *that* anything has been done. As this places me against all those (probably the majority) who see her as somehow redeemed or triumphant at the end, I had better make my case. In doing so I do not mean to set aside as irrelevant the play's real complexities: the self-serving mendacity and perhaps genuine moral confusion of Orsino; the fascinating contradictions in the character of the Count, who is as close to being a purely evil figure as one might imagine, but who has a consummate grasp of theology and seems more fixedly to believe in and trust the God he invokes than anyone else in the play; the odd recantation of Marzio; Beatrice's possible flutterings of faith at the end, or any of the other ambiguities whose resonances separate for us the truly tragic from the merely melodramatic. I believe, however, that there is a clear and wholly articulated pattern of integrated action and theme culminating inexorably in the damnation of Beatrice, and that the other elements humanly and dramatically enrich but do not negate it.

We begin with the Count's self-established character as so jaded by ordinary sins and crimes as to require a voluptuousness in the torment of his victims beyond most men's conceiving. Anyone can kill, but that is simple and final, and he likes more complex and prolonged torture. He boasts that "I rarely kill the body, which preserves, / Like a strong prison, the soul within my power" (1.1.114–15). But if there is pleasure in tormenting the living soul, the ultimate pleasure must be to accomplish the eternal torment of another's soul by bringing it into damnation. It is a concept that Shelley had entertained as an evil epitome as early as the juvenile *Zastrozzi*, in which the title figure, who often sounds like a finger exercise for the later Count Cenci, rages that "revenge is sweeter than life," and, even if he were to die in its execution, he would "taste superior joy in recollecting the sweet moment of [Verezzi's] destruction. Oh! would that destruction could be eternal!"[17] It is also the declared goal of the Count for Beatrice. He has some doubts about his ability to achieve it, when Lucretia tells him of the angelic voice proclaiming to Beatrice his forthcoming death, and he laments that "I must give up the greater point, which was / To poison and corrupt her soul" (4.1.44–45). But he immediately takes heart again in the hope that "Beatrice shall, if there be skill in hate, / Die in despair, blaspheming" (4.1.49–50), from which there can be only one possible eternal outcome; and he confidently predicts that, "As she shall die unshrived and unforgiven, / A rebel to her father and her God, / . . . Her spirit shall approach the throne of God / Plague-spotted. . . . I will make / Body and soul a monstrous lump of ruin" (4.1.89–90, 93–95). But Beatrice is a girl of spirit and of transcendent virtue, and Lucretia reports to the Count that "She bids thee curse; / And if thy curses, as they cannot do, / Could kill her soul . . ." (4.1.167–69), at which point the Count abruptly cuts her off.

Now it is one thing to curse and threaten but quite another to manipulate the Divine Will. God does not punish the innocent or the victims of others' sins. We might ask, what makes the Count think that the incestuous rape he plans for his daughter, and later effects, will threaten her immortal soul? Well, perhaps he knows his daughter better than we do, for he predicts that "her stubborn will / . . . by its own consent, shall stoop as low / As that which drags it down" (4.1.10–12). And he further predicts that "what she most abhors / Shall have a fascination to entrap / Her loathing will" (4.1.85–87). If we suppose this to refer, as it perhaps but not necessarily does in the Count's mind, to the incestuous act, it is clearly out of keeping with the angelic nature we have so far seen in the play. If, on the other hand, and as the Count perhaps does not but perhaps does anticipate (considering the angelic message just delivered to him), it refers to parracide and the arrogant assertion of its justification, it is entirely accurate. The one thing needful, of course, is the warping of a hitherto perfect nature toward that end. And this is the turning point of the play and of my argument. It is precisely because of her purity and of the value she places upon it that Beatrice can be brought to the ruin the Count has wished for her. There are ladies, Lot's daughters for example, who do not scruple at a bit of incest. But such is the purity of Beatrice that she feels herself to have been horribly polluted by her father's assault, and it is this extreme of goodness, once violated, that leaves her suggestible to the idea of father-murder. Had she begun as a more venal person, she could not suffer and react as she does.

Once committed to the idea of murder, however, both before and after the fact, she maintains a coolness and toughness that would have been the envy of Lady Macbeth. Stuart Curran objects to the tendency of critics for the past century to see the play only in terms of Beatrice's character, and he has a little poker-faced fun with the idea that she was naughty for lying about having murdered her father.[18] Surely the point of *all* of Beatrice's actions, however, lies not in their individual qualities but in their multifaceted revelation of what happens to her character—and what happens is that her heart is hardened and she becomes what her father was at the beginning of the play.[19] One may extenuate the murder, as Donald Reiman does, by saying that Beatrice was pushed into evil action by the evil that was done her,[20] but one may not say that, irrespective of the physical facts, she remains a spiritual innocent. Still less may one say, with Stuart Curran, that evil was the only good available to her if she were to escape having her goodness converted into evil, and that the evil she does preserves her goodness—a self-contradiction as dubious as the passage in Shelley's "On the Devil, and Devils" on which Curran founds his argument. It may be said that the idea is nonsense but that we must accept it because it is

Shelley's nonsense. With all due respect, I think not. Curran cites the following from Shelley's essay, "On the Devil, and Devils":

The benevolent and amiable disposition which distinguished his adversary [Lucifer], furnished God with the true method of executing an enduring and a terrible vengeance. He turned his good into evil, and, by virtue of his omnipotence, inspired him with such impulses, as, in spite of his better nature, irresistibly determined him to act *what he most abhorred,* and to be a minister of those designs and schemes of which he was the chief and the original victim.[21]

Now, the problem here is that, even if we allow Shelley his dismissal of free will, we still know, as Shelley knew, that Lucifer fell everlastingly, that God succeeded in his "plot," if one sees it in Shelleyan terms. I am perfectly willing to join Curran in the use of this passage as a commentary on the play, but I must then ask that its logic be applied faithfully and not be used to excuse Beatrice from consequences that even the second citizen of heaven could not escape. Shelley doesn't say that Lucifer escaped damnation, he says that the means used to bring it about were unfair. He does himself play fair in his drama, however. Lacking that possibility of omnipotence in Count Cenci which could make Beatrice harbor unclean thoughts "in spite of" her better nature, Shelley provides a machinery that will enable the Count to *use* her better nature as an instrument of damnation.

The fact is that hardness of heart, or obstinacy in sin, manifests itself as a refusal to repent of sins committed, without which repentance there can be no salvation. And that is the condition in which Beatrice goes to her execution. Shelley perfectly understood the nature and penalty of that condition, and had at least as early as the writing of *St. Irvyne*.[22] In *The Cenci,* before it is a hundred lines along, he makes the Count boast that "I am what your theologians call / Hardened" (1.1.93–94). And Shelley makes it clear that Beatrice understands how much more damnable is this spiritual condition than any individual sin when he has her say that "Worse than a bloody hand is a hard heart" (5.2.133). Notice, to avoid the trap of other meanings, that the Count's usage is in terms of theological definition. Beatrice also knows the theological definition and its implications, for she sends her mother to tell her father of a spirit voice that has announced to her the Count's imminent death, and further, "Even now the accusing angel waits to hear / If God, to punish his enormous crimes, / Harden his dying heart!" (4.1.35–37). Shelley keeps hammering away at an idea that is not customary with him but that is, as he says in his preface, appropriate to the historical time, place, and commitment of his characters. And why should he do so unless to make us understand what it means when Beatrice, whose brother calls her "lost" upon learning of her determination to murder their father, counsels him that he too must harden his heart and join the plot? (3.1.387–90). This is the same Beatrice who commits the sin of despair in undertaking the parricide, and of presumption in assuring Marzio and her mother that God will forgive the crime (4.3.56; 4.4.24–25). This is the Beatrice who, like her father, exults in the death of one of her own blood; who, like her father, asserts the complicity of God in the event; and who, like her father, boasts of indifference to consequences; the Beatrice who is willing to have Marzio twice tortured when she denies knowledge of what he has confessed on the rack; who berates her mother and brother mercilessly for having confessed the truth under torture; who blames God for having allowed her to suffer in the first place; who never, ever, shows the least sign of that repentance without which redemption from her triply mortal sin is impossible; and who, when counselled by her mother to "Trust in God's sweet love," replies that her mother's "words strike chill" because she has never seen any evidence of divine efficacy in human affairs, and therefore, much as she would like to trust God, her "heart is cold" (5.4.75–89).

There is much more, but the heart that hardens whenever such critical criteria are used will not be persuaded by it. If theological criteria, however much insisted upon by Shelley, should not be acceptable, perhaps one might admit that Beatrice's reiterated fear that her conviction will blacken the name of an otherwise stainless house is as grotesquely untrue to what we know of that house as is her reiterated assertion that God knows her to be guiltless. If she does not go blaspheming to the grave, as the Count had hoped and as I see her quite clearly doing, she goes to it very much out of touch with both temporal and spiritual reality. In any case, I am so powerfully compelled to read the play as a tragedy of character destroyed through the instrumentality of its own initial goodness, that I find it very hard to read any of Beatrice's postmurder speeches without a strong and detailed sense of their intentional irony. Shelley's repeated assertions that he had written a play unlike his other works, and his inability to understand why it was considered generally to be immoral, suggest that he too felt, regardless of his private commitments, that he had produced a work conformable with the traditional moral codes of his society.

But I began this essay by defining the view of evil that is its subject as a modern phenomenon, one which found its first full literary expression in the literature of Romanticism but which is even more deeply embedded in today's consciousness. Indeed, in the post-Watergate era it may well take at least a full generation to outlive the habitual and virtually instinctual sense that government is the poisoned well described by Godwin almost two hundred years ago. I shall be more brief in dealing with the literature of our own time, however, as befits my relative ignorance of it and my sense of limited reader patience.

For the appearance of the idea in the novels of our own century one could scarcely find a better starting point, for succinctness as well as chronology, than Mrs. Gould's reflection, in the eleventh chapter of *Nostromo* (written in 1902–04), that "there was something inherent in the necessities of successful action which carried with it the moral degradation of the idea." The Platonic echoes here bring to mind *The Great Gatsby* of two decades later, whose protagonist "saw that the blocks of the sidewalks really formed a ladder and mounted to a secret place above the trees"[23] and who "sprang from his Platonic conception of himself" (p. 99). The degradation of the divine idea in mortal action consistently turns good into its evil opposite in the novel. The "fresh, green breast of the new world" that the first Dutch sailors saw (p. 182) becomes the valley of ashes under the sightless eyes of Doctor T. J. Eckleburg (p. 23); Dan Cody had gone west with the dream of wealth, found it, and "brought back to the Eastern seaboard the savage violence of the frontier brothel and saloon" (p. 101); Meyer Wolfsheim perverts the promise of the land of opportunity into the opportunity to "play with the faith of fifty million people—with the single-mindedness of a burglar blowing a safe" by fixing the World Series of 1919 (p. 74); and Gatsby himself incarnates his imperishable dream in the unstable element of Daisy Fay and so draws himself into a life of vulgarity and crime. There is no value, goal, or wonder that is not corrupted into its opposite. One feels in the degradation of all things, from puppies to people to continents, an absolute and irrevocable pessimism, to be redeemed, if at all, only by the beauty of that human energy that Fitzgerald's favorite, Keats, once saw as dignifying even the sordidness of a quarrel in the streets. What gives the novel its peculiarly oppressive quality is the pervasive sense that it cannot be otherwise. The cumulative weight of many episodes, characters, and digressions finally persuades us, as it must have Fitzgerald himself before he could have written the magnificent final paragraphs, that the fault is not in ourselves but in the stars. We are creatures made to dream and to move in the actual world toward fulfillment of those dreams, but there is an economy of scarcity in the actual world, as there is not in the dream world. There simply is not enough love or greenery to go around. If we would live on the fresh green breast of the new world, we must ignobly cut down its trees and convert them into houses and firewood. If we would preserve the object, we must ignobly give up the dream of life that it inspires in us. The novel leaves us with no way to avoid the degradation of the good, short of giving up the idea of it.

Although the evil-out-of-good hypothesis has become pervasive in modern life, I can think of no recent literary work that treats it on the comprehensive scale of *Gatsby*. If I may risk a generalization to which there are innumerable exceptions, I think that we have increasingly come to see the fault as neither in ourselves nor in the stars but in the "system" whose institutions collectively constitute what we think of as the social machine. Parts originally designed as separate goods seem to have unexpectedly cohered into an oppressive whole. Having fallen away from metaphysic toward this perception, we have become tinkers and social mechanics, and the artists who speak to and for us have given us back that image of ourselves. I have chosen three novels of the recent past that seem to me illustrative of that view, Ken Kesey's *One Flew Over the Cuckoo's Nest* and Anthony Burgess' *Clockwork Orange*, both of which appeared in 1962, and Michael Chrichton's *Terminal Man* of a decade later. I take them as representative because all have enjoyed large general sales and have been widely studied in college and university literature courses and because each has won the popular approval implied by book-club distribution or adaptation to film. All of these books tend to locate the corruption of the good in institutions and outside the individual wills of either the institutions' victims or their proprietors.

In *One Flew Over the Cuckoo's Nest*, for example, if Randle Patrick McMurphy fights the system that has corrupted psychiatry into a coercive instrument of social conditioning, there is indeed an affirmation of human will and its efficacy, even if McMurphy must die in order to pass his message of resistance on to others. But the most active and most frequently visible representative of the system is Big Nurse, and we come finally to know that her devotion to the system is grounded in her extraordinary repression or sublimation of her sexuality. She is, in other words, something of an automaton or psychic zombie, not willing or choosing her role so much as being compensatorily thrust into it. Whether Kesey intended her to be the human equivalent of a heartless and mindless system of mind control, or embodied in her the idea that the social machinery for the maintenance of "normality" is the invention of psychic cripples and freaks, the fact remains that cripples and freaks do not choose to be so—a fact that we recognize by our having made those two cruel words virtually taboo in ordinary discourse. But if one does not choose, then no one is really to blame, and there is as much sadism as justice in the satisfaction we feel when Big Nurse finally does get *hers*.

In *Clockwork Orange* the system is again the villain, and virtually everyone in the society has dehumanized himself in order to maintain his place within it. There is no lack of individual will, but it is what Auden called will's negative inversion, the will of each to extirpate in himself and others all individual tendencies that do not serve his own commitment, the commitment thus absorbing the self instead of becoming an expression of it. The psychiatrists condition conformity into the individualists; the social workers' concern is not with their clients' human needs but with their identification as successful or failed "cases" on their own professional records; the radical political activists do not hesitate to compromise the freedom of individual human beings in their own quest for the ideal abstraction of liberty; the clergy employ theological argument in order to deprive others of that free will that is at the heart of their theology; each and all preserve the continuity of their individual commitments by using the disciplines appropriate to them for the negation of their original ends. Like Kesey, Burgess holds out the possibility that a lucky or determined few may escape the corrupting machinery of the system, but only at the cost of becoming increasingly alienated and isolated from the mass of their kind. Neither suggests that the perverse parody of the good that is embodied in the system may itself one day be corrupted back to its original purity.

In Michael Chrichton's *Terminal Man* the world view is less hopeless insofar as we are shown imperfections in the science and conflicts among the scentists. Not everyone in the novel agrees that the technical ability to implant in Harry Benson a computerized device to counter his attacks of psychomotor epilepsy is the best human way to deal with the disease. And as readers we find ourselves perversely but humanly cheering for Harry, or for his autonomic nervous system, as he, through it, learns to detect and override the electronic counterforce. We know that this "victory" will be disastrous for Harry, and for the innocent victims of the violence engendered by his attacks, but we want the man to beat the machine. And then come the questions. The autonomic nervous system being just that (the human will in abeyance when Harry's involuntary neural processes fight the machine, but in control as long as the humanly designed and programmed machine does its work), are we not simplistically sentimentalizing the concept of humanity when we identify it with one defective human being who has lost the ability to will his actions? Are not the will and skill of humanity more finely shown in all those who toil to create the device that will leave Harry free to make his own choices of action? But, once the humanly created machines are cut loose from their makers and begin independently to do the work they were created for, who is in charge, man or machine? Or does that matter, if the human purposes are met? However we answer these questions to ourselves, they are cut short in the novel when Harry's body overcomes the implanted device and he goes on another unwilled rampage. But we are not left free to think the questions resolved by the narrative action, because the novel has a dimension in the future as well as the present. Dr. McPherson's "Form Q" project envisages the supercomputer of the future, to be miniaturized by the use of living nerve tissue linking the hardware components, and finally to be implanted in a human being, as a supplement to his own brain, to create the greatest intelligence in the world. And we naturally ask, at what sacrifice to that person's humanity? And toward what human end? But it does us no good to entertain these imponderables, even though we have witnessed in the novel the failure of a much simpler operation, because every element in the novel persuades us that we have seen not a reversal of direction in this failure but a temporary setback. Knowledge is available, and we have faith that knowledge in itself is good. We also believe that, diligently applied, it will solve human problems and fulfill human goals. It is our humanity that tells us so, and though our history tells us another human truth, that our knowledge is vulnerable to error, abuse, or simple ignorance of its own limits, we can never know what we might be and do until we have tried.

Perhaps it is in the naiveté of that simple faith that our present difficulty lies, in the faith that if one tries everything possible, something might work. But no matter what the good envisaged, every good that does not work has the potentiality of such catastrophes as Harry Benson's, and often on an enormously greater scale. More important, however, is that the final corruption, the final evil to have emerged from our attempts to improve the human lot, is revealed by Chrichton's book as the imminent loss of free will. We shall soon be no longer able to make choices because the demonstrable superiority of our technology to its creators in the solution of an increasing number of definable human problems will soon leave us no measure for distinguishing the good from the merely practicable. Principled choice will become as impossible for us as for a machine programmed to play a random-numbers game. Damned if we do, and damned if we don't.

Having argued that the perception of evil as taking its origin in the good arose as a major literary theme in the Romantic period and continues as a premise in contemporary consciousness, nothing could please my sense of symmetry more than the following remarks by Peter Conrad in a recent issue of the *Times Literary Supplement:*

In a sense twentieth-century culture has been a prolonged, perplexed inquest into Romanticism, at one level officially disowning it, at another democratizing it in drugs, magic, astrology, self-exploratory suicide and the overtaking of culture by pop music, which recreates electrically in amplified form Sterne's vibrant sensorium of the world. Though we are the last romantics, it is also true that we are all romantics now. Romanticism has successfully universalized itself, with the aid of affluent technology— what began at the end of the eighteenth century as a new sense of human individualism has now turned against that individuality, coaxing it into visionary delirium or inciting it to communal hysteria. The peculiar and painful sense of exclusion and ironic self-division of Byron and Hölderlin has become the spiritual uniform of every undergraduate; impassioned radicalism has likewise become obligatory and in so extending itself lost its integrity and become a violent defence of privilege.[24]

There is much more in this vein, but we need not hear it any more than we need dispute it. For Mr. Conrad, and one hears the echo of many other voices in his, Romanticism *is* the envisioned good that has brought our evils upon us. One might wish to play the Blakean devil and redefine his terms, but, rhetoric aside, one sees what he means. Perhaps one could be more charitable, however, and recognize that, whatever the transitory social phenomena may be, there is a dilemma built into Romantic thought structure which focuses but does not itself create the pathos of our human position. As Morris Dickstein has finely put it, "Through imagination the poet becomes a creator, a lawgiver, a god; yet by virtue of that largeness of vision he sees all the more acutely that he is a mortal man."[25] To such realization, rage might be a fit response, or tears. Still, if we have any of the ironist in us at all, nothing should bemuse us more than the spectacle of Mr. Conrad's fixing blame for our current social and moral deformities on those Romantic artists who first perceived and creatively embodied the process that defines our modern moral dread.

NOTES

1. "The Principles and Practice of Hedonic Psychology," *Psychology Today*, (Jan. 1973), p. 53.

2. *Enquiry Concerning Political Justice and Its Influence on Morals and Happiness*, ed. F. E. Priestley (Toronto: University of Toronto Press, 1946), I, xxiv. For ease of reading I have eliminated the apparatus of outline form used by Godwin and recast his remarks in paragraph form.

3. Quoted in *Newsweek*, 9 Sept. 1974, p. 26.

4. "The Uprising of Caliban," in *Interpretations and Forecasts: 1922–1972* (New York: Harcourt Brace Jovanovich, 1973), p. 348. The essay was originally published in 1954.

5. Comment on his play *The Borderers*, available in many places but taken by me from *The Poetical Works of Wordsworth*, ed. Thomas Hutchinson, rev. Ernest de Selincourt (London: Oxford University Press, 1946), p. 897.

6. While there are legitimate ambiguities in translating *moeurs*, I follow the suggestion of Roger D. Masters, *The Political Philosophy of Rousseau* (Princeton: Princeton University Press, 1968), p. 205n., that "morals" is the nearest English equivalent, although Rousseau does also discuss social manners as evidence of the deceit engendered by the arts.

7. *Caleb Williams*, ed. David McCracken (London: Oxford University Press, 1970), p. 72.

8. The attack was denied in a curious pamphlet by the painter Henry Fuseli, published anonymously in 1767, who insisted that Rousseau was attacking the abuses of the arts and sciences, not the things themselves. Despite the claims made by a modern editor for "the extremely high estimation that was accorded to Fuseli by his contemporaries" (Karl S. Guthke, ed., *Remarks on the Writing and Conduct of J. J. Rousseau*, Augustan Reprint Soc., No. 82 [Los Angeles: William Andrews Clark Memorial Library, 1960], p. ii), the evidence does not suggest that even Fuseli's friend William Blake was converted or that any other important writer read the pamphlet.

9. Stuart M. Sperry, "Byron and the Meaning of 'Manfred'," *Criticism*, 16 (1974), 189–202, persuasively argues that *Prometheus Unbound* was heavily indebted to *Manfred* in both structure and theme, which is of course the direction in which influence would have had to flow if one work influenced the other. By "Shelleyan" I do not mean to suggest influence but merely to characterize certain elements of structure and tone. Following Bostetter and Bloom, Sperry sees the essential conflict of *Manfred* as internal, between aspects of the self, in terms different from but not contradictory to mine. His emphasis is on the working out of the conflict within the play, mine on its implied preconditions.

10. Ibid., pp. 198–99.

11. Some months after this was originally written, Jonas Spatz, in "The Mystery of Eros: Sexual Initiation in Coleridge's 'Christabel,' " *PMLA*, 90 (1975), 107–16, argued that Geraldine should not be seen as an external evil but as the projection of a necessary stage of psychic growth. Specifically: " 'Christabel' traces its heroine's attempt to come to terms with her sexuality, to recognize its essential role in her love for her absent knight and in their approaching marriage, and to progress from adolescence to womanhood. Geraldine is the projection of that sexuality, with its desire, fear, shame, and pleasure . . . . In Christabel's dreams, Geraldine is the woman she at once yearns and fears to become" (p. 111). I am much impressed with

the way Spatz builds his argument and have already adopted it as my favorite alternative to my own.

12. All quotations, cited by line in the text, are from Ernest Hartley Coleridge, ed., *The Poems of Samuel Taylor Coleridge* (London: Oxford University Press, 1912).

13. Samuel Taylor Coleridge, *The Table Talk and Omniana*, preface by H. N. Coleridge (London: Oxford University Press, 1917), p. 259.

14. Available in many places, e.g., the Spatz article previously mentioned, and Arthur H. Nethercot, *The Road to Tryermaine: A Study of the History, Background, and Purposes of Coleridge's "Christabel"* (1939; rpt. New York: Russell & Russell, 1962), p. 43. It originally appeared in Gillman's *Life* of Coleridge.

15. All Shelley citations refer to Roger Ingpen and Walter E. Peck, eds., *The Complete Works of Percy Bysshe Shelley*, 10 vols. (New York: Scribner's, 1926–30), hereafter cited as Julian. *Prometheus Unbound* and *The Cenci*, cited in the text by act and line, both appear in volume two.

16. In my view, the most balanced discussion of the play remains that of Robert F. Whitman, "Beatrice's 'Pernicious Mistake' in *The Cenci*," *PMLA*, 74 (1959), 249–53, to which my remarks here might be considered an addendum, though he has no knowledge of nor complicity in them.

17. Julian, V, 18–19.

18. *Shelley's Cenci: Scorpions Ringed with Fire* (Princeton: Princeton University Press, 1970), p. 24.

19. Carlos Baker, *Shelley's Major Poetry: The Fabric of a Vision* (Princeton: Princeton University Press, 1948), pp. 148–50, anticipates me in noting the comparability of the Count's and Beatrice's "hardness." If the past were recapturable, it would not surprise me to discover that I first began to think of the play as I do because of his analysis. As he does not consider "hardness" in the theological context provided by the Count, however, he and I see Beatrice's character somewhat differently.

20. Donald H. Reiman, *Percy Bysshe Shelley* (New York: Twayne, 1969), p. 94. It would be unfair to Reiman to suggest that he finds Beatrice guiltless, as he is quite aware of her moral shortcomings, but he does tend to see them in the light of misjudgment on her part, rather than as a state of sin, and he seems to imply (p. 93) that she is finally redeemed.

21. Cited in Curran, pp. 137–41.

22. E.g., "He shrunk not at the commission of crimes; he was now the hardened villain; eternal damnation . . . awaited him"; and, "Wolfstein . . . shuddered at the darkness of his future destiny. He strove to repent of his crimes; but . . . as often as repentance presented itself to his mind . . . a dark veil seemed to separate him for ever from contrition." Julian, V, 124,169.

23. F. Scott Fitzgerald, *The Great Gatsby* (1925; rpt. New York: Scribner's, 1953), p. 112, hereafter to be cited directly in the text.

24. Peter Conrad, "The Religion of Romanticism," *TLS*, 23 May 1975, p. 550.

25. *Keats and His Poetry: A Study in Development* (Chicago: University of Chicago Press, 1971), p. 194.

MICHAEL GOLDMAN

The Ghost of Joy:
Reflections on Romanticism and
the Forms of Modern Drama

An actor appears on a stage. The moment is innately interesting; all
plays begin well. This fact is crucial for understanding the "form"
or "structure" of drama, whatever general name, that is, we give to
the principle of maintained interest that seems to hold a play together—the whatever-it-is that lets excitement lead to excitement,
that makes us feel moment calling to moment in a satisfying and
significant way. For the promise of interest, and hence the source of
any particular principle of interest, is already present in that first
moment. Imagine the following exercise: write the *shortest possible*
opening sequence of a play that would succeed in boring an audience. What would the minimum time be, I wonder? Thirty seconds?
Twenty? Not much less, at any rate. The point is, it takes time for
drama to bore us. The first word of a poem—as we first receive
it—cannot be interesting in itself; the first moment of a play is; and
thus we may seek in that first moment a quality which speaks to the
uniqueness of drama as an art.

A man who is acting stands in a place set aside for acting. The
innate interest springs from the appeal of acting itself, from the
promise that the special kind of behavior we call "acting" will continue, transmitting to us its special kind of pleasure and energy. We
may think of this energy as a kind of hauntedness. Primitive drama
is almost exclusively concerned with the activity of ghosts and the
impersonation of the dead. This has less to do with any religious
"origin" of drama than with an essential feature of acting—the actor
is inevitably a person who appears to be both himself and not
himself, a figure specially liberated and set apart because he inhabits or is inhabited by another's identity. In this respect an actor is
like a ghost, and it is no wonder that society has turned to acting
and drama in its effort to grapple with the brooding presence of its
dead. Conversely, if the appeal of acting has to do with the quality
of hauntedness, then the continuing interest of a play has to do
with the ways in which we feel this hauntedness exercised and
transmitted, with who or what is haunting whom. Ghosts spook
us—they transmit an unsettling and volatile energy to us and en-

courage us to haunt as we are haunted. Like Orestes or Hamlet or Oswald Alving, the haunted man becomes something of a ghost himself. When method actors look for the "spine" of a play, and, indeed, when we employ any method to identify what unifies a play's action as dramatic experience (and not, say, as theme), what we are seeking is a source of haunting for the play as a whole, the principle or premise which keeps the histrionic energy alive through a whole performance by providing an echo throughout the play of that strange displacement of the actor's being that is involved in acting a part.

Characters in modern drama are typically haunted by a feeling of being cut off from the joy of life, or indeed from life itself, a feeling of being dead. This is a Romantic feeling, and in this essay I wish to put forward the notion that the history of modern drama is essentially that of adapting this feeling to dramatic representation. The adaptation is a difficult one, and modern drama becomes successful only when it learns to treat the difficulty itself as an expressive device. I should add that I make my claims in an undogmatic and exploratory spirit, and that my plan here is not to offer a comprehensive and detailed analysis, but a series of reflections that I hope will stimulate further discussion. I aim simply to explain what I mean as clearly as I can, and then to point to certain connections and patterns in the modern repertory that support my notion and that are, I think, illuminated by it.

First we must return to the feeling I have described, of being cut off from the joy of life. The feeling is romantic because it is the negative reflex or unfulfilled aspect of the romantic project of self-fulfillment. Like the feeling of being dead, the quest for self-fulfillment is hardly original with the Romantic era, but certain terms of the quest become paramount as the era dawns, above all a particular notion of where fulfillment lies, of how the self defines itself and how the joy of life is recognized.

A major defining impulse of Romanticism is the drive to conquer inner space, to possess internally a transcendent quality of being. This is often sought through action in the external world: revolt, travel, the pursuit of sublimity or freedom; but the ultimate reference of such activity is internal. The Romantic quest is validated by an expansion, possession, or transfiguration of the self. Inner space is no Romantic discovery, of course, but the shift of emphasis, the new notion of what the space is for, and perhaps of the effort required to explore it, is radical and seems to gain momentum as the Romantic era approaches. From our point of view, the shift is elusive, for two reasons. First, the traditional Western emphasis on inner discovery—as we find it, say, in Plato, or St. Augustine, or Shakespeare—is easily assimilated to our post-Romantic (or still-Romantic) reading of the world. Second, we are apt to project the Romantic reading backward onto self-absorbed literary heroes from the past—Homer's Achilles, say. In consequence, it is easy for us to miss the revolutionary character of the Romantic emphasis. Western thought has always been concerned with the individual and his private vision, but in the Romantic period private experience takes on a new articulation, a new primacy, which it retains today. When Janis Joplin's face fills the screen and describes the experience of singing, "You get inside yourself—and that becomes the entirety," she makes a statement that, with a little effort and translation, would have been perfectly intelligible (if not acceptable) to Shelley, say, as a description of a kind of satisfaction, a kind of awareness of self. But I suspect that it would be nearly unintelligible to anyone before Rousseau. Joplin is talking about the artistic process and the value of art. Both, she is certain, flow from the search for a pleasure to be found and won inside the self, a life within, realer and truer than anything outside.

This must be contrasted with the search for pleasure and achievement as it is understood in earlier periods. A stress on the life within appears, for instance, in Elizabethan literature, but the relation between inner and outer realms is quite different; and this applies to both the secular and religious perspectives. When Tamburlaine caps his great encomium to the restless human soul by defining its highest achievement as "the sweet fruition of an earthly crown," the phrase is apt to strike a modern reader oddly, as falling curiously short of the powers and ambitions evoked. We are likely to think of the sweet fruition of the artist or guru or philosopher as being greater because more inward, hence more profound. Tamburlaine's conclusion sounds odd to us because we no longer believe in the ultimate significance of outer kingdoms. Now, it is true that Tamburlaine's phrase might have struck some members of the Elizabethan audience as deficient, too—but only because they would have been thinking of the *heavenly* crown which was the soul's true goal. For the Elizabethan, there could be no doubt that the splendor and activity of the individual's inner world only pointed to the glory of some outer kingdom, whether earthly or heavenly. Shakespeare's heroes venture deep into the inner world and bring back news of the ripeness to be gained there, but, for even the most inward of them, that ripeness exists only in coordination with the outer world, usually the world of political achievement, in which the hero also lives in a primary way. Hamlet complains about having to set right the particularly ugly situation in Denmark; it is only Romantic criticism that imagines him to be complaining about having to act at all. We are accustomed to finding the external world deprecated in traditional Christian literature, but this is always and only in favor of a better world, which is distinguishable from the merely internal world of the individual. The kingdom of God is within us, to be sure, but it is larger and other than we are. Only in our era do we find the outer world deprecated in all its forms, the kingdom of God itself but a metaphor for the properly self-delighted soul. And in this sense at least, our era begins with the Romantics.

II

The heroes of Wordsworth and Keats, of Shelley, Byron, Goethe, Stendhal, Ibsen, and Chekhov are seeking sweet fruition in the Romantic sense. They may seem to find it in world traveling, or a life spent in nature, or the fight for freedom, or a high position in the church, or financial power, or building homes for human beings, or in sexual adventures, or even ecological adventures (like Dr. Astrov or Faust). These all may be vehicles for sweet fruition. But it is the sweet fruition itself, the expansion of the self into its internal kingdom, that they are after, and not whatever earthly or unearthly crown may help them to it.

What is new, then, is that the conquest of an inner realm is seen as an end in itself and not as a sign of having conquered an external one. For drama, the consequences are immense, though they take several decades to become apparent. The most obvious result is that characters are provided with a new type of intention. Consider, for example, the spine of *Ghosts,* as Francis Fergusson describes it: "to control the Alving heritage for my own life."[1] The last phrase is crucial. Some of the minor characters, like Engstrand, seem to be satisfied with putting the inheritance to good use in the external world, but this is a sign of their limited vision; it is why they are minor. What the heroine, Mrs. Alving, wants from the inheritance is "the joy of life," and this can only be verified internally. The orchard in *The Cherry Orchard* works well as a dramatic symbol because its flowering loveliness—like that of the forests Astrov loves in *Uncle Vanya*—stands for an inner achievement that seems to elude all the characters. To possess the orchard itself, as Lopakhin discovers, guarantees nothing. Like the Lyubovs, he cannot keep what is his. The central concern of the heroes of Ibsen, Strindberg, and Chekhov is always romantic in this sense. They aim, finally, to make something happen inside, to clear or refurnish a place in their secular souls.

This shift in focus changes the nature of drama because it changes the meaning of the stage. One quality of the acting area which stems directly from the peculiar hauntedness of acting, is that the area has always been felt to be a place where inner and outer worlds are powerfully superimposed. In all societies, the stage is perceived as a highly charged condensation of the outside world. It is like places the audience knows, or is marked by important features of place in the known world (the bull's-eye altar-center of the Greek theater, the hierarchical pageant-facade of the Elizabethan). At the same time, by the very nature of the dramatic occasion, the stage is charged with the special significance of the heightened life of acting. It is a place where crucial events will happen, a scene where the life of a few people can be projected into actions and statements that are clear and whole. In classical Greece and Elizabethan England, the structure of the scene glowed with the potential excitement of acting, with the felt receptivity of the stage to the thrusting inner world of acted characters. Now, for contrast, think of Romantic drama, the theater of Schiller and Hugo— and of its successor, modern realistic drama, the theater of Ibsen and Hauptmann. On the first of these stages, we see Romantic heroes in antique, pseudo-Shakespearean settings. On the next, Romantic heroes in tasteless parlors. In both cases, the outer worlds cannot glow with the possibilities of the inner, because the inner cannot fulfill its possibilities upon them.

The characters of high Romantic drama charge round a quasi-Elizabethan stage, stumbling upon opportunities for Romantic poetry, but not at all at home in the world of dramatic action the Elizabethan stage requires. Some great isoladoes, like Kleist and Büchner, manage to make of this failure to connect a compelling, if spasmodic stage poetry of absence, of ancient gestures like a dive into the void. But the Romantic drama proper is a spectacle of poets thrashing about in costume on an exhumed stage, speaking all the more loudly—and at times beautifully—for the silence of the painted world around them. Büchner's and Kleist's heroes seem to stagger or dream their way through busy theatrical worlds, like the Shakespearean-historical clamors of *Danton's Death* or *The Prince of Homburg*. What distinguishes their achievement from any of their contemporaries is that they are thus able to express—and to make dramatic meaning out of—the incompatibility of the Romantic hero's concerns with the external traffic of the stage.

We must bear this in mind when we come to consider Ibsen's "realistic" dramaturgy. Part of the sensation of forward movement we get from an Ibsen play comes from the steady solution of problems of plausibility, of matching the haunting thrust of the main characters to some notion of familiar social behavior and to a probable sequence of events. But the solution is never quite perfect; it never leaves the reader entirely comfortable. And for Ibsen, I would suggest, this is just the point. It was not only the awareness of a new external reality that governed his realism. It was not simply that people now lived in flats and used the telegraph and the railway, as opposed to living in palaces and riding on horseback. What mattered most was that this new reality could function as an irritant within the work of art itself. As a resistance to action and expression, it could suggest a tragic defect in the very impulse toward joy and self-fulfillment by which Ibsen's heroes were defined.

Here we may have a clue to the apparent unsatisfactoriness of the artist characters in Ibsen's later plays. There is always something grotesque and unlikely about their projects and achievements. Solness' "home for human beings" with a funny tower on top, Rubek's "Resurrection" with animal figures in the foreground, even Lovborg's *History of the Future*, have always struck critics as curiously awkward, defective as realism and heavy-handed as symbolism. It is as if Ibsen's weight of meaning could not quite be borne by any plausible book or statue or architectural design. My suggestion is that, in all these cases, the oddness in the portrait expresses the inadequacy of any contact between the romantic individual and the matter of the world. The ordinary home with the tower on it, the statue of the nude surrounded (and somehow "pushed to the background") by animals—a statue moreover that has been exhibited "all over the world"—these make us feel something unsatisfactory, a sense of disproportion or absurdity in what we are asked to think of as the highest possibilities of individual expression. Like Borkman's empty, grandiose dreams, or Mrs. Alving's great campaign for the joy of life (which consists, finally, in trying to convince her son's half-sister to become his mistress in order to take his mind off his syphilitic decline) they have the effect of yanking the stage out from under the hero.

In one form or another, this is the major pattern in Ibsen, and it stands at the heart of his realism. From the earliest prose plays, the climactic moments are those in which the individual's outlet to the world goes up in smoke. The orphanage burns down and reveals that Mrs. Alving cannot make an orphan of her son. The monument to Capt. Alving that was supposed to exorcise his baleful influence is destroyed; his influence is more virulent than ever. In *A Doll's House*, the letter from Krogstad plunks into the letter box but fails to produce the "wonderful thing" that Nora has hoped for. Both these climaxes deliberately remind us of the well-made play, of a dramaturgy that lets issues resolve themselves in neatly patterned change in the external world, but if (as reviewers from time to time complain) these contrivances "creak," in Ibsen it is the deliberate creak of a machine that has made nothing happen. Mrs. Alving and Nora turn to the world, to others, for an action that will expand their souls, and the world does not respond. *A Doll's House* remains unique among Ibsen's plays because it contrives to suggest that the world might respond; Nora runs off (with Ibsen, one might say) into a night of hope. But we have only to compare that final scene with the rest of Ibsen's plays to see what the hope amounts to. Onstage, in fact, all we can see is Helmer, and his hope for a wonderful resurrection is answered by the slam of the door; there is nothing creaking here.

The spectacular sunrise on the mountains at the end of *Ghosts*, the fire in the orphanage, the ominous letter box of *A Doll's House*, Ekdal's "hunting" garret in *The Wild Duck*, the snow-covered hillside in *Borkman*—these are all scenic devices whose literal character renders them at odds with the psychological expansiveness of the characters on stage. They express the characters' situation, to be sure, and sometimes very profoundly, but they do not join with them, they do not receive and extend the characters' actions as, say, the crowns in *Tamburlaine* or the carpet in the *Agamemnon* do. There is a seam in Ibsen that always shows between the inner life of his characters and their condition. James notices it in his famous review of *John Gabriel Borkman*. "If the spirit is a lamp within us," he observes, "glowing through what the world and flesh make of us as through a ground-glass shade, then such pictures as *Little Eyolf* and *John Gabriel* are each a *chassez-croisez* of lamps burning, as in tasteless parlors, with the flame practically exposed."[2] But the seam—the incompatibility of lamp and shade, of haunted hero and tasteless parlor—is not a sign of defective workmanship. It is the essential mark of Ibsen's tragic dramaturgy, the point where the romantic project fails to connect with the outer scene. It expresses the drama of the romantic self in its necessarily unsatisfactory commerce with the world.

III

Near the end of Pirandello's *Enrico IV*, the hero has a speech which offers a fine example of both the dramatic problem posed by the romantic project and the type of solution modern drama has found. The speech combines a profoundly ambiguous notion of reality with what appears to be a powerfully expansive and emphatic statement of individual transcendence. By doing so, it makes us feel both the haunting romantic drive toward a joy which escapes the formal constraints of life in society and a puzzling blockage which renders the drive unrealizable. Enrico has turned on his guests with scorn and contempt. In a series of big speeches, he seems bent on demonstrating the superiority of his conscious masquerade to the general falseness of the lives around him. Then, ostensibly in the same vein, he introduces an unexpected reminiscence:

I remember a priest, certainly Irish, a nice-looking priest, who was sleeping in the sun one November day, with his arm on the corner of the bench of a public garden. He was lost in the golden delight of the mild sunny air which must have seemed for him almost summery. One may be sure that in that moment he did not know any more that he was a priest, or even where he was. He was dreaming. . . . A little boy passed with a flower in his hand. He touched the priest with it here on the neck. I saw him open his laughing eyes, while all his mouth smiled with the beauty of his dream. He was forgetful of everything.[3]

The little boy with a flower: it is a romantic intervention *par excellence*, a touch of nature breaking through the rigidities of convention, the body shocked and freed by immediate, sensual contact with life. Enrico continues:

He was forgetful of everything. . . . But all at once, he pulled himself together, and stretched out his priest's cassock; and there came back to his eyes the same seriousness which you have seen in mine; because the Irish priests defend the seriousness of their Catholic faith with the same zeal with which I defend the sacred rights of hereditary monarchy!

The sequence is surprising. At the touch of the flower, the priest goes from the golden delight of his dream to the grim seriousness of his priestly role—from freedom, life, and pleasure to repression and rigidity. The effect is not far from the terrible climaxes of Ibsen—the moment of intensest contact with the longed-for, dreamed-of joy of life guttering, because of the contact, into absolute inhibition.

Indeed, I would call this the model sequence of modern drama. Here is the paradigm: First, we are caught up in the campaign of the individual soul to break through to reality in what the soul perceives to be an unreal world, a campaign on the side of joy, of an inner flowering, a campaign that seems to be leading to a breakthrough. And then comes the moment of breakthrough, in which the campaigning soul plunges into—an absence of some sort. In the nineteenth century, this is usually represented as an absence of joy, of fulfilled life. Later dramatists tend to treat it as an absence of reality. But whether it be Mrs. Alving discovering that the joy of life is impossible, or the revolutionaries in *The Balcony* learning that their war against illusion can only be sustained by illusion, or Brecht's Shen Te finding that she can only be a good woman by masquerading as a bad man, the final revelation opens a fissure between the individual drive that makes for the play's action—that "haunts" the main actor—and the world in which he tries to act.

Pirandello is perhaps the first dramatist to make this sequence explicitly question the nature of reality. In the speech just discussed, Enrico's train of thought undercuts his claim to have made a superior contact with the real. He argues that he is free, but he concludes in images of entrapment. He resembles the priest not in the brief moment of release, but in the long career of rigidity. Though he strikes the pose of the triumphant revenger, the liberated hero exposing the madness of a society he disdains, the play regularly shows him as trapped in his posture of liberation. All his life, Enrico has longed for human contact and been terrified of exclusion from life. His solution to the problem has been the masquerade, which has excluded him even more absolutely. Behind his performance as emperor lies a restless search for freedom. Speaking as emperor at the end of the first act, he has seen himself as dead and begged for resurrection:

It isn't enough that [the Pope] should receive me! You know he can do *everything—everything* I tell you! He can even call up the dead. [*Touches his chest.*] Behold me! Do you see me? There is no magic art unknown to him. Well, Monsignor, my Lady, my torment is really this: that whether here or there [*Pointing to his portrait almost in fear.*] I can't free myself from this magic. I am a penitent now, you see; and I swear to you I shall remain so until he receives me. But you two, when the excommunication is taken off, must ask the Pope to do this thing he can so easily do: to take me away from that; [*Indicating the portrait again.*] and let me live wholly and freely my miserable life.　　　　　　　　　　　　　　　　　　　　　　　　　　(P. 172)

Two acts later, the climax of the play, like the story of the dreaming priest that precedes it, shows that Enrico cannot be reawakened. His impulse to grasp life issues in emptiness suggesting the real function of the theatrical metaphor in *Enrico IV*. In the course of the play, role-playing comes to stand for an inhibition, a limit on the real life which, we are led to feel, lies behind the masquerade. But the action is contrived so that we feel—just as the impulse breaks through—that there is nothing but the masquerade available to the actor. Enrico, as is often pointed out, has no "real" name; we know him only by the name of the eleventh-century emperor he pretends to be. The point is not that all life is a masquerade. This is the type of "Pirandellism" that Pirandello is always trailing before us as a sort of philosophical red herring. The point is not a point at all, but an experience—the experience of breaking through to an emptiness that is charged with our longing for fullness. Enrico's masquerade is a device for exploring, in theatrical terms, the romantic impulse to private fulfillment.

The moment before he kills Belcredi, Enrico has roughly grasped Frida in his arms, and so we see him at the end not as a romantic hero defying society, but as an aging man grotesquely embracing a woman young enough to be his daughter, the daughter by another man of the woman he once loved. This sudden and disturbing version of the primal scene brutally mates reality and fantasy. The sad reality behind the masquerade and the pathetic fantasy behind the real embrace are both made visible. This is Enrico's reentry into real life—a painfully actual version of his grand desire. It may remind us of the similar scene that stands at the center of *Six Characters,* when the father approaches the step-daughter in Mme. Pace's brothel. *Six Characters,* too, is about the desire for "life," as the Characters keep telling us. In his preface to the play, Pirandello explicitly associates this desire with romanticism. More than that, he associates his presentation of the characters' desires, his success in making a play out of the *failure* of a play to be made, with the failure of romantic desire to make contact with reality:

I have presented [a drama] . . . in which . . . there is a discreet satire on romantic procedures: in the six characters thus excited to the point where they stifle themselves in the roles which each of them plays in a certain drama while I present them as characters in another play which they don't know and don't suspect the existence of, so that this inflammation of their passion—which belongs to the realm of romantic procedures—is humorously "placed," located in the void.   (Pp. 373–74)

Modern drama's greatest successes are largely of this kind. They show the failure of romanticism through theatrical forms in which one kind of dramatic procedure fails and is contained in another. The effect is to "locate" the self in the void.

IV

Whenever we wish to inquire about the career of drama in a given period, we will always do well to inquire after the fate of *Hamlet* in that period. For in writing *Hamlet,* Shakespeare managed to hold a mirror up to the nature of drama. In the Romantic era,

Hamlet, naturally enough, became a Romantic. But in transforming Hamlet into that extremely influential Hamlet-like image of itself, the era gave away a number of its secrets.

The Romantic Hamlet is a man set down in a world not of his own making and, perhaps even more significantly, a man who is ponderously disturbed, if not bewildered by this fact. Whether he be described as a delicate vase into which an oak tree has inadvertently been inserted (Goethe) or a procrastinating philosopher brutally constrained to practical action (Coleridge), Hamlet is seen by the Romantic imagination as a man at odds with the very conditions of existence in a real world. Indeed we might say that the Romantic imagination regards Hamlet as a poet unfairly and tragically forced to make an appearance in a play.

Hamlet is at his most Romantic when he claims that he has that within him which passes show. With this statement he places "real life" beyond the reach of theater. It is a position Shakespeare's Hamlet quickly learns he must abandon—for four-and-a-half acts of intricate action and play-acting—but the Hamlet of the Romantic imagination clings to it. If all that matters most to Hamlet is inaccessibly *within*, then he can never get beyond the withdrawal of his first appearance at Claudius' court. And this is the attitude in which Romantic criticism freezes Shakespeare's prince—the soulful adolescent brooding at the feast. Once more, the portrait points to the difficult relation between Romanticism and drama.

This is not to say, of course, that Romantic critics did not believe in action. In his discussion of *Hamlet*, Coleridge insists that "action is the chief end of existence," and Goethe's Faust finds happiness redeeming swampland. This will remind us, if we need reminding, that the nineteenth century was an age of projectors and revolutionaries, of adventurers with an itch for changing the order of the world. It will remind us of Borkman and Solness. In every case, however, the romantic itch for action expresses a yearning for inner fulfillment. The sweet fruition, even for Faust, is internal, an event inside the spirit. Ibsen differs from Goethe and Coleridge here only in that he firmly grasps the absurdity of the itch for action, the incompatibility between homes for human beings and the restless inner expansionism of the romantic project. It is not, I think, that Ibsen saw more clearly than Coleridge or Goethe, or that he came later and knew more. He *had* to see the incompatibility because his genius was dramatic. On any living stage, the Romantic Hamlet is an absurdity, a whirlwind of passion disconnected from the world around him, a bad poet in an inflated closet drama, beating his sensibilities in vain.

Goethe's characterization of Hamlet as "a costly vase" provides a key to the defects of the Romantic stage, to the inability of its great poets to produce real drama. Hamlet, in Goethe's metaphor, is a beautiful container, shattered by misuse. The image implies a conception of dramatic character as something to be displayed or exclaimed over, something that remarkably indicates the rarity of its composition—Hamlet as a delicate vase, not the oak tree it contains, certainly not a Renaissance prince.

Like Coleridge, Goethe too saw Hamlet's inability to act as a sign of failure. Hamlet lacked "the strength of nerve which makes the hero," but my point is that the hero desiderated here is just another kind of vase, sturdier than the Hamlet variety, displaying, shall we say, the strength-of-nerve pattern. On the early nineteenth-century stage, such heroes are inevitably less interesting than a Prince of Homburg or a Danton—than characters who fall back deliberately and dangerously into the void, who puzzle over their discontinuity with the stage world they move in. The romantic project was neither a mistake nor an aberration, and I hope that nothing I have said suggests that it was. On the contrary, it was a necessary step into the labyrinth of being—and one result of it was a new and rich critical sensitivity to the inwardness of Shakespeare's heroes. Its gift to the drama was a new source for haunting, the imperious hunger for inner space, a flight from spiritual deadness which ultimately transformed every object on the realistic stage into a ghost, a persecuting agent of the dead external world. But it took some time to discover the forms by which this haunting could be released in dramatic action.

V

Romantic man invented a secret place, the ego, and then set out to explore it. It was like a cavern or a heaven or a beautiful day or a sublime landscape, but it was different from all these in that it was inaccesible, or accessible only to its inventor, "I." And "I" seemed simultaneously imprisoned in his secret place and excluded from it. The Romantic egoist was doomed to explore his secret place in secret, though not in silence. Any traffic with the ego was subject to a fundamental interruption. Nothing could be brought into the cavern in its own state, as grace, say, could be brought to the Christian soul, victories to the hero, realms to the king, friends to the social man. All such had now to be translated into the currency of the secret place, which was by its nature private, coined and counted only by the Romantic individual in his private cave.

The art of Romantic man was a public form of this currency, a scrip one might say, a way of communicating value, of speaking to other privacies about the private cave. Today, we are accustomed to translating all art into such terms, and very likely it *is* an aspect of all art, at least all sophisticated Western art, but, in truth, there is little we can do to avoid thinking this way. We cannot escape the Romantic translation because we cannot escape our past. For the purposes of this essay, however, it is only necessary to note how the public forms of art became firmly related to the inaccessible privacy of the artist. The full purport of the privacy and the problems it raised were perhaps not immediately clear. Wordsworth could think of the poet as a man speaking to men, and thus, quite honestly, offer his unprecedented exploration of private experience in terms that linked it to a kind of Horatian conversation. But the solitaries who inhabit Wordsworth's landscapes like features in it, and the conversations in which Wordsworth and his interlocutor are clearly speaking different languages, tell a different story. The Wordsworthian conversation is extraordinary, like nothing before it in English poetry, but he talks with men as he might with a flower or a rock. It is not that their speech is less meaningful or less respected than his own; it is simply other. And it speaks finally of the otherness of his private place. The poet who talks of a man speaking to men is the same as the boy who had to cling to a tree to keep the world from disappearing.

The contradictions already implicit in Wordsworth become crucial in the work of succeeding generations. The ambiguous privacy of the poet and his driven, unsatisfactory commerce with a dissolving world—these are themes the art of the period 1780–1830 bequeathed to the modern era. In one fashion or another, they make themselves felt in all the experiments of modern drama. We feel them at play in Enrico Quattro's struggle to make contact with the world, and in the struggles of Borkman, or Miss Julie, or Peter Handke's Kaspar. Much more explicitly, they form the basis for one of the great innovative dramas of the modern repertory—Brecht's first play, *Baal. Baal* is about a poet, a most un-Wordsworthian one in personal style, to be sure, but he too seems both locked in the depths of private experience and haunted by a desire to embrace the ungraspable world. It is fitting to close with a look at this prodigal, refractory work, which has always proved so resistant to analysis. *Baal* was conceived as a counter-play to Hanns Johst's *Der Einsame,* an Expressionist paean to the Romantic playwright, Grabbe. As such, it gives us a figure whose absorption in the personal is so complete as to be monstrous. At the beginning of the play, we see Baal surrounded by a throng of bourgeois poetry-lovers. They react to him as might an audience at some more conventional play—like Johst's—about the glories and sorrows of a stereotyped Romantic artist. But Baal neither responds nor performs as they wish. He takes what he wants from them—food, drink, the promise of an assignation. Quickly, he alienates them all. They leave, angry and troubled. At the end of the scene, the stage is empty except for Baal, who "goes on drinking."[4]

Baal haunts his play—and holds it together—by this endless capacity for ingestion. Like any Romantic artist, he values himself for what he contains, and he wishes to contain not only multitudes, but all—trees, sky, rain, death. There is some suggestion in the play that this desire amounts to a wish, on the poet's part, to incorporate the mother—if so, it is a brilliant insight into the romantic project with its dissatisfied yearning after death, apocalypse, self-generation, the womb. In any case, the movement toward ingestion is also a movement to dissolution. Scenically and structurally, the play seems to dissolve. There are no resistances; everything flows into Baal, and the more he dominates, the more he decays. His haunting power comes from the way he goes beyond whatever is extreme, whatever is romantic in those who surround him. He estranges them, and the audience, ever further by rejecting any of the pieties or limits by which we ordinarily accommodate the limitless romantic absorption in self to acceptable behavior in the world.

At the end of the play, Baal crawls out of a shabby workman's hut, dying, calling not on God, but on "dear Baal." For Brecht, this marks the fate of the private ego, grown absolute and terrifying in its asociality. Does Baal want to live more than he wants to die? It is not clear, but the absolute absorption in self that he represents is inseparable from his restless drive toward dissolution. Brecht's own artistic career is a brilliant, hopeless struggle to be free of the Romantic legacy. Throughout it, he remains profoundly ambivalent toward *Baal*, constantly trying to redefine the play in notes which serve only to emphasize the unsettling tensions it embodies. And Baal's destructive, restless, stirring, self-absorbed personality keeps recurring in his plays, never quite tamed by the distancing devices that surround it.

Writing near the end of his life, Brecht tries to assimilate *Baal* to the Marxist usefulness of epic theater. He finds it difficult, and prefaces his remarks with a wry warning: "*Baal* is a play which could present all kinds of difficulties to those who have not learned to think dialectically." Denying that the play is "a glorification of unrelieved egotism," he pictures Baal as "standing out against the demands and discouragements of a world whose form of production is designed for exploitation rather than usefulness." It is an unpersuasive argument, and Brecht himself seems unsatisfied with it. Finally, he asks us simply to accept *Baal* as a kind of weak spot in his oeuvre: "I have left the play as it was, not having the strength to alter it. I admit (and advise you): this play is lacking in wisdom."[5]

The conclusion is dismissive, but in the course of his remarks, Brecht makes an observation that is of great importance to our discussion. By emphasizing the unredeemed capitalism of the world Baal moves in, Brecht manages to hint at a significant and troubling relation between *Baal* and modern social thought, which also bears upon its relation to Romanticism. As a revolutionary play, Brecht suggests, *Baal* may be taken to have the following moral: "Humanity's urge for happiness can never be entirely killed."

This is a perplexing commentary on a play whose self-obsessed hero seems infinitely remote from the fraternal optimism of a phrase like "Humanity's urge for happiness." But is the distance so great? Just as the figure of Baal carries to extremes and thus subverts the cheerful glorification of the Romantic artist, so Baal's monstrous asocial appetite is an extreme expression of the Romantic notion of happiness as a purely internal achievement. The urge for happiness in this sense is ultimately subversive of any society or even of any coherent life in the world. In this, *Baal* is also very much in the mainstream of the modern theatrical investigation of romantic possibilities. In the twentieth century, drama has pursued to the source—more doggedly and deeply perhaps than any other form— the great promise of an internal kingdom that the revolutionary desires of the eighteenth and nineteenth centuries opened for our imagination. The link between the political and personal is crucial here—and not a little disturbing. "Bliss was it in that dawn to be alive," writes Wordsworth, and surely a great reason why it was bliss for a young Romantic to be alive as the French Revolution began was that the fraternal dreams of the Revolution and the more private dreams of the Romantic ego on the verge of new self-discovery seemed for a moment to be one. Freedom, for both self and society, was the promise in the air. Modern tragedy, based as it is on the failure of the Romantic project, strikes at the hopeful social vision that informed the blissful dawn of the modern idea of liberty, the political version of Mrs. Alving's "joy of life." As O'Neill's Larry Slade says, surveying the ragged, drunken wrecks about him in the first act of *The Iceman Cometh*, "It's a great game, the pursuit of happiness."

NOTES

1. *The Idea of a Theater* (Princeton: Princeton University Press, 1949), p. 150.

2. Henry James, *The Scenic Art: Notes on Acting and the Drama,* ed. Allan Wade (New York: Hill and Wang, 1957), p. 293.

3. *Naked Masks,* ed. Eric Bentley (New York: Dutton, 1952), p. 205. Hereafter cited in the text.

4. There are many versions of *Baal.* Some of the difficulties in deciding on a preferred text are discussed by Ralph Manheim and John Willett in the introduction and notes to the first volume of their edition of Brecht's *Collected Plays* (New York: Vintage Books, 1971). I follow Brecht's first published version of 1922, which has been translated by Eric Bentley and Martin Esslin (New York: Grove Press, 1964).

5. Manheim and Willett, pp. 345–46.

RICHARD HAVEN

Some Perspectives in Three Poems
by Gray, Wordsworth, and Duncan

Any poem is potentially a Pandora's box for the speculative reader. For a poem embodies an attempt of a human mind to find articulate form for emotional and intellectual experience, a process central, complex, and still far from understood—still, that is, far from being comprehended by the human mind attempting to find articulate form for the emotional and intellectual experience of the creation of art. As critics and historians of literature, we employ terminologies, paradigms, theoretical positions, which enable us to limit our concern to a few of the infinite variables and to disregard some mysteries, and thereby to discern or impose an order, to appear to be in control. Since omniscience is not within our grasp, such illusions of order and control are necessary to us, as in other ways they are necessary to a poet, if we are to attain to a momentary pause in which we may be able to see and speak.

In this essay, I should like to depend for some measure or illusion of order and control not so much on a critical position as on the common ground that seems to me to be provided by three poems from three different periods: Gray's "Elegy Written in a Country Churchyard," Wordsworth's "Lines composed a few miles above Tintern Abbey," and Robert Duncan's "The Fire, *Passages* 13."[1] In the first two cases, both poem and poet are generally familiar and have been widely discussed. The third, being contemporary, is less so, and I shall consider that poem in conjunction with the author's remarks in his introduction to *Bending the Bow*, the volume in which it appears. I do not propose to trace a line of descent or influence or to offer three variations on a theme. The three poems are in most respects very different. But they seem to me to share— the first two obviously, but the third as well—a significant structural affinity, which, I think, derives from the situation of the poet in relation to his world, his language, and his audience. Using this as a foothold, I hope to be able to consider a number of variables that differentiate the poems without too great a sacrifice of coherence. And while it would indeed be naive to pretend that valid general conclusions about the periods which produced the three poems could be erected on so narrow and selective a foundation, I hope also to suggest thereby differences in the intellectual, attitudinal, and verbal situation of the poems which could be given broader application.

In the introduction to *Bending the Bow*, Duncan writes that "The Fire" is one of "a series [of poems] that extends in an area larger than my work in them. I enter the poem as I entered my own life, moving between an initiation and a terminus I cannot name" (p. v). Any poem also has within itself, as does any sentence, an initiation which must be named and moves toward a terminus which must in some manner be named if the poem ends and which may not be named if the poem merely stops. In any poem as in any sentence, the point of initiation and the terminus may be considered both in terms of what is named and in terms of how it is named.

The three poems under discussion all belong to the rather large class of what are sometimes called circular poems, poems, that is, in which in some sense the point of initation and the terminus are the same. One common variety of these is the poem that ends with a repetition or modification of an initial line or stanza. Another, widespread during the Romantic period and since, is that in which initiation and terminus are provided by the situation of the speaker who, wherever his thoughts may stray in the interim, begins and ends as one speaking in a particular time and place.

This latter category includes most of those poems to which Meyer Abrams has given the name Greater Romantic Lyric,[2] a type of which Wordsworth's "Tintern Abbey" is a prime example. It also with a little stretching includes Gray's "Elegy" which begins and ends in a country churchyard, though with some modification of speaker and time. Duncan's poem ends with a slightly different arrangement of the thirty-six words with which it begins, which appear to present neither a speaker nor his situation, and might thus seem to belong to the first category. I think, however, that the difference in this instance is in the manner of the naming of the point of initiation and the terminus rather than in the nature of what is named, and that the three poems may in this respect fruitfully be considered together.

In the essay I have alluded to, Abrams defines the Greater Romantic Lyric as a poem which presents

a determinate speaker in a particularized, and usually a localized, outdoor setting, whom we overhear as he carries on, in a fluent vernacular which rises easily to a more formal speech, a sustained colloquy, sometimes with himself or with the outer scene, but more frequently with a silent human auditor, present or absent. The speaker begins with a description of the landscape; an aspect or change of aspect in the landscape evokes a varied but integral process of memory, thought, anticipation, and feeling which remains closely intervolved with the outer scene. In the course of this meditation the lyric speaker achieves an insight, faces up to a tragic loss, comes to a moral decision, or resolves an emotional problem. Often the poem rounds upon itself to end where it began, at the outer scene, but with an altered mood and deepened understanding which is the result of the intervening meditation. (Pp. 527–28)

This definition will be useful as a point of reference, but I quote it here because it raises an additional issue. Abrams speaks of a process of thought and feeling "closely intervolved with the outer scene," clearly implying that thought and feeling are "inner." This is slippery ground not only because it assumes a dualism which has been a problem at least since Descartes, but also because both outer scene and inner meditation are parts of a poem which as a whole may be thought of either as an inner experience or as an objective, outer, verbal artifact. But like many distinctions that may not correspond to absolute verities, this is one which in some form or other we need to make. We think of the outer scene as "actual," as something public which may be shared by a number of individuals, which may be pointed to. An inner meditation may not be pointed to or shared except insofar as it can be and is given an outer, public form. Similarly, language that is understood is shared, is public, and the inner experience embodied in language is given a public dimension rather as the speaker has a public dimension as a figure in the outer scene.

The distinction between "outer" and "inner" may be thought of as a distinction between "public" and "private." But "public" and "private" may have another related but somewhat different relevance. Abrams describes the speaker as carrying on a colloquy "sometimes with himself or with the outer scene, but more frequently with a silent human auditor, present or absent," and his thoughts are evoked, not by the words or actions of another, but by "an aspect or change of aspect in the landscape." The speaker is, in other words, effectively, if not actually, solitary. The outer scene that is the setting for the inner meditation is a private place at least implicitly distinct from more public scenes of human activity. Gray is alone in his churchyard with the owl, the beetle, and the graves. Wordsworth describes only his natural surroundings, though when he turns to find confirmation in the light of her "wild eyes," we discover the presence of a silent human auditor. Duncan does not describe a scene in any conventional sense, but as we shall see, his words evoke a natural, peaceful setting, a place of cool water and green vegetation, sunlight and shadow.

In these poems the setting, which serves as both initiation and terminus, is thus an outer dimension and also, as a place of solitude, the emblem of an inner place of thought. By implication it may also be a means of mediating between inner and outer, private and public. Each of the three poems I have chosen involves a discovery or a pursuit of order, and in all three, the wider public world offers some threat of disorder. Gray's churchyard is remote from "the madding crowd's ignoble strife," and Wordsworth feels secure from "evil tongues, rash judgments, . . . the sneers of selfish men, . . . [and] all the dreary intercourse of daily life." Duncan looks for refuge from the fire, the strife and violence of the world of the 1960s. But each begins with a place of order and ends with a place of order.

I have mentioned a speaker and a setting. In Gray and Wordsworth, if not in Duncan, we are led to think of such a speaker and setting as providing a point of initiation and a terminus outside the poem. Gray's lines, we are told in the title, were "written in a country churchyard," and with even greater particularity, we are informed that Wordsworth's were "composed a few miles above Tintern Abbey, on revisiting the Banks of the Wye during a tour, July 13, 1798." But so far as the issues I have mentioned are concerned, it does not very much matter whether we think of Gray at Stoke Poges or Wordsworth in the Wye Valley or Duncan in, perhaps, some remembered scene from his Iowa childhood. What does matter, what does differentiate the poems is the manner in which place and speaker are created or re-created in the language and syntax that constitute the initiation and terminus within the poem, that provide the poles between which the speaker's meditation moves.

Let us turn then to Gray. If we think of these poems as an initiation and a terminus with an intervening meditation, we may consider each as having three movements, in the first of which speaker and setting are introduced and a relation between them established. In the "Elegy," the first four stanzas locate the speaker in time and space and describe the outer scene. The speaker is explicitly present only once, in the "me" of line 4:

> The curfew tolls the knell of parting day,
>   The lowing herd winds slowly o'er the lea,

> The ploughman homeward plods his weary way,
> And leaves the world to darkness and to me.

It is obvious but nonetheless important that the speaker here is determinate without being individualized. A first person pronoun necessarily means a determinate speaker, but he may speak as one of a class rather than as an individual. That we so hear this speaker is assured by the next line, "Now fades the glimmering landscape on the [not my] sight" (5), as well as by the fact that the pronoun does not recur elsewhere. It is also important that the form of the pronoun is objective rather than subjective. The poet is active in composition. The speaker, we may say, is active in that he speaks. But syntactically, he is not active: nowhere is the first person pronoun the subject of a verb except later in the words of the "hoary-headed swain" where it has a different reference. Here in the first stanza, "me" provides not an agent but a focus. A partial focus, in time, is provided by the four verbs in the present tense, but this would be true if the fourth line were something like "The lighthouse casts its beams across the sea." "To me" gathers the otherwise discrete images of curfew, herd, and ploughman into a single pattern in space as well as time. And this is maintained in the following three stanzas by "now," "yonder" tower, "those" elms, and "that" yew-tree. "Me" provides a determinate point of view, a perspective which orders what is perceived. But it is simply that of a conscious being at a particular point in time and space.

It is equally obvious that the setting is typical rather than individual. Gray certainly knew and may have had in mind the churchyard at Stokes Poges. But as the speaker in the poem has no characteristics that identify him as Gray, so the setting is generalized even in the title to *a* country churchyard, and the poem describes only what might, at the right season of the year, well have been seen and heard at dusk in any country churchyard. The description is generic and objective, of the world composed of sights and sounds familiar, from experience or literature or painting, to any observer or auditor, and thus recognizable and nameable. None of them is peculiar to one place, nor is their combination.

The first four stanzas admittedly make statements which do more than give a temporal and spatial pattern of typical objects in a typical scene. They do not, however, serve to individualize either the scene or the speaker. Apart from sights and sounds recognized and named (curfew, herd, ploughman, owl) and brought together in time and space, and apart from the few and typical perceptual details added (lowing, winds slowly, plods), the statements are either tautological ("now fades the . . . landscape on the sight") or inferential from the type named ("the ploughmen homeward plods his weary way") or from literary or artistic conventions ("the moping owl does to the moon complain"). In saying this I do not intend to denigrate Gray's aesthetic achievement, which is not here my concern, but rather to suggest a kind of structure that the stanzas exhibit, a structure whose principles are syntactical (including spatial and temporal relations in verbs and adverbs) or conventionally inferential and not, either objectively or subjectively, experiential. The structure, in other words, does not derive from a particular inner consciousness or a particular outer scene, but from the language, the syntax, and associations already familiar to the poet or speaker and his auditor or audience. And I would suggest further that this verbal structure that is the setting for "me" is at least as significant a determinant of the course of the whole poem as is the churchyard as a setting for "Gray," that the patterns established in the opening stanzas dominate the second section of the poem (stanzas 5–23), and that in the final section, it is to such patterns that the speaker, redefined as the youth,[3] is adapted.

In the Greater Romantic Lyric, Abrams says, "the speaker begins with a description of the landscape; an aspect or change of aspect in the landscape evokes a . . . process of memory, thought, anticipation, and feelings which remains closely intervolved with the outer scene." In the "Elegy," the knell of the curfew, the weariness of the departing ploughman, the darkness, the solitude, and the graves evoke such a process, and the graves and the storied urns and animated busts in the nave are "intervolved" with a meditation which culminates in the imagined grave of the speaker-youth. (This does not imply that the poem evolved in fact from these images to this meditation, but this is the order in which the poem works.) To the perceived here and now, the speaker adds a past and eventually a future, and he invokes a world wider than that of a single village in whose churchyard he stands. The past is not, however, as in Wordsworth, a remembered and personal but an inferred and typical one. As the setting was seen as general and generic, so too are the lives of those who may here be buried. It is in terms of this generic and inferential thinking that the speaker is able to define a position and an attitude. These moldering heaps are recognized as—that is, known to be—"rural village graves," and they contain therefore not individuals but "rural villagers," the poor and the obscure. Monuments within this or any church, tombs of the well-born, the rich, and the famous, are similarly the tombs of any such and therefore of all. Individuals are subsumed under types, particulars are comprehended by generalizations, all men may be divided into those in churchyard graves and those in marble tombs, and these again are merged by their common mortality. Once the name is found, multiplicity is controlled and order appears to a "me" who does not need to be restated. And thus the meditation, like the description, is able to proceed in a coherent linear sequence of general formal statements which comprehend the human condition as the description comprehended the landscape.

In another but otherwise similar poem, we might have found in the opening section not only a more individualized but a more assertive first person. And in the concluding section, we might expect not only a return to the outer scene, to here and now, but also to a first person with a renewed or altered consciousness of itself *in* the here and now. In turning to the melancholy youth and his epitaph, Gray does turn from the general to the particular instance, but only so that the particular, the individual, the "I" in fact, may be assimilated to the general. Whether as is often assumed Gray intended the youth as a self-portrait or, less plausibly, a portrait of Richard West, the figure in the poem is highly formalized and idealized,[4] deriving more from a literary, i.e., verbal, tradition than from any direct experience of a self or another. The youth is as much a type as the village Hampden and Milton, and his only identity is the identity he acquires as an instance of a type.

This assimilation of the individual to the type has been prepared for by the fact that the solitary individual speaker has spoken only as a generalized observer, and this preparation has been reinforced by the shift in pronoun from the "me" of line 4 to the "thee" of line 93 and to the "him" of line 98. Whatever the speaker's subjective knowledge of himself might be imagined to be, he describes himself only through the impression which might be made on another observer, the "hoary-headed swain." That observer infers: he sees the youth "smiling *as in* scorn" and "drooping . . . *like* one forlorn, *or* crazed with care, *or* cross'd in hopeless love" (105–08, italics added). But he, and we, are given no direct access to the youth's inner self. And even such inference disappears from the anonymous epitaph, the lines cut in stone over the grave to which all paths lead, lines which give the youth and thus the speaker whatever continuing existence they can have in the public material world in which stone outlasts both flesh and consciousness. Whatever in his being was particular, private, and transitory, the epitaph refuses to disclose, as does the poem as a whole. The solitary speaker's private meditation in a country churchyard has been embodied in public language as the being of the youth has been embodied in the epitaph. And in both cases, which are the same case, the process is one in which the private particular achieves communicable existence by being assimilated to the available and public patterns of language and of history.

Of course an essential element in the effect of Gray's remarkable poem is the awareness on the part of poet and reader of what the public and general excludes, that it is painful to resign "this pleasing anxious being," that the epitaph should elicit, the poem evoke, a sympathetic sigh. But there is no sense that the general is therefore invalid. The awareness leads not to revolt but to sadness. It is important that we have a sense of a speaker in the poem, and that we attribute to the youth some self-consciousness not visible to the hoary-headed swain. But it is also important that the outer order would be as little affected by the removal of the speaker as it is by the death of the youth, or as the poem would be by the removal of the first person pronoun in line 4. If there were no first person— if the voice were wholly disembodied—it would affect our response to the poem, but it would not affect the order embodied in it.

The situation in Wordsworth's "Tintern Abbey" is clearly different. If, in the description in the first 22 lines of the poem, we consider the setting in itself, that is as distinct from the speaker, we find that it is both less particularized and less ordered than is Gray's. "Waters," "steep and lofty cliffs," "wild secluded scene," "landscape," "sky"—these terms and those which follow are even more general than "curfew," "herd," "ploughman," and "tower." And whereas the form of Gray's sentences leads us to imagine spatial relation between the objects named, to "picture" the scene, Wordsworth's do not. Without the speaker, the scene is formless, chaotic.

But of course in "Tintern Abbey" we can separate setting from speaker only by a conscious effort that violates the poem. Gray's verbs relate noun to noun; Wordsworth's relate noun to first person pronoun: "I hear," "I behold," "I view," "I see." Even where the subject of the verb is not "I," the construction still conveys a subjective relation: "cliffs, / That on a wild secluded scene *impress / Thoughts*" and "*connect* the *landscape* with the *quiet* of the sky" (5–8, italics added). The pattern is described as one which cannot exist independently of the perceiver, and it is this which constitutes the particularity of both speaker and setting. In the subtitle, the setting is given a name and the time a date in terms of the public calendar. But in the poem, the date is relative to the speaker ("five years after the time I was first here") and the scene is particular in that it is the same scene that he saw on the previous occasion. The emphasis is on the demonstrative pronouns (*these* waters, *these* cliffs, *this* dark sycamore) which relate the nouns to the pronoun ("these where I am, which I see") rather than on the nouns themselves.

Statements of the form "I am aware of . . . " include a grammatical subject and object and seem to posit a distinction between the conscious observer and the object or scene observed. But Wordsworth's predicates do not, as might appear, denote the outer scene so much as events in consciousness, whether the impressions of the opening description or the processes and states of mind with which he continues. Instead of an observer describing a public order and placing himself in that order, we have a description of self-observation, a description of what has occurred in the speaker's mind in the past, of what is occurring "now . . . while here I stand" (58–61), and briefly of what "I dare to hope" (65) may occur in the future. And it is here in moments of experience that an order is found, felt rather than conceptualized, that enables him to stand with "cheerful faith" against the disorders of "the dreary intercourse of daily life" (131).

Wordsworth is not preaching solipsism. The "beauteous forms" which are "felt" and which pass "into my purer mind / With tranquil restoration" (22–30), the "presence which disturbs me" (94), the "Nature" which has formed his thoughts, his heart, his moral being—to all these he attributes a more than subjective origin. But except as they are known in a particular experience, they are difficult to name. Gray's terms are general or abstract but exact. Wordsworth's are not so much general as vague: "forms," "presence," "something." And they are not, as in Gray, part of a verbal structure which appears to reflect an outer order. Rather, and it is this which gives meaning to what would otherwise remain vague, the verbal structure follows, re-creates, the observed experiential process.[5]

Wordsworth thus offers two possible bases for order. One is the continuity of individual consciousness that permits the conjunction and overlapping of past and present experience and the consequent projection of future experience, not because experience can be stated and preserved in words but because states of mind can revive and coexist. It is this continuity and conjunction which underlies the movement of the second section of the poem. The other is unity of consciousness in a given moment, which is taken to be also a consciousness of unity and which permits Wordsworth to postulate a "something . . . deeply interfused" (96). In Gray, there is an order of public and historical reality to which all men are subject and a corresponding order of language to which the speaker and poet submit. As a result, there need be no distinction between public and private discourse. In his solitude, Gray speaks of what is there for all to see when rightly named. What is there in Wordsworth for all to see is, at the outset, a man gazing at the Wye Valley on July 13, 1798, and at the end that man speaking to his sister. But Wordsworth speaks not of what is there to be named for all to see but of what there may be for some at least to sense or feel. He must depend on being able to assume or evoke a kindred sense or feeling in another consciousness. In the "wild eyes" of his sister, he can "read" his "former pleasures" and "behold . . . what I was once" (117–20) and the possibility that she will become what he is now. It is to her consciousness, and by implication that of the reader, that he must point and only there that his epitaph can exist "if I should be where I no more can hear / Thy voice" (147–48).

Essential and numerous though their differences may be (and I have not begun to exhaust the subject), Gray's "Elegy" and Wordsworth's "Tintern Abbey" obviously touch at a number of points which make their juxtaposition not unreasonable. It is much less obvious that the same can be said when we add the third poem, Robert Duncan's "The Fire, *Passages* 13." The subject matter of the poem appears explicitly topical, even political, and argumentative. The second of the three sections, instead of evolving from and recurring to the images of the first, introduces descriptions of pictures by di Cosimo and Bosch and extended quotations from Ficino and Whitman. Most importantly, there is not, as in the "Elegy" and "Tintern Abbey," a speaker who is an explicit character within the poem, a figure in a landscape who serves to connect the world of private consciousness with the public world of objects and events. The only obvious similarity is that this is a poem which again begins with at least a suggestion of a peaceful and rural scene, to which at the end it returns, and that the second section is some sort of meditation on an aspect of the human condition in which the speaker finds himself involved. But superficial though this resemblance may initially appear, I think it is not merely whimsical to say that the determinate speaker and localized setting are not far away, that there is an intimate relation between the setting and the language of the first section and the meditation which follows, and that we may discover some things about Duncan's poem by approaching it from the perspective provided by the other two.

The first of the three movements of "The Fire" consists of thirty-six words arranged in six lines (or six columns):

jump	stone	hand	leaf	shadow	sun
day	plash	coin	light	downstream	fish
first	loosen	under	boat	harbor	circle
old	earth	bronze	dark	wall	waver
new	smell	purl	close	wet	green
now	rise	foot	warm	hold	cool

The concluding section consists of the same words in a different order: the last column read from bottom to top has become the first line, and so on—a mirror image turned through ninety degrees. These rows of words with which the poem begins and ends provide a point of departure and return, a kind of location for the central section of the poem.

The first section of the poem does not constitute a description in a conventional sense. It does not convey a structured picture as in Gray or a structured impression as in Wordsworth. But it is apparent that all the words could have been used in or drawn from such a description. The difference is in the absence of an ordering and limiting syntax, and this in turn means that there is no embodiment either of an eye which fixes things in relation to each other or of an "I" which apprehends things in relation to itself. Because the words are syntactically unconnected, they are free to enter into various associations. The effect is strangely relaxed, though not at all static, like images refected in rippling water. I hope it is not too fanciful to suggest that the return to the same words in the last section gives a sense of something like the reestablishment of such images in water after they have been disturbed by the throwing of a stone or a gust of wind.

It is not that the words have no order or a merely arbitrary one. They have, in the first place, a metrical order. All but seven of the thirty-six words are of one syllable, and the remainder are two-syllable words with the accent on the first. We have thus six-beat lines in which the predominance of one-syllable words has the slow monumental effect of the spondee, relaxed and made more flowing by the few unstressed syllables. To an ear attuned to English verse, a six-beat line is usually the longest that does not break down into shorter units, and an even number of beats has a slightly more continuous, flowing effect than an odd number. That there are six lines as well as six words and six beats to a line gives the passage an aural as well as a visual sense of symmetry and completeness.

This aural order leads the reader to apprehend the words as a group, to let them associate within his own mind, to produce a sense of place or places, and of atmosphere. And this in turn conveys a sense of a consciousness whose images these are, of a speaker, if you will, though not one who here appears as a figure in the scene or who is conceived as "I" or "me."

The second section of the poem is a vision of an order ("Pan's land, the pagan countryside") that is threatened and of the disorder that threatens it. The order is described first in relation to Piero di Cosimo's painting "A Forest Fire," which portrays disruption but in which Duncan sees also the depiction of harmony:

> seeking refuge wherever,
>
> as if in Eden,   in this   panic
>
> lion and lamb lie down,   quail
>
> heed not the eagle in flight before the flames high
>
> over head go.
>
> We see at least the man-faced roe and his
>
> gentle mate;   the wild boar too
>
> turns a human face.   In whose visages no terror
>
> but a philosophic sorrow shows.   The ox
>
> is fierce with terror, his thick tongue
>
> slavers and sticks out panting
>
> to make the gorgoneion face.   (16–27)

The artist "inherits the *sfumato* of Leonardo da Vinci— / there is a softening of outline, his color fuses," and produces

> featherd, furrd, leafy
>
> boundaries where   even the Furies are birds
>
> and blur   in higher harmonies Eumenides;
>
> whose animals, entering a charmd field
>
> in the light of his vision, a stillness,
>
> have their dreamy glades and pastures.   (45–50)

There is the same magic which in David's song calmed "Saul in his flaming rage" and in the music of Orpheus produces "chords and melodies of the spell that binds / the many in conflict in contrasts of one mind" (35–38).

Opposed to this is a vision of disorder, of "Hell . . . an opposing music," first in an unidentified picture by Bosch in which

> The faces of the deluded   leer, faint, in lewd praise,
>
>   close their eyes in voluptuous torment,
>
>   enthralld by fear,   (56–58)

and further reflected in the modern world of

> the daily news: the earthquakes, eruptions,
> flaming automobiles, enraged lovers, wars against communism,
> heroin addicts, police raids, race riots. . . .   (60–62)

In this world,

>   Satan looks forth from
>   men's faces:
>   Eisenhower's idiot grin, Nixon's
>   black jaw, the sly glare in Goldwater's eye, or
>   the look of Stevenson lying in the U.N. that our
>   Nation save face •   (78–83)

Finally,

> My name is Legion   and in every nation   I multiply.
>
>   Over those who would be Great Nations   Great Evils.
>
>   They are burning the woods, the brushlands, the
>
>   grassy fields razed;   their
>
>   profitable suburbs spread.
>
>   Pan's land, the pagan countryside, they'd
>
>   lay waste.   (110–16)

And we return to the reordered thirty-six words of the opening section.

Clearly this second section of the poem which I have briefly described does not make use of the setting in the manner of Gray or of Wordsworth. It is not "an aspect or change of aspect in the landscape" which evokes a process of thought, nor does that process of

thought remain "closely intervolved with the outer scene," to repeat Abrams's words. Rather it seems to be the two pictures, one of
them identified and the other easily imagined by anyone familiar
with Bosch's work, and some current events which provide points
of departure for the thoughts in the poem. But there is a relationship and one that may well be considered in conjunction with the
earlier poems. There would seem to be some affinity between the
first and third sections of the poem, and the order and harmony,
the *sfumato*, that Duncan finds in di Cosimo. The beginning of the
second section both links the opening lines with the description of
"A Forest Fire" and modulates from the lack of syntax in the opening section of the poem to the more conventional patterns of the
second section.

> blood   disk
>
> horizon   flame
>
>
> The day at the window
>
> the rain at the window
>
> the night and the star at the window
>
>   Do you know the old language?
>
>   I do not know the old language.
>
>   Do you know the language of the old belief?
>
>   From the wood we thought burning
>
> our animal spirits flee, seeking refuge wherever,
>
>   as if in Eden. . . .   (7–17)

The phrase "the language of the old belief" may have many ramifications for Duncan, with his theosophical background and esoteric knowledge, but within the poem it seems associated with the
sfumato and the "magic Pletho, Ficino, Pico della Mirandola prepared, / reviving in David's song." It also, in view of its transitional
position, seems to be associated with the language of the opening
section. If the old language and the old belief are associated with
the world of natural and magical harmony, with "Pan's land" which
is threatened and laid waste in the present, then the opening and
closing passages are surely, if perhaps among other things, an at-

tempt to render in the words but not the syntax of the language that we do know, something of that land, that order and harmony. If, without the old language and the old belief, the rendering can only be partial, it is at least not distorted by conflicting forms of thought and language.

More importantly, it is the first and third sections which enable the whole poem to parallel the achievement which Duncan attributes to di Cosimo. Within the painting, the conflict of terror and refuge, fire and Eden become contrasts within one harmony. In the poem, the conflict between the harmony of the painting and the disorder of the world in which "Satan looks forth from men's faces" becomes a contrast within the totality of the poem. It is the sense of order, and of an order which does not oppose this to that, which emerges from the first section and to which in the final section we return, which offers the possibility of a further music in which the opposing harmony and discord may play a part.

Bending the Bow, in which "The Fire" appears, is a collection of Duncan's poems written in the 1960s, in a world permeated by the malaise engendered by the cold war and Vietnam. The introduction to the volume begins with a section entitled "The War" describing the situation of a poet in that world, in which

we enter again and again the last days of our own history, for everywhere living productive forms in the evolution of forms fail, weaken, or grow monstrous, destroying the terms of their existence. . . . Now, where other nations before us have flounderd, we flounder. To defend a form that our very defense corrupts. We cannot rid ourselves of the form to which we now belong. (P. i)

Gray, though aware of the disorder of the madding crowd's ignoble strife, saw no such corruption. Wordsworth, disillusioned with the new political dawn he had thought was breaking, could nevertheless find within himself and in his past a cheerful faith against which no disorder "shall e'er prevail." For this poet, Duncan,

a boy raised in Iowa has only this nightmare, crawling forward slowly, this defeat of all deep dwelling in our common humanity, this bitter throwing forth of a wall of men moving, in which his soul must dare tender awakening or else close hard as an oak-gall within him. Only this terrible wounded area in which to have his soul-life. He turns from us, my very words turn from their music to seek his deaf ears in me. All my common animal being comes to the ox in his panic and, driven by this speech, we imagine only man, *homo faber*, has, comes into a speech words mean to come so deep that the amoeba is my brother poet. (Pp. i–ii)

Gray speaks as one remote from the arena of ignoble strife, from a tranquil and solitary spot in which he may contemplate permanent and symmetrical patterns of life and death. He has not needed to withdraw from familiar forms or language, nor need he fear the lack of auditors with whom he shares them. Wordsworth has withdrawn from France, from London, from the "din of towns and cities" and the "dreary intercourse of daily life" to where he may find both what he was and is, where he may sense the "motion and the spirit that impels" both nature and the mind of man. This is a more private and inward retreat than Gray's, a more than physical soli- tude. But seeing in his sister's eyes that what he was, she is, and what he is, she will be, he can know that what he speaks of himself can be shared by another.

For Duncan, familiar forms "fail, weaken, or grow monstrous" and he does not see in eyes around him the light of shared aware- ness. He describes the poet and his audience in the figure of an antiwar demonstration, in which "we few standing here" are con- fronted by "the advancing line of men on guard," by "hostile readers" with whom "it seemd futile at first to speak," but of whom he is also a part. "We were, in turn, members of a company of men, moving forward, violently, to overcome in themselves the little company of others kneeling and striving to speak to them, a refusal of all common speech that strove to maintain itself before us" (p. ii). Duncan too assumes a common humanity but walled away be- hind incomprehension and hostility rather than accessible as in Dorothy.

What would I have tried to tell them? That we were unarmd? That we were not the enemy, but men of their kind? In the face of an overwhelming audience waiting for me to dare move them, I would speak to those alike in soul, I know not who or where they are. But I have only the language of our commonness, alive with them as well as me, the speech of the audience in its refusal in which I would come into that confidence. The poem in which my heart beats speaks like to unlike, kind to unkind.   (P. iii)

The "language of our commonness" does not mean the accep- tance of "forms which have failed, weakened, or grown monstrous" but the speech in which "the amoeba is my brother poet." Poetry is the generation of new forms, "the ever forming of bodies in lan- guage in which breath moves, . . . a field of ensouling" (p.ii) and, like all creation, a "configuration of It in travail: giving birth to Its Self, the Creator, in Its seeking to make real—the dance of the particles in which stars, cells and sentences form" (p. vii). If the auditor or reader is to be reached, it is by language which will involve him in the dance. "In the confrontation, had we danced, taking the advance of the soldiers by the number in ranks into the choreography of the day, or, members of the dance, sat where we were, tensing the strings between the horns for the music's sake, the event the poem seeks might have emerged" (p. iv).

To include the soldiers in or from their ranks in the choreography of the poem would be to overcome the conflict, to permit a new form by dissolving the boundaries of an existing one, as in di Cosimo's boundaries "blur in higher harmonies Eumenides." In "The Fire," the magic in art and music creates a "spell that binds / the many in conflict in contrasts of one mind." It is a spell that produces order by liberation rather than restraint. "The part in its fitting," Duncan writes in his introduction,

does not lock but unlocks; what was closed is opend. Once, in the scale of Mozart, a tone on the piano key-board could be discordant; then, in Schön-berg's scale, the configuration uses all the keys, only the tone row is set. But the harmony, the method of stringing, in which conflicts are trans-formd in their being taken as contrasts, I mean to take in the largesse of meanings. It is in the movement of the particles of meaning before ideas that our ratios arise. (P. iv)

And "The Fire" as a whole attempts a harmony in which the oppos-ing music, the conflict, of Eden and hell, di Cosimo and Bosch, demonstrator and soldier, poet and audience become contrasts.

For Gray, order appears in a world conceptualized and verbal-ized. For both Wordsworth and Duncan, the basis of order is some-how beyond or prior to conceptual structure, in the motion and the spirit that "rolls through all things," in the "It in travail" which in all creation is "giving birth to Its Self." But in Wordsworth, the apprehension of that "motion," that "presence," has, we are asked to believe, occurred outside the poem; the speaker in the poem who describes his experience denotes a character and an apprehension which could exist if the poem did not. For Duncan, the "It" is manifest in the writing of the poem—the poem itself is the scene of Its activity.

Back of my person, my creaturely being, as words shift from words of my mouth, expressing, to words of the poem, creating, Man His-Her-Self, my immediate Creator, moves—the poet, His-Her agent—and would force me to some agony of my resources I dare not come to sufficient for the birth of the Created Self. In this figure, my own breath becomes a second, the breath of the poem. Olson's "the breathing of the man who writes" made anew in the breath of the line. But there is the third: the inspiration, the

breath of Creation, Spiritus Sanctus, moving between the creator breathing
and the breath of his creature.   (P. viii)

The poem is not subject to or derived from patterns perceived or
conceived outside itself but is a place of liberation where new harmonies can occur.

Working in words I am an escapist; as if I could step out of my clothes and
move naked as the wind in a world of words. But I want every part of the
actual world involved in my escape. I bring the laws that bound me into an
aerial structure in which they are unbound as outlines of a prison
unfolding.   (P. v)

As "the old orders passed from belief into the imagination," it
has come that it is in poetry that reality may be explored.

The real universe of Christendom had so become an imaginary world by
the thirteenth century that Dante could enter it in a poem as primary vision
and explore even its mysteries in the structure of his rimes. . . . Now, as
the cry *God is dead!* out of Romantic poetry deepens the crisis of Protestant
theologies a hundred years later, in poetry God is resurrected. All this
making of universes in language becomes resonant with the living reality
of His passion. Father Son and Spirit, with the saints and the Virgin,
Mother of God, become authorities of the Imagination in which Logos is
Beginning. The persons of It have revealed themselves in Eternity as the
authors of the gods.   (P. viii)

The identification of speaker and setting which we have seen
variously in Gray and Wordsworth, the formal and familiar syntax
of language, fix elements in a pattern and involve selections and
relations prior to the process of the poem. But for Duncan,

the artist, after Dante's poetics, works with all parts of the poem as *polysemous*, taking each thing of the composition as generative of meaning, a
response to and a contribution to the building form. The old doctrine of
correspondences is enlarged and furtherd in a new process of responses,
parts belonging to the architecture not only by the fittings—the concords
and contrasts in chronological sequence, as in a jigsaw puzzle—by what
comes one after another as we read, but by the resonances in the time of
the whole in the reader's mind, each part as it is conceived as a member of
every other part, having, as in a mobile, an interchange of roles, by the
creation of forms within forms as we remember.   (P. ix)

In the poem, the work of art "in which conflicts are transformed in
their being taken as contrasts," in which a "largesse of meanings"
is possible, the poet

strives not for a disintegration of syntax but for a complication within syntax, overlapping structures, so that words are freed, having bounds out of bound.

So, the artist of abundancies delites in puns, interlocking and separating figures, plays of things missing or things appearing "out of order" that remind us that all orders have their justification finally in an order of orders only our faith as we work addresses.   (P. ix)

It is awareness of the insufficiency of our orders, a recognition that "these imperatives of the poem . . . exceed our proprieties," that provides "a life-spring of dissatisfaction . . . from which the restless ordering of our poetry comes" (p. x).

How Duncan's position in the poetry of our time may come to be seen, I should not wish to predict. It does seem to me that the introduction to *Bending the Bow* stands now as a kind of manifesto for his own work, and that "The Fire" exemplifies that manifesto. It further seems to me that both, however significant or eccentric they may appear to various readers, reflect concerns which he shares with many others of his generation, different though their responses may be—concerns involving the situation of a poet in relation to himself, to his world, his language, and his audience. How far that situation has really changed since the time of Gray or the time of Wordsworth is another question. That it has been seen as having changed is evident. Because the situation has been seen by poets as having changed, it has called forth changes in response which affect the language and structure of particular poems. It is aspects of those changes which I believe poems such as I have discussed may reveal without forcing us to disregard largesse of meanings or to attempt to confine poems within the formulae of our proprieties.

NOTES

1. *Complete Poems of Thomas Gray*, ed. H. W. Starr and J. R. Hendrickson (London: Oxford University Press, 1966), pp. 37–43; *Poetical Works of William Wordsworth*, ed. Ernest de Selincourt and Helen Darbishire (London: Oxford University Press, 1952), II, 259–63; *Bending the Bow* (New York: New Directions, 1968), pp. 40–45. Subsequent page and line references in the text are to these editions.

2. "Structure and Style in the Greater Romantic Lyric," in *From Sensibility to Romanticism: Essays Presented to Frederick A. Pottle*, ed. Frederick W. Hilles and Harold Bloom (New York: Oxford University Press, 1965), pp. 527–60.

3. I accept without discussion the arguments against F. H. Ellis's finding of multiple characters in the poem, arguments summarized and extended by Frank Brady in

"Structure and Meaning in Gray's *Elegy*," Hilles and Bloom, pp. 177–87.

4. See Brady, p. 186.

5. There have been many discussions of this aspect of Wordsworth's poetry. A clear and concise account in terms of "Tintern Abbey" is by R. O. C. Winkler, "Wordsworth's Poetry," in *From Blake to Byron*, ed. Boris Ford (Harmondsworth, Middlesex: Penguin, 1957), pp. 165–69.

II. Individual Writers

GEORGE BORNSTEIN

Yeats and the Greater Romantic Lyric

In the second part of "The Tower" Yeats—as persona—paces on the battlements of his tower, stares at the landscape, and sends imagination forth to encounter it. That series of actions dramatically places him in a central Romantic line of symbol, theme, and form; like Thoor Ballylee itself the poem becomes an elaborate stage set for Yeats to sport upon in his true role of modern Romantic. The tower as symbol derives partly from Shelley, as Yeats acknowledged in the related "Blood and the Moon": "And Shelley had his towers, thought's crowned powers he called them once."[1] Yeats adopted both the symbol itself and the notion of varying it from poem to poem which he found in his precursor. Correspondingly, "The Tower" seizes upon the high Romantic theme of mind encountering the world through imagination. And finally, the second part of "The Tower"—and indeed the whole poem, for the underlying pattern would hold even without the overt triple division—is a Greater Romantic Lyric, in which poetic movement follows a special course of imaginative mental action. Yeats discovered his great mature subject in his relation to what "The Tower" calls "images and memories," and a characteristic means of developing it in the Greater Romantic Lyric. This essay first examines that traditional mode, then pursues the grounds of Yeats's reworking of it in "The Tower, II" and finally surveys his other innovations in that form.[2] In focusing primarily on later poems I do not mean to scant Yeats's early Romanticism but simply assume that topic to be sufficiently established already.[3] My subject here is Yeats's transformation of a Romantic mode—and accompanying Romantic themes—in some of his finest mature work, including "The Tower," "In Memory of Major Robert Gregory," and "The Second Coming."

I

In the Greater Romantic Lyric, Coleridge, Wordsworth, Keats, and to a lesser extent Shelley evolved a structure suitable to their individual conceptions of mental action: in Meyer Abrams's definition, a speaker in a landscape undergoes "an out-in-out process in which mind confronts nature and their interplay constitutes the poem." The first poem in the new genre, Coleridge's "Eolian Harp," illustrates the pattern: a particular speaker begins by describing the landscape round the cottage with detached affection (out), progresses through an increasingly rapt meditation in which he identifies more and more with his own revery (in), and then breaks off imaginative involvement to return to the original scene in a new mentality (out). While Abrams's interest in the doctrine of such poems causes him to describe the "in" phase as a "meditation" through which the speaker "achieves an insight, faces up to a tragic loss, comes to a moral decision, or resolves an emotional problem,"[4] I would substitute "vision" for "meditation" to emphasize the poem's structure as determined by shifting mental modes from observation to increasingly active imagination and then to its subsidence in an interpretive conclusion. In these terms, the poem's structure is description-vision-evaluation. "The Eolian Harp," for example, moves from Coleridge describing his cottage to his imagining first a fairy world, which in turn modulates into a projection of a more general world of "the one Life within us and abroad"; he then imagines himself in a noontime revery on a sunny hillside and finally rises to highest imaginative intensity in envisioning "all of animated nature" as organic harps swept by an Intellectual breeze. He then breaks off the vision and returns to the cottage, where faith, memory, and reason conspire to repudiate his imaginative power for having challenged Christian orthodoxy. Seen doctrinally, the poem "comes to a moral decision"; seen psychologically, it moves through different faculties in a searching presentation of genesis, fulfillment, and exhaustion of imagination.

Like all Greater Romantic Lyrics, "The Eolian Harp" is a poem of the act of the mind. But the genre provides a structure, not a straitjacket, and admits a variety of actions within its basic tripartite pattern. Four representative poems serve as reference points for mapping the grounds on which Yeats built his tower vision—Coleridge's "Frost at Midnight," Wordsworth's "Tintern Abbey," and Keats's "Ode to a Nightingale" and "Ode on a Grecian Urn." Situation, use of memory, and two structural innovations point our attention in "Frost at Midnight," which is in effect a Prayer For My Son. Like Yeats's "A Prayer for My Daughter," a variant on the pattern whose combination of the Atlantic with "Gregory's wood and one bare hill" recalls Coleridge's "sea, hill, and wood," the poem invokes growth in a future environment favorable to imagination for the poet's child, in contrast to the father's own experience. Coleridge's poem opens with a favorite Yeatsian situation—a man meditating at midnight inside his rural home, as in "All Souls' Night" or the more generally nocturnal "In Memory of Major Robert Gregory," two more of Yeats's Greater Romantic Lyrics. Unlike "Eolian Harp," this poem shifts into memory for its first "in" section, where Coleridge creates an image of his past self in remembering dreams prompted by a grate in childhood. Structurally, the vision comes in two parts punctuated by a return to the present, here a brief address to his "Dear Babe," before imagining a future of Hartley's communion with "lovely shapes and sounds intelligible." As Yeats will later sometimes do, Coleridge ends within his vision in impressive rhetoric.

"Tintern Abbey" follows "Frost at Midnight" in offering two visions, making the pattern out-in-out and then back in again, and stresses memory as much as imagination. As in "Coole Park 1929" (a structurally simpler Greater Romantic Lyric) and in "The Wild Swans at Coole" (which in its original stanzaic order tried to be one as far as its theme of failed imagination would permit), dynamism derives from confrontation with a place important to the speaker in the past. Wordsworth first describes the scene, then imagines a near past when he remembered it and a further past when he first encountered it, comes back to the present, and then imagines a future for Dorothy. His diction rather than his technique of using memory to prepare for imaginative action claims our attention here. He speaks of animated mental images—"the picture of the mind," "beauteous forms," and being "laid asleep in body and become a living soul"—just as Coleridge calls on "flitting phantasies" and "shapings of the unregenerate mind." Although Yeats would have hated the poem's praise of nature, he habitually used similar phrases,[5] most notably "the mind's eye," and interpreted Romantic references to images, phantoms, and other shapes more literally than their creators did. The point is not that he borrowed terms from, say, Wordsworth, but that a drive to render similar mental action causes related phraseology among writers in this genre.

Keats's two odes return to a normative three-part pattern with obvious links to Yeats's later work but also with those differences of stance which made Yeats cleave more unto Shelley. Unlike Yeats, Keats remains in the present tense, for his poems depict an ongoing struggle to transform current experience rather than to invoke memory. "Ode to a Nightingale" speaks a parable of sympathetic imagination—first bodily quiesence, then imaginative projection into the nightingale ("already with thee"), and final collapse of the vision with a bell-like forlorn "to toll me back from thee to my sole self." This Keatsian out-in-out pattern of interaction with a natural object remained alien to Yeats, who created visions apart from nature. In the Byzantium poems, his desire to reincarnate himself in a golden bird of art both recalls and "corrects" Keats's limitation of merger within natural rather than aesthetic boundaries. But even while divorcing human life from cold pastoral, Keats did allow his imagination to interact with art. In "Ode on a Grecian Urn" he first describes the urn (out), then enters into his vision to imagine a town not actually on the urn (in) at his highest intensity, and then withdraws again to a more distanced perspective (out). That is, he substitutes an art work for an actual landscape to prompt his Greater Romantic Lyric, as Wordsworth did in "Elegiac Stanzas" on Peele Castle. Yeats does not, though poems like "A Bronze Head" or "The Municipal Gallery Revisited" display similar devices. Most strikingly, his imagining of the halfway house in "Lapis Lazuli" parallels Keats's image of the Grecian town—neither exists in the artistic object, but only in the poet's mind. Yeats took from Keats as much as he could without changing from creative to sympathetic imagination.

The Romantics channeled so much creative energy into the new genre because it followed the shape of imaginative experience. More than displaying the results of imaginative creation, it allowed the following through of a mind moving from description or ordinary perception to vision and then back again. Abrams has quoted Coleridge on the return upon itself as a device making for wholeness: "The common end of all *narrative,* nay, of *all,* Poems . . . is to convert a *series* into a *Whole:* to make those events, which in real or imagined History move on in a *strait* Line, assume to our Understandings a *circular* motion—the snake with it's Tail in its Mouth."[6] Experience thus assumes the shape of ouroboros, the tail-eating snake. Equally important, it becomes a cycle and harmonizes with the cyclicity that haunts Romantic thought about both societies and individuals. Often this cyclicity takes a special shape: vision breaks off at its intensest moment and the poet returns to his ordinary state, whether in "The Eolian Harp," "Grecian Urn," or "Nightingale." Inability to sustain imagination in the poems matches our experience in life. Wordsworth minimized the discrepancy and drew new strength from his experience, while Keats stressed the discontinuity. At his most extreme a Keatsian poet is not sure which state is real, the imaginative or the ordinary, and is plagued by doubt and questioning, often ending the poem with an interrogative ("Do I wake or sleep?"). Yet despite the persona's questions, these poems ratify vision de facto, for in all of them vision is more important than natural landscape. The poems exist to present the visions, and interest centers on acts of mind, not narrative description of nature. Significance springs only from mind—the landscapes do not possess meaning in themselves but only that meaning which the poet gives them by his own mental processes. The banks of the Wye interest us only because of Wordsworth's experiences there, and we do not know at all from the poem precisely where Keats encounters his nightingale.

II

Yeats wrote Greater Romantic Lyrics only in his maturity, when he had cast off derivative Romanticism of the nineties and was creating a modern variety. The form suited the intermittent pulsations of his own imagination, and its circular shape harmonized with his antinomies and gyres. By moving into and then out of vision he could hold in a single poem reality and justice, or actual and ideal. Likewise, doubts generated by discontinuity between states matched his own vacillations. Yet he did not simply imitate his predecessors. Instead, he stepped up the importance of vision over nature even further, diminishing description of external scene and preserving only as much of nature as imagination needed. For him vision became a literal summoning of images in nature's spite. In effect, he crossed visionary autonomy from Blake and Shelley with poetic structure from Wordsworth, Coleridge, and Keats, and he infused both stance and form with his own sensibility. The resultant hybrids included many of his best poems between 1918 and 1929.

"The Tower" (VP 409) makes the form an arena for a romantic grappling with the despondency of aging. Unlike Wordsworth, the poet still has both flaming imagination and fervent sense. For Blake, those would have been enough,[7] but Yeats here fears waning of emotion, the third term he introduced into his exposition of Blake. His temptation is abstract argument, for his years demand the philosophic mind, which he conquers through vision. The first five lines of part two present an orthodox beginning for a Greater Romantic Lyric: a speaker looks at a landscape and "send[s] imagination forth" to encounter it. The next line signals a Yeatsian innovation, in calling "images and memories" from the landscape. Were the speaker Keats, he would identify with objects in the scene; were he Wordsworth, he would summon images and memories of his past self. Since he is Yeats, he calls up images and memories mostly of others. With their arrival the "in" part of the lyric begins.

These images divide the great symbols of passion and mood Yeats admired in the Romantics into paired creator and follower—

Mrs. French and her serving man, blind poet Raftery and the man drowned in Cloone bog, and Yeats's own characters of old juggler and tricked Hanrahan. Despite his Shelleyan situation on the tower, Yeats here repudiates his youthful Intellectual vision of ascent to the ideal which he had founded upon Shelley. Mrs. French's servant, the drowned man, and Hanrahan all carry over ideal moonlit visions into the actual world ("the prosaic light of day") and so end in disaster. Opposed to that, Yeats now wants moon and sunlight to "seem / One inextricable beam" encompassing antinomies into which all things fall without kindling a mad lust to live only by the moon.

The vision builds to its climax in Yeats's questioning of those images of passion—did they too rage against old age as he does? Just here, in line 101, we suddenly realize what Yeats has done. He has called up the images literally and they stand in front of him:

> But I have found an answer in those eyes
> That are impatient to be gone;
> Go, therefore; but leave Hanrahan.

We understand that Wordsworth imagines his past self near Tintern Abbey, or that Keats imagines himself with the nightingale; but what are we to understand by Yeats addressing images here as though they were present? We can make sense of this in two ways: first, he has slipped into revery and these images "in the Great Memory stored" (line 85) have now entered his individual consciousness. If we do not believe in the Great Memory, then we can say that he has called up images from his own conscious or subconscious memory (Yeats in fact knew a fair amount about the characters in this poem), or else simply created them outright, and in the intensity of his vision addresses them as if they were present, which they are in the mind.

Whatever explanation we choose, the speaker modulates out of vision in questioning Hanrahan, his own creation. His second question signals the change: "Does the imagination dwell the most / Upon a woman won or woman lost?" The "you" in the following line refers more to Yeats himself than to Hanrahan, for this is another of Yeats's continual self-reproaches about his failed relation to Maud Gonne. The lines of the poem,

> If on the lost, admit you turned aside
> From a great labyrinth out of pride,
> Cowardice, some silly over-subtle thought
> Or anything called conscience once . . .

parallel the mixture of pride, timidity, over-subtlety, and conscience in a passage about Maud in the original draft of his auto-
biography:

And in all that followed I was careful to touch [her] as one might a sister. If
she was to come to me, it must be from no temporary passionate impulse,
but with the approval of her conscience. Many a time since then, as I lay
awake at night, have I accused myself of acting, not as I thought from a high
scruple, but from a dread of moral responsibility, and my thoughts have
gone round and round, as do miserable thoughts, coming to no solution.[8]

That love, linked by Yeats to his early Romanticism, signifies the
same mistake made by the servant, drowned man, and even Hanrahan, yet its memory is so strong that even the memory reduces him
to their condition. With realization in the poem that passion still
remembers what was so fugitive, Yeats's obstinate questionings
cease. Yet in making this tangent to the Intimations ode he veers off
into his own orbit, for he refuses the Wordsworthian comfort of the
philosophic mind and, spurred by the renewed sense of loss on
which his poetry depends, makes his will in triumph of imagination. Exaltation carries over into the third section, until it subsides
again in the closing lines and leaves the poet where he began,
though with a difference.

The images summoned in this poem provide one gauge for
Yeats's claim to have corrected Romanticism by fastening its visions
to a national landscape, and thus reinvigorating them. Unlike
Greater Romantic Lyrics of the Romantics themselves, "The Tower"
could not be transferred to another setting. Mrs. French, Raftery,
and Mary Hines, the bankrupt ancient master of the house, and
others all lived in *this* landscape. Yeats's elevation of major and
minor Irish figures into heroic roles has stirred a large controversy
in which both its defenders and its attackers overstate their cases.
On the one hand, Yeats's allusions to Mary Hines, or, say, to
Maeve, do not make his poems any easier for non-Irish readers (and
perhaps not always even for Irish ones); they are, in fact, obstacles
to understanding. On the other hand, critics who simply condemn
the habit, and Yeats's exaggerated claims for it, miss the point. In
"The Tower" he uses them to move away from Romantic subjectiv-
ity which made earlier Greater Romantic Lyrics depend only upon
the poets' minds and not their environments. Mrs. French and Raftery, or elsewhere MacGregor Mathers or William Horton, are not
immediately meaningful for everybody, but they do, at least, link
private vision to something beyond the poet himself. In *A Vision*
Yeats boasted that he had improved on Blake by turning historical

characters into elements of his mythology and so made it more accessible. A romanticist might respond with some truth that the representativeness of Wordsworth's or Keats's mind makes them in fact more accessible than Yeats's quirky Celts, but I think it also true that Yeats's poems do gain both force and a measure of seeming impersonality from his tactic, which the character of his imagination badly needed. Though original Romantics may not have required this attachment, Yeats himself clearly did.

Yeats habitually addresses such images as if they were present and often claims that he sees them "in the mind's eye." That phrase takes us back to Hamlet, not thin from eating flies but as visionary prince:

> Hamlet: My father—methinks I see my father.
> Horatio: O, where, my lord?
> Hamlet: In my mind's eye, Horatio.

Yeats used the expression particularly often from about the time of *Responsibilities* through *The Tower,* when it appears in half a dozen poems and frequently in his prose. He connected it especially to seeing images of human forms, for which the allusion to Hamlet provides a cunning context. In Shakespeare's play Hamlet uses his mind's eye to see a mental image of his dead father, but he is shortly to encounter a real ghost. In Yeats's poems speakers summon figures which could be mental images but which also seem, like ghosts, to exist independently. The Shakespearian echo allows us to interpret the images as we choose, with Yeats himself remaining as gnomic as the Delphic oracle.

Because Yeats's chief innovation in the Greater Romantic Lyric was to make vision into a summoning of images, we need to look more closely at these images seen in the mind's eye before turning to more of his work in that genre. They are usually great figures of passion or of mood, like the Romantic questers so dear to Yeats. We meet the first as a completed poet-figure associated with a tower in a sort of Greater Romantic Lyric in prose, related as an incident from a tour of the Appenines:

I was alone amid a visionary, fantastic, impossible scenery. It was sunset and the stormy clouds hung upon mountain after mountain, and far off on one great summit a cloud darker than the rest glimmered with lightning. Away south upon another mountain a mediaeval tower, with no building near nor any sign of life, rose into the clouds. I saw suddenly in the mind's eye an old man, erect and a little gaunt, standing in the door of the tower, while about him broke a windy light. He was the poet who had at last, because he had done so much for the world's sake, come to share in the dignity of the saint.[9]

Yeats goes on to combine the figure with Jesus in an ecstatic rhapsody in which the old man, a mixture of Athanase and Ahasuerus, becomes a prototype of the poet as successful quester and mage. The passage's embryonic doctrine of poet and mask exfoliates later in "Ego Dominus Tuus" (1917), where Hic argues that Dante "made that hollow face of his / More plain to the mind's eye than any face / But that of Christ" (VP 368). Ille's correction of Hic's oversimple account of how poets create their masks concerns us less than how the masks or images are perceived by observers—in the mind's eye as figures of impassioned questing.

Three other poems in which images appear to the mind's eye ring changes on the theme of intense desire. In "The Magi" (1914) they are searching again for the divine union of celestial mystery and bestial floor, while in the last section of "Meditations in Time of Civil War" (1923) they are troopers calling for vengeance on the murderers of Jacques Molay. Clearly, the images can represent misdirected as well as admired passion, for Yeats's note to "Meditations" identifies the troopers' cry as "fit symbol for those who labour for hatred, and so for sterility in various kinds" (VP 827). A mixed tone pervades the description of William Horton, first image summoned in the Greater Romantic Lyric "All Souls' Night" (1921). Like early Yeats, Horton had known "that sweet extremity of pride / That's called platonic love" (VP 471). After the death of his lady (Audrey Locke) he fixes "his mind's eye . . . on one sole image," a fusion of her and God.[10] Despite Yeats's ambivalence toward Horton's (and his own) form of quest, concentrated intensity still makes Horton fit auditor of the poem's "mummy truths."

Besides great figures of passion and mood, the mind's eye could summon figures of self-possessed mastery or symbols from esoteric Yeatsism. To the first group belong Major Robert Gregory and his literary forerunner, the fisherman. In "The Fisherman" Yeats calls up an image of a Connemara man who does not exist but is "a dream" as ideal audience for the cold and passionate poetry he wanted to write. Here Yeats gives us a simple account of his genesis—he simply imagined the man. His accounts of the origin of images were not always so direct, whether in poetry or in prose. The Great Memory which he invoked in "The Tower" and the Spiritus Mundi of "The Second Coming" found fuller description in *Per Amica Silentia Lunae*, where Yeats described his own practice of symbolic meditation:

Before the mind's eye, whether in sleep or waking, came images that one was to discover presently in some book one had never read, and after looking in vain for explanation to the current theory of forgotten personal memory, I came to believe in a Great Memory passing on from generation to generation. But that was not enough, for these images showed intention and choice. . . . The thought was again and again before me that this study had created a contact or mingling with minds who had followed a like study in some other age. . . . Our daily thought was certainly but the line of foam at the shallow edge of a vast luminous sea; Henry More's *Anima Mundi*, Wordsworth's "immortal sea which brought us hither."[11]

The Great Memory gets into the poetry, but the guardedly expressed (not "I believed" but "the thought was before me") remainder does not, except possibly for the Spiritus Mundi of "The Second Coming." The sphinx vision there, like the related one seen by the mind's eye in "The Double Vision of Michael Robartes," will appear in our chronological survey of Yeats's Greater Romantic Lyrics. We have learned enough of the mind's eye and its images to continue.

III

Yeats wrote eight Greater Romantic Lyrics between 1918 and 1929. They divide into four pairs: "In Memory of Major Robert Gregory" (1918) and "All Souls' Night" (1921) summon images of the dead; "The Second Coming" (1920) and "The Double Vision of Michael Robartes" (1919) conjure images from the Great Memory; "The Tower, II" (1927) and "Meditations in Time of Civil War, VII" (1922) stress the tower top; and "Coole Park, 1929" (1931; written 1929) and "The Crazed Moon" (1932; written 1923) offer landscapes uncommonly symbolic even by Yeats's standards. All relate to Romanticism in form and often in theme and symbol as well, as we saw in "The Tower." The earliest of them, "In Memory of Major Robert Gregory," prefigures both the tower symbol and the stanzaic pattern of that poem, for it takes place in the "ancient tower" and uses the same *a a b b c d d c* rhyme scheme which Yeats derived from Cowley's elegiac ode on William Harvey and based two other Romantic poems upon, "A Prayer for My Daughter" and "Byzantium." The Coleridgean situation of Yeats's elegy recalls "Frost at Midnight," while its place in the overall order of Yeats's poems recalls Shelley, for it follows "The Wild Swans at Coole," whose basic image derives from an encounter between poet and swan in *Alastor*.

Mental action in "In Memory of Major Robert Gregory" (VP 323) follows the program of description-vision-evaluation, but a brief return to the present divides the vision itself into two parts, one of Lionel Johnson, John Synge, and George Pollexfen, and the other of Robert Gregory himself. Typically, for Yeats, the vision reverts to the past, counterpointing the spatial out-in-out with a temporal present-past-present sequence. He begins with meditative description of his present situation in the tower, whose subdued symbolic suggestion still alerts us for imminent imagination. In the initial vision, images of "discoverers of forgotten truth" and "companions" come to the speaker's mind. All of them are figures of passion or mood: Johnson brooding on sanctity and dreaming of consummation, Synge finding at last an objective correlative to his heart in passionate and simple Aran islanders, and Pollexfen forsaking physical sport for astrological search. A relapse into the present to mention "all things the delighted eye now sees" prepares for the sustained vision of Robert Gregory. Though described as ideal "soldier, scholar, horseman," Gregory appears mostly as artist, particularly if we remember that the eighth stanza, on horsemanship, was added to the poem later at his widow's request. In accomplishing all "perfectly," Gregory resolves the split between active and contemplative, becoming the kind of possible subject for a poem suggested at the end of Stevens' "Of Modern Poetry." The vision culminates in the eleventh stanza where Yeats subordinates Gregory to symbolic ignition of the combustible world. The question, "What made us dream that he could comb grey hair?" signals the exhaustion of imagination at its intensest moment and prepares us to shift back "out" into evaluation.

The final stanza deserves more attention than it usually receives. Its first two lines, which return us to the original scene, oppose the wind of nature (not inspiration) to mind and suggest that mind creates its images to counterbalance nature, to resist a violence from without by a violence from within. The speaker then reveals his original plan—not just to call up Synge (whom "manhood tried"), Pollexfen (whom "childhood loved"), or Johnson (whom "boyish intellect approved"), but to *comment* on them "Until imagination brought / A fitter welcome." Imagination thus redeems the decay implicit in the chronological sequence love-approve-test. Yeats's always erratic punctuation obscures the syntax here. A comma instead of semicolon after "each" in the first two printings[12] makes it culminate the previous sequence—he thought to comment until imagination would enter in. This Yeats has done most fully for Gregory but also in miniature for Johnson, Synge, and Pollexfen, whom he has turned into images of intensity. But, the last two lines suggest, thought of Gregory's death interrupted a lengthier sequence by discharging Yeats's passion ("heart"). This exhaustion of the heart recurs as problem in "The Tower"; here it marks the end of a remarkable reworking of a Romantic mode.

Similar structure holds together the more abstruse "All Souls' Night," written two years later and eventually made into an epilogue for *A Vision*. Again the speaker summons a trio of dead contemporaries—Horton, Florence (Farr) Emery, and MacGregor Mathers, all of whom appear as images of the esoteric students Yeats imitated as Athanase. Since the mental action resembles that of the Gregory elegy,[13] we may focus on the meaning of "the dead." In the earlier poem, the figures were dead in a double sense: they had physically died, and they had become artistic images in the poem, part of the artifice of eternity opposed to time. This Shelleyan association of death with completion or fulfillment, which had informed Yeats's poems of the nineties, spills over into "All Souls' Night," where the ghostly (a deliberate Yeatsian pun) images become fit auditors for Yeats's "mummy truths," both of the poem and of *A Vision*. As creations of imagination they can share Yeats's own imaginative communications. As conclusion to the *Tower* volume, the poem neatly reverses the situation of the initial "Sailing to Byzantium," when Yeats had wanted to be instructed by the spirits; as a result of lessons learned in poems like "The Tower," he can now summon spirits to be instructed by him in imagination's truth. That is, the volume as a whole resurrects flagging passion and harnesses it to imaginative vision. A different kind of action informs the next pair of Yeats's Greater Romantic Lyrics.

Like "The Double Vision of Michael Robartes," Yeats's famous "The Second Coming" calls up impersonal images rather than those fashioned from the poet's past. Yeats ascribes their source to Spiritus Mundi, which in a note to another poem from *Michael Robartes and the Dancer* he defines as "a general storehouse of images which have ceased to be a property of any personality or spirit" (VP 822). The poem's brevity reveals its structure as a Greater Romantic Lyric clearly:

> Turning and turning in the widening gyre
> The falcon cannot hear the falconer;
> Things fall apart; the centre cannot hold;
> Mere anarchy is loosed upon the world,
> The blood-dimmed tide is loosed, and everywhere   5
> The ceremony of innocence is drowned;
> The best lack all conviction, while the worst
> Are full of passionate intensity.

> Surely some revelation is at hand;
> Surely the Second Coming is at hand.   10
> The Second Coming! Hardly are those words out
> When a vast image out of *Spiritus Mundi*
> Troubles my sight: somewhere in the sands of the desert
> A shape with lion body and the head of a man,
> A gaze blank and pitiless as the sun,   15
> Is moving its slow thighs, while all about it
> Reel shadows of the indignant desert birds.
> The darkness drops again; but now I know
> That twenty centuries of stony sleep
> Were vexed to nightmare by a rocking cradle,   20
> And what rough beast, its hour come round at last,
> Slouches towards Bethlehem to be born?   (VP 401–02)

The transition from description to vision comes midway in line 11, while that from vision to evaluation occurs immediately after line 17. But here Yeats prepares for vision not by passive revery or negative capability but by working himself into a prophetic frenzy. He adopts the stance of seer, and what he describes is not an actual landscape but a metaphoric one: we do not feel that a falcon flies off before his eyes any more than that he literally sees a blood-dimmed tide. Instead, he depicts the state of Europe as if from the top of a mile-high tower, from which he can see as far as the Germans in Russia—whom he mentioned in the original draft.[14] Scholarly quarrels about identity of falcon and falconer—whether Christ and man, nature and spirit, logic and mind—should not be allowed to obscure the emblem's significance, loss of control. It matches loss of rational control in the speaker's mental action as he moves to a rhetorical crescendo preparatory to vision.

Because the image seen in the mind's eye comes from Spiritus Mundi, Yeats does not have to recall it personally; consequently, he can increase urgency by writing the entire poem in the present tense. The vision section carries over the passionate tone of the quasi description to a displacement only in space and not in time. A here-there-here movement matches the familiar out-in-out structure. This vision of antithetical Egyptian Sphinx heralding the end of primary Christianity replaces the erratic falcon with birds once again wheeling in formation. Although Yeats often exults at the end of "scientific, democratic, fact-accumulating, heterogeneous civilization,"[15] commentators err in seeing that attitude in the poem. The vision "troubles" the speaker's sight; it is the sphinx whose eye is "blank and pitiless."

With the end of vision the speaker's return to himself completes the doubling action built into the poem by the paired birds, the title itself, and the repeated phrases "turning," "is loosed," "surely," "the Second Coming," and "is at hand." The change reminds us why the Greater Romantic Lyric attracted Yeats so much: its return upon itself suits his true subject, which is more his relation to his vision than the vision itself. Typically, the vision leaves the speaker in a state of partial illumination. Now he knows not only that a nightmarish coming is at hand, but also that it was caused by the rocking cradle of Jesus. This means, I think, not just that the gyres are reciprocal (living each other's life and dying each other's death), but that the new god appears savage because seen through the mental set of Christian civilization and its derivatives. The final question is genuine, not rhetorical; in Yeats's system we know that something is coming but we do not know precisely what, nor can we, for we are bound by the old civilization. Nor does the speaker rejoice, for his phrase "rough beast" suggests horror rather than delight.

"The Second Coming" is Romantic in more than form; it is shot through with Blakean and Shelleyan echoes in theme and diction. Behind the poem lurks "Ozymandias," with its picture of a monumental ruin in a desert, while Harold Bloom has identified the source of the center which cannot hold in the rejection of natural love by the Witch of Atlas.[16] Likewise, the phrase "stony sleep" comes from Blake's *Book of Urizen,* where it describes Urizen's transitional phase between his Eternal state and his rebirth as fallen man.[17] But reworking of the Last Fury's speech in act one of *Prometheus Unbound* dwarfs even those in significance:

> The good want power, but to weep barren tears.
> The powerful goodness want: worse need for them.
> The wise want love; and those who love want wisdom;
> And all best things are thus confused to ill.   (1.625–28)

> The best lack all conviction, while the worst
> Are full of passionate intensity.   (VP 402)

As many commentators, including the present one,[18] have pointed out, Yeats reverses the thrust of Shelley's apocalyptic lines by making them a prelude to another cycle rather than to (possibly temporary) transfiguration. Here, we may note the difference in mental action. Prometheus frustrates the Fury's plan to torture him with a vision of human suffering by unexpectedly drawing strength from it: "The sights with which thou torturest gird my soul / With new endurance, till the hour arrives / When they shall be no types of things which are." A vision of heroic and selfless virtues follows in the songs of the six spirits, preparatory to the poem's later apocalypse of love. In "The Second Coming," however, the comparable lines create a frenzy in the speaker which prepares him for a vision of the rough beast to come, after which he reverts to his original state, having grown in knowledge but not in power. There is a fatalism in the poem which Yeats's *Vision* system often prompted, in which the quest for Unity of Being turns into a quest for knowledge instead, whether "mummy truths" of "All Souls' Night" or half-knowledge of "The Second Coming." Against this, Yeats sets ironic self-criticism as in "The Phases of the Moon" or images of Unity of Being like the dancer in "Among School Children."

"The Double Vision of Michael Robartes" (VP 382) summons images from Spiritus Mundi or the Great Memory and returns us to Yeats's concern with the poet's relation to Unity of Being. In a Greater Romantic Lyric which begins and ends in the ruins of a chapel restored on the Rock of Cashel by Cormac MacCarthy in the twelfth century, Robartes sees "in the mind's eye" two visions—in terms of the system, the first of phase one and the second of phase fifteen. In the second, a girl emblematic of Unity of Being dances between Sphinx (this time a Grecian one, representing knowledge) and Buddha (love). Because all three have overthrown time, like other images in Yeats they seem both dead and alive. In the third movement of the lyric (out), Robartes's attention focuses on the girl who "outdanced" thought. He identifies her with a dream maiden forgotten when awake, one of the Shelleyan ideals of Yeats's youth, whom in later life he preferred to identify with Homer's Helen or Dante's Beatrice. Unlike her, he is caught not between perfect knowledge and perfect love but rather in the human tension between objective thought and subjective images. He faces this predicament both in life and in the two opposing states which form the poem. With vision fled, his gain is knowledge of a personal ideal, not of impersonal forces as in "The Second Coming." Development toward that ideal is the one freedom offered by Yeats's system, though he allows others outside of it. The lyric ends with his Romantic "moan" of recognition and equally Romantic resolve to render the experience artistically. Like a miniature *Prelude* or *Milton*, "The Double Vision of Michael Robartes" describes an action which is a prelude to poetry.

Yeats's next pair of Greater Romantic Lyrics, "The Tower, II" and "Meditations in Time of Civil War, VII," strike a middle ground between the personal images of dead friends in "In Memory of Major Robert Gregory" and "All Souls' Night" and the impersonal ones of inhuman extremes in "The Second Coming" and "The Double Vision of Michael Robartes." Both poems make the tower top into a symbolic outpost on the border between self and soul. Yet unlike "The Tower," discussed above, "Meditations"[19] draws its images not from past associations of the landscape but from an analogous event in history—the murder of Jacques Molay, Grand Master of the Templars, which it counterpoints with figures derived from Gustave Moreau's visionary painting "Ladies and Unicorns." They become the ingredients of one of Yeats's most moving struggles against the hatred inherent in the age and in some of his own thought. As he stands upon the tower top, images of first the troop of murderers and then the procession of ladies swim "to the mind's eye." In terms of the poem's title, the first represent "Phantoms of Hatred" and the second those "Of the Heart's Fullness." The imagination tries to counter images of hatred with those of fullness, but as even they yield to "an indifferent multitude . . . brazen hawks . . . Nothing but grip of claws," the poem modulates out of vision into its third and final section. There Yeats descends from the tower top, regrets his separation from friends and public approval, but still resignedly affirms his continued allegiance to "the half-read wisdom of daemonic images." That moment becomes all the more poignant for its frank avowal of human cost.

Although Yeats paired "The Crazed Moon" with "Coole Park, 1929" in *The Winding Stair,* he had written it in 1923, shortly after the other Greater Romantic Lyrics on *Vision* themes. Like them, it can be read in terms of Yeats's system: in a late phase, the moon shines only on moonstruck, disorganized gropers, in contrast to her exuberant children of earlier phases, who danced in order. Further, the later children grow murderous as the gyre approaches conclusion, and they long maliciously to rend whatever comes in reach. But the poem can also be read more literally, as a Greater Romantic Lyric of mental action:

> Crazed through much child-bearing
> The moon is staggering in the sky;
> Moon-struck by the despairing
> Glances of her wandering eye
> We grope, and grope in vain,
> For children born of her pain.
>
> Children dazed or dead!
> When she in all her virginal pride

> First trod on the mountain's head
> What stir ran through the countryside
> Where every foot obeyed her glance!
> What manhood led the dance!
>
> Fly-catchers of the moon,
> Our hands are blenched, our fingers seem
> But slender needles of bone;
> Blenched by that malicious dream
> They are spread wide that each
> May rend what comes in reach.   (VP 487–88)

The three stanzas reenact the familiar triple pattern, matching out-in-out with present-past-present. The speaker first describes the current state of the old moon, then creates a vision of the moon in virginal pride inspiring both passion ("stir") and order ("dance"), and finally returns to the present with perceptions of our vain groping's goal—malicious destruction. The landscape here is remarkably insubstantial even for Yeats; one feels as though the speaker were charting a symbolic Romantic landscape rather than an actual scene. Polysemously, the moon can refer to a natural object, the twenty-eight phases of *A Vision*, historical development in clock time, or imagination withering from exultance to despair. In his current condition, the speaker's only triumph is to re-create past glory from memory.

Yeats transfers that theme to his favorite Irish setting in the following poem of *The Winding Stair*, "Coole Park, 1929." The poem contributes to the book's running modern adaptation of Romanticism, following the Shelleyan tower of "Blood and the Moon" and literary history of "The Nineteenth Century and After" and "Three Movements," picking up the Greater Romantic Lyric form of "The Crazed Moon," and anticipating Romantic self-avowal in "Coole Park and Ballylee, 1931" and Romantic artifice in "Byzantium." He returns to the Coole-Ballylee region for the national ballast with which he habitually sought to weight Romanticism. The landscape's significance derives neither from mere personal experience nor from the arbitrary mythology of *A Vision*, but from its importance to actual historical figures, albeit ones transformed by Yeats's imagination. These historical types, which include the younger Yeats himself, become quasi-objective analogues to Romantic symbols of passion and mood.

The poem opens with a conventional enough beginning for a Greater Romantic Lyric: in a specific landscape at nightfall, the speaker meditates on a bird's flight and even identifies the surrounding trees as a sycamore and a lime.[20] Although the swallow may pick up the Neoplatonic echoes[21] which Yeats associated with Romanticism in general and Shelley in particular, its overt development in the poem follows orthodox Romantic use of singing birds to symbolize artists and their works. The ensuing portions champion freedom from oppressive nature, which Yeats always commended in Romanticism, in explicating why the speaker fixes his eye on works constructed "in nature's spite."

With the vision of former glory in the second stanza, the speaker reverts to the past. Noble Hyde, meditative Synge, and impetuous Shawe-Taylor and Hugh Lane, with Yeats himself in ironic companionship, become heroic figures whose action indicates the poem's real symbol of passion and mood, Lady Gregory herself. Her character most rouses Yeats's intensity of vision as he moves in the third stanza from remembering the past to creating the powerful image of swallows whirling in formation around her true north. The concluding couplet, with its off-rhyme of "lines" and "withershins" and suggestion both of gyres and of imaginative *kairos* replacing natural *chronos*, exhausts his imagination in a momentary blaze.

Superficially, the "here" of the final stanza seems to signal the close of a conventional Greater Romantic Lyric. We expect completion of normative here-there-here, out-in-out, and present-past-present movements. But Yeats plays against our vain anticipation, for "here" turns out to be placed in an imagined future. It is as if Wordsworth's "Tintern Abbey" or Coleridge's "Frost at Midnight" omitted their return to the present which separates their vision of the past from that of the future. Instead, Yeats moves directly from past to future in imagining later travelers, scholars, and poets (or perhaps the ghosts of those mentioned in stanza two) taking their stand at a ruined Coole and paying tribute to Lady Gregory. By replacing a return to self with a return to vision, Yeats shifts our attention away from the speaker and toward his overt subject. We end in contemplation of Coole rather than of Yeats's relation to it.

Yeats's adventures with the Greater Romantic Lyric show a sensibility with affinities to Shelley and Blake reworking a poetic form developed principally by Coleridge, Wordsworth, and Keats. The resultant collision exploded the original importance of nature to the form. For Yeats vision became the summoning of images and, in the highest case, active creation of them *de novo*. He pruned his natural descriptions radically, reducing them to a minimum and exploiting their national associations. This transformed his predecessors' concern with tension between mind and nature to tension between mind and images. That dialectic suited his antinomial correction of the emphasis on ideal beauty in his earlier works; through it, he could reach a poetry of insight and knowledge rather than of longing and complaint. The resultant Greater Romantic Lyrics of mental action form one branch of Yeats's mature and innovative Romanticism.

NOTES

1. *The Variorum Edition of the Poems of W. B. Yeats,* ed. Peter Allt and Russell K. Alspach (New York: Macmillan, 1957), p. 480. Hereafter cited in the text as VP followed by page number. Cf. Yeats's note to *The Winding Stair:* "In this book and elsewhere I have used towers, and one tower in particular, as symbols and have compared their winding stairs to the philosophical gyres, but it is hardly necessary to interpret what comes from the main track of thought and expression. Shelley uses towers constantly as symbols" (VP 831). Yeats had traced Shelley's use of towers in "The Philosophy of Shelley's Poetry."

2. An abbreviated text of this essay was read at the Midwest Modern Language Association Meeting in Chicago, November 1975. A still longer version will form part of a larger study, *Transformations of Romanticism in Yeats, Eliot, and Stevens.* I am grateful to the American Council of Learned Societies for a fellowship in support of this work.

3. I have already given my views on Yeats's early romanticism in *Yeats and Shelley* (Chicago: University of Chicago Press, 1970); Harold Bloom uses a different approach to arrive at many similar and some quite different views in his *Yeats* (New York: Oxford University Press, 1970). The two books are in part complementary.

4. "Structure and Style in the Greater Romantic Lyric," in *From Sensibility to Romanticism: Essays Presented to Frederick A. Pottle,* ed. Frederick W. Hilles and Harold Bloom (New York: Oxford University Press, 1965), p. 528.

5. Cf. "pictures of the mind" in "In Memory of Eva Gore-Booth and Con Markiewicz" (VP 475).

6. "Structure and Style in the Greater Romantic Lyric," p. 532. Ellipses mine.

7. A. Norman Jeffares has even suggested a possible echo in "The Tower" of Blake on bodily decay; see his *A Commentary on the Collected Poems of W. B. Yeats* (Stanford: Stanford University Press, 1968), p. 258.

8. W. B. Yeats, *Memoirs,* ed. Denis Donoghue (London: Macmillan, 1972), p. 133. See pp. 33 and 84 for Yeats's conception of his youthful love as romantic.

9. *Essays and Introductions* (New York: Macmillan, 1961), p. 291.

10. Horton's contemplation of an image links this poem to the more recondite "Phases of the Moon" (1919), where the creatures of the full moon, or phase fifteen, fix the mind's eye "upon images that once were thought" (VP 375).

11. *Mythologies* (London: Macmillan, 1962), pp. 345–46.

12. In *The English Review* and *The Little Review,* 1918.

13. It moves out-in-out, with a parallel present-past-present pattern.

14. See Jon Stallworthy, *Between the Lines: Yeats's Poetry in the Making* (Oxford: The Clarendon Press, 1963), p. 17.

15. This phrase comes from Yeats's own note to "The Second Coming" (VP 825).

16. *Yeats,* p. 320.

17. Margaret Rudd first noticed this in her *Divided Image: A Study of William Blake and W. B. Yeats* (London: Routledge & Kegan Paul, 1953), p. 119. There is an interesting discussion in Bloom, *Yeats,* p. 319.

18. In *Yeats and Shelley,* pp. 195–98.

19. VP 425. See VP 827 for Yeats's note.

20. Yeats's prose draft for the poem began: "Describe house in first stanza." Parkinson has a valuable discussion of the evolution of the poem, in *W. B. Yeats: The Later Poetry* (Berkeley and Los Angeles: University of California Press, 1964), pp. 80–81, followed by a longer one of "Among School Children."

21. Jeffares compares Pythagoras' use of a swallow image; see *A Commentary,* p. 344.

A. WALTON LITZ

Wallace Stevens' Defense of Poetry:
La poésie pure, *the New Romantic,*
and the Pressure of Reality

Poets have always been on the defensive, at least since the time of Plato, but few can have found themselves under such intense pressure from without and within as Wallace Stevens in the mid-1930s, when he was laboring on *Ideas of Order* and *Owl's Clover*. Having abandoned the writing of poetry in 1924 for a variety of complex reasons, both personal and aesthetic,[1] Stevens returned to his art in the early 1930s as a "most inappropriate man / In a most unpropitious place."[2] The general impact upon the human spirit of economic and political disasters, and the popular demand that the poet take an active role in social reform, placed Stevens under almost intolerable strain. Stanley Burnshaw's Marxist review of *Ideas of Order*, and Stevens' exaggerated response to it, were merely the most obvious signs of an anxious struggle which ran deep in his poetry and prose of the 1930s. At the climax of his work on *Harmonium*, Stevens had felt himself a part of the contemporary literary world, both in subject and technique; in his highly personal way he belonged to the Modernist movement that dominated the early 1920s. But as he warmed himself back to artistic life in the early 1930s with the poems of *Ideas of Order*, Stevens felt isolated and out of fashion. Of the many "orders" he sought in the 1930s, a sustaining "defense of poetry" was his most compelling need.

We can take the measure of Stevens' uncertainty at that time by comparing the confident poems of *Harmonium* with the more tentative "ideas of order" of 1931–35. In 1921, when Stevens was at the height of his early imaginative powers, "The Snow Man" and "Tea at the Palaz of Hoon" were published side-by-side in a dazzling series of poems called "Sur Ma Guzzla Gracile."[3] Taken together the two poems map out the extreme coordinates of *Harmonium*: in "The Snow Man" bare landscape dominates the poetic spirit, demanding a "mind of winter" which will see and hear "Nothing that is not there and the nothing that is" (CP 9–10), while in "Tea at the Palaz of Hoon" the nonlocalized setting and exotic detail are totally favorable to the inventive imagination.

111

Not less because in purple I descended
The western day through what you called
The loneliest air, not less was I myself.

What was the ointment sprinkled on my beard?
What were the hymns that buzzed beside my ears?
What was the sea whose tide swept through me there?

Out of my mind the golden ointment rained,
And my ears made the blowing hymns they heard.
I was myself the compass of that sea:

I was the world in which I walked, and what I saw
Or heard or felt came not but from myself;
And there I found myself more truly and more strange.   (CP 65)

In *Ideas of Order*, by contrast, the sumptuous Imagist landscape of
"The Snow Man" has given way to the monotonous sound-scape of
"Autumn Refrain" (CP 160), where the evasive "words about the
nightingale" of traditional Romanticism are replaced by the
"skreaking and skrittering residuum" of minimal reality; and "that
mountain-minded Hoon," the creator of his own world, finds himself bereft of forms.

The truth is that there comes a time
When we can mourn no more over music
That is so much motionless sound.

There comes a time when the waltz
Is no longer a mode of desire, a mode
Of revealing desire and is empty of shadows.

Too many waltzes have ended. And then
There's that mountain-minded Hoon,
For whom desire was never that of the waltz,

Who found all form and order in solitude,
For whom the shapes were never the figures of men.
Now, for him, his forms have vanished.

("Sad Strains of a Gay Waltz," CP 121)

In a time of social chaos and disbelief, the poet lives in a world
without shadows, without imaginative other selves. Like the "An-
glais Mort à Florence," Stevens was faced in the 1930s with a diminished world where he could no longer stand alone.

Perhaps the poem most expressive of Stevens' uncertain mood,
his need for a new defense of poetry, is "Mozart, 1935," the only
poem in the canon which bears an explicit dateline.

Poet, be seated at the piano.
Play the present, its hoo-hoo-hoo,
Its shoo-shoo-shoo, its ric-a-nic,
Its envious cachinnation.

If they throw stones upon the roof
While you practice arpeggios,
It is because they carry down the stairs
A body in rags.
Be seated at the piano.

That lucid souvenir of the past,
The divertimento;
That airy dream of the future,
The unclouded concerto . . .
The snow is falling.
Strike the piercing chord.

Be thou the voice,
Not you. Be thou, be thou
The voice of angry fear,
The voice of this besieging pain.

Be thou that wintry sound
As of the great wind howling,
By which sorrow is released,
Dismissed, absolved
In a starry placating.

We may return to Mozart.
He was young, and we, we are old.
The snow is falling
And the streets are full of cries.
Be seated, thou.   (CP 131–32)

Here, as in "Lions in Sweden" (CP 124–25), the word "souvenir" is
used in Baudelaire's sense: a once vital feeling or image which has
become a piece of poetic bric-a-brac through the changes of time.
"Be thou the voice" echoes Shelley's "Ode to the West Wind,"

> Be thou, spirit fierce,
> My spirit! Be thou me, impetuous one!

but without Shelley's belief in the possibility of some transcendent
metamorphosis. All that is left of the great Romantic *ars poetica* is
the naked personality of the poet, isolated in an unsympathetic
environment. If he is to construct a new defense of poetry, a modern variation on the themes of Sidney and Shelley, the poet must

build it out of the fragments of a shattered tradition, yet make it strong enough to withstand the pressures of contemporary reality.

In his poems and essays of the 1930s, as well as in the early "Adagia,"[4] Stevens is looking for a satisfactory definition of the poet's role, trying to locate the sources of "nobility" in an age without order or form. At first this search was tentative and even muddled, filled with false starts, but by the time he had written *The Man with the Blue Guitar* and the frankly "theoretic" poems in *Parts of a World,* Stevens had sketched the outline of a sustaining poetic, which was then fleshed out and refined in the essays and long poems of the 1940s. In the course of this heroic self-examination he developed a vocabulary which may appear vague or self-indulgent to the uninitiated reader, but which is validated through repeated use in the poetry and prose: words such as "nobility," "purity," "transparence," "imagination," "the central," and "romantic" take on a special reality of their own. However, in the years of doubt and experimentation, when *Ideas of Order* and *Owl's Clover* were works-in-progress, Stevens was trying out various terms and mottoes with obsessive frequency, shifting their connotations until he could find their exact properties. It is almost as if he believed that certain traditional terms contained magical powers and would reveal their meaning for his time and place if used often enough. Among these obsessively repeated terms, which would ultimately take on the force of personal metaphor, "pure poetry" and "the romantic" stand out. This essay will explore the sources and permutations of these terms, with the double aim of illuminating Stevens' transitional poetry and providing a background for the grand poetics of his last years.

When the second and augmented edition of *Ideas of Order* was published in 1936, the dust jacket contained a statement by Wallace Stevens which read in part:

The book is essentially a book of pure poetry. I believe that, in any society, the poet should be the exponent of the imagination of that society. *Ideas of Order* attempts to illustrate the role of the imagination in life, and particularly in life at present. The more realistic life may be, the more it needs the stimulus of the imagination.

The term "pure poetry" may have been intended as provocation in an age of social realism, and certainly the left-wing critics took it as such; but it was also a crucial term in Stevens' evolving aesthetic. In December 1936, in a lecture at Harvard on "The Irrational Element in Poetry" (OP 216–29), he used the term as the keystone in his first public justification of his own poetry. Written at the time when he had finished *Owl's Clover* and was beginning work on *The Man with the Blue Guitar*, the lecture displays all the faults of *Owl's Clover* that Stevens was to cast off in his next poems. It is diffuse, rhetorical, and somewhat anxious in tone. The "irrational" of the title is connected with the "subman" of "Sombre Figuration" (*Owl's Clover*, Part 5), and testifies to Stevens' passing belief (a flirtation with fashionable psychology) that the imagination was an "activity of the sub-conscious" (L 373). In the course of answering the rhetorical question, "Why does one write poetry?" Stevens revealed one of the sources for his notion of pure poetry by referring to Abbé Henri Bremond's address to the Institut de France in 1925.

In his discourse before the Academy, ten years or more ago, M. Brémond elucidated a mystical motive and made it clear that, in his opinion, one writes poetry to find God. I should like to consider this in conjunction with what might better be considered separately, and that is the question of meaning in poetry. M. Brémond proposed the identity of poetry and prayer, and followed Bergson in relying, in the last analysis, on faith. M. Brémond eliminated reason as the essential element in poetry. Poetry in which the irrational element dominated was pure poetry. M. Brémond himself does not permit any looseness in the expression pure poetry, which he confines to a very small body of poetry, as he should, if the lines in which he recognizes it are as precious to his spirit as they appear to be. In spite of M. Brémond, pure poetry is a term that has grown to be descriptive of poetry in which not the true subject but the poetry of the subject is paramount. Pure poetry is both mystical and irrational. If we descend a little from this height and apply the looser and broader definition of pure poetry, it is possible to say that, while it can lie in the temperament of very few of us to write poetry in order to find God, it is probably the purpose of each of us to write poetry to find the good which, in the Platonic sense, is synonymous with God. One writes poetry, then, in order to approach the good in what is harmonious and orderly.   (OP 221–22)

Bremond's lecture, which was elaborated in *La Poésie pure* (1926) and *Prière et Poésie* (1926), became the focus for an intense critical debate in France that did not subside until the early 1930s.[5] At one time or another most of the important French poets and critics joined the argument, including Valéry and Ramon Fernandez (this may help to explain the "accidental" appearance of Fernandez in "The Idea of Order at Key West"). Valéry was in some ways the initiator of the debate, with his 1920 "Avant-propos" to Lucien Fabre's *Connaissance de la Déesse*, and his continuing concern with the definition of pure poetry gave the issue international currency. His famous 1928 essay "Poésie pure" first appeared in English in

the *New York Herald Tribune*, 15 April 1928. Paul Souday published
a partisan account of the early phases of the debate in the *New York
Times Book Review*, 29 November 1925, and Mario Praz put forward
the Crocean viewpoint (essentially hostile to Bremond) in *The Criterion* (1928).[6] The lingering force of the debate in England and America is evidenced by Robert Penn Warren's essay "Pure and Impure
Poetry" (1942), delivered at Princeton as a *Mesures* lecture the year
after Stevens read "The Noble Rider and the Sound of Words," and
by T. S. Eliot's "From Poe to Valéry" (1948), which presents
Valéry's poetic as the culmination (and termination) of a century-
long movement toward poetic self-consciousness and aesthetic autonomy.[7] Eliot sees the progress from Poe to Valéry as an approach
toward the theoretical goal of *la poésie pure*, a goal which—like all
theories in Eliot's critical world—is unobtainable in practice.

This process of increasing self-consciousness—or, we may say, of increasing consciousness of language—has as its theoretical goal what we may call
la poésie pure. I believe it to be a goal that can never be reached, because I
think that poetry is only poetry so long as it preserves some "impurity" in
this sense: that is to say, so long as the subject matter is valued for its own
sake. The Abbé Brémond, if I have understood him, maintains that while
the element of *la poésie pure* is necessary to make a poem a poem, no poem
can consist of *la poésie pure* solely. But what has happened in the case of
Valéry is a change of attitude toward the subject matter. We must be careful
to avoid saying that the subject matter becomes "less important." It has
rather a different kind of importance: it is important as *means:* the *end* is the
poem.[8]

Stevens obviously knew the English and French traditions of *la
poésie pure* in great detail; his affinities with Mallarmé's concept of
"purity" have already been examined by Michel Benamou.[9] He
must have realized that he, like Valéry, was a true inheritor of the
traditions, but he could not accept without modifications the practice and theory of any one precursor. He could not accept the sterility of Mallarmé's "ideal nakedness," nor Bremond's religious mysticism, nor Valéry's emphasis on the purity of language, nor the
fuzziness of conventional English usage (in George Moore's 1925
Anthology of Pure Poetry the term seems synonymous with direct
lyricism, and the examples range from Skelton to Swinburne). Stevens had to isolate from the critical traditions those elements which
could satisfy his special needs, and weld them onto his nascent
theory of the heroic in poetry. And in this obscure process of adaptation and change, Benedetto Croce appears to have played a cata-
lytic role.

Croce's 1933 Oxford lecture, *The Defence of Poetry*, is first cited by Stevens in "The Noble Rider and the Sound of Words" (1941), but its influence on his poetic thought stretches back to 1934–35. "Is it possible to discuss aesthetic expression without at least discussing Croce?" Stevens asked rhetorically in 1941, while giving advice on the planning of the *Mesures* lectures at Princeton (L 385); for Stevens himself it does not seem to have been possible. One can imagine his delight in reading the 1933 *Defence of Poetry*, since Croce places his discussion against a contemporary background of vanished "lofty motives" and a diminished "sublime." "The old religion loses every day more of what respectability it still possessed," Croce observes: "This is the dense atmosphere in which we are stifled, which painfully chokes and crushes every freedom of heart, every delicate sensibility, every quickness of mind."[10] It does not matter that Croce is deliberately exaggerating; the background fits well enough with Stevens' own plight in the 1930s. Against this sense of impending disaster Croce sets the "magic of poetry," in a famous passage which Stevens quotes in part in "The Noble Rider and the Sound of Words" (NA 16).

If . . . poetry is intuition and expression, the fusion of sound and imagery, what is the material which takes on the form of sound and imagery? It is the whole man: the man who thinks and wills, and loves, and hates; who is strong and weak, sublime and pathetic, good and wicked; man in the exultation and agony of living; and together with the man, integral with him, it is all nature in its perpetual labour of evolution. . . . Poetry . . . is the triumph of contemplation. . . . Poetic genius chooses a strait path in which passion is calmed and calm is passionate.   (706)

In response to the question "What do we in fact expect of poetry, and what can it give?" which is also the recurrent question in Stevens' dialogue with himself, Croce produces a modern variation on the defenses of Shelley and Schiller. Like them, he believes that poetry has an ennobling power, that it is (to quote from one of Stevens' "Adagia") "a purging of the world's poverty and change and evil and death" (OP 167). But—again like Stevens—Croce cannot accept the view of poetry as a universal transcendent force, and puts forward in its stead a profound yet circumscribed claim for pure poetry.

We may indeed invoke it [poetry] for the regeneration and refreshment and spiritual renewal of human society, but only in accordance with its own essence, not as if it could replace or spontaneously generate the other powers, capacities, and relations of man. In short, we must only look upon it as one among other paths leading to a single goal.   (707)

These limitations would not satisfy the Stevens of *The Man with the Blue Guitar* and after, who was to make claims for poetry as sweeping and grand in their way as those of Shelley. But in the more compromised world of *Ideas of Order,* where a slight transcendence or momentary point of order is all that can be expected, Croce's *Defence* must have given Stevens sanction and encouragement.

It also helped him to define the nature of pure poetry, which Croce thought the "only proper object of aesthetic consideration to-day" (702). Croce distinguished between a normative "pure poetry," where feeling and image (or, in his terms, intuition and expression) are inextricably fused, and an "impure" corruption of the concept which "excludes, or pretends to exclude, from poetry all the meaning of words, concentrating on the mere sound" (703). Thus the term "pure poetry" can be either ennobling or pejorative, depending upon usage and context, a distinction which explains a passage in Stevens' letter to Ronald Lane Latimer of 31 October 1935:

I was on the point of saying that I did not agree with the opinion that my verse is decorative, when I remembered that when HARMONIUM was in the making there was a time when I liked the idea of images and images alone, or images and the music of verse together. I then believed in *pure poetry,* as it was called.   (L 288)

Two months later, in correspondence with Latimer, Stevens could use the term in a wholly laudatory sense. It is as if he delighted in teasing the ambiguities out of the word "pure," a process which helped him to define his own aims.

In the French debate over *la poésie pure* a central issue was the reinterpretation of Racine; and his famous line of "pure music," which Gautier loved to declaim, "La fille de Minos et de Pasiphaé," became a crux. Those who took the extreme position of *ut musica poesis* found the line "meaningless" but supremely expressive, the quintessence of pure poetry, while more temperate exponents sought to analyze the relation between sound and sense. In this argument Croce's attitude was unequivocal.

[The verse] is certainly beautiful, but not in virtue of the physical combination of its sounds. One might make infinite other combinations of such sounds without producing any effect of beauty. It is beautiful because these sounds, these syllables and accents, bring before us, in an instantaneous imaginative fusion, all that was mysterious and sinister, all that was divine and fiendish, all that was majestical and perverted, both in the person and in the parentage of Phaedra. And this is expressed by two epic names, that of the royal Cretan legislator and that of his incestuous wife, at whose side rises, in our imagination, the brutal figure of the bull.   (705)

Pure poetry, in the pure sense of the term, is certainly "sounds," and certainly it is not sounds which have a logical meaning like the sounds of prose. That is to say, it does not communicate a conception, a judgment, or an inference, nor the story of particular facts. But to say it has no logical meaning is not to say it is a mere physical sound without a soul. . . . [Poetic intuition] is something infinite that has no other equivalent than the melody in which it is expressed, and that may be sung but never rendered into prose.   (704)

In this second passage the deepest affinities between Croce and Stevens are revealed, in language reminiscent of "The Idea of Order at Key West," where the voice of the singing girl is not "sound alone," a musical rendering of the "voice of the sea," but a poetic intuition expressed in an autonomous word pattern. When read as displaced literary criticism, another defense of poetry, "The Idea of Order at Key West" links Stevens with Sidney and Shelley and Croce. From Sidney among others he derived the classical term "maker," and the notion that the poet, although bound by the general responsibilities of mimesis, can grow through his invention into "another nature." From Shelley he took the belief that poetry is "the expression of the imagination," an inner harmonization of outer impressions that can prolong and intensify immediate sensations. Both these views lie behind the poem's "idea," but Stevens rejects traditional theories of imitation and expression in favor of a poetic closer to that of Croce. As an autonomous creation which, through its fusion of feeling and imagery, alters our perception of the external world, "The Idea of Order at Key West"—like the song it celebrates—is a work of pure poetry, in which poetry itself becomes the subject.

> It was her voice that made
> The sky acutest at its vanishing.
> She measured to the hour its solitude.
> She was the single artificer of the world
> In which she sang. And when she sang, the sea,
> Whatever self it had, became the self
> That was her song, for she was the maker. Then we,
> As we beheld her striding there alone,
> Knew that there never was a world for her
> Except the one she sang and, singing, made.   (CP 129–30)

The claims made for pure poetry in *Ideas of Order* are often provisional and cautious, as Stevens acknowledged in a letter of December 1935. "There must be pure poetry and there must be a certain amount of didactic poetry, or a certain amount of didacticism in poetry. Poetry is like anything else; it cannot be made suddenly to drop all its rags and stand out naked, fully disclosed" (L 302–03). This sense of pure poetry as merely one of several activities of the mind is best expressed in an aphorism from the mid-1930s:

To give a sense of the freshness or vividness of life is a valid purpose for poetry. A didactic purpose justifies itself in the mind of the teacher; a philosophical purpose justifies itself in the mind of the philosopher. It is not that one purpose is as justifiable as another but that some purposes are pure, others impure. Seek those purposes that are purely the purposes of the pure poet.   (OP 157)

The Stevens of *Owl's Clover* (1935–36) was obsessed with the desire to seek "the purposes of the pure poet" in an unpropitious time, and in part three of "The Greenest Continent" he tests the proposition (already defended in parts one and two) that, as he later told Henry Church, "pure poetry is rather older and tougher than Marx and will remain so" (L 340). "The Greenest Continent" is probably the least successful part of *Owl's Clover*, flawed throughout by Stevens' ambiguous attempts to handle the contemporary themes of imperialism and the white man in Africa; but the "basis of the poem," as Stevens would explain to Hi Simons in 1940, was the defense of the pure poet.

One way of explaining this poem is to say that it concerns the difficulty of imposing the imagination on those that do not share it. The idea of God is a thing of the imagination. We no longer think that God was, but was imagined. The idea of pure poetry, essential imagination, as the highest objective of the poet, appears to be, at least potentially, as great as the idea of God, and, for that matter, greater, if the idea of God is only one of the things of the imagination.   (L 369)

This desire to make pure poetry a central fiction was complicated by Stevens' long-held belief that the imagination changes from time to time and place to place: the consciousness of Europe is different from that of Africa, and therefore the imaginations of the two places are different. Yet the "extreme poet" will press the theory, although he may not be able to support it fully, that "the idea of pure poetry: imagination, extended beyond local consciousness, may be an idea to be held in common by South, West, North and East" (L 370). Faced with the empty heaven of Europe, where Marxism and Fascism vie for shabby ascendancy, Stevens in the last section of "The

Greenest Continent" fabricates a provisional, central fiction which may suffice for a time. This fiction is "Fatal Ananke . . . the common god," whose "starless crown" rules over all.

> The voice
> In the jungle is a voice in Fontainebleau.
> The long recessional at parish eves wails round
> The cuckoo trees and the widow of Madrid
> Weeps in Segovia. The beggar in Rome
> Is the beggar in Bogotá. The kraal
> Chants a death that is a medieval death. . . .
> Fateful Ananke is the final god.   (OP 59)

Stevens told Hi Simons that the concept of Ananke was "an importation from Italy" (L 370), and in the Stevens manuscripts the source is made plain. Stevens had used a quotation from Mario Rossi, the Italian scholar, as the epigraph, for "Evening Without Angels":

the great interests of man: air and light, the joy of having a body, the
voluptuousness of looking   (CP 136)

and with his interest in Rossi aroused he had obtained Rossi's address and entered into correspondence. A letter from Rossi of April 1934, commenting on the epigraph, introduced the term "Ananke," and Stevens copied part of the letter into his commonplace book, adding an observation of his own:

"I dont think indeed man has only such interests. I meant to say that amongst human interests, the simple pleasures of life—living pure, as it were—have a paramount importance . . The glory and glamour of the world is enough in itself to make man happy with his destiny . . Poetry and pleasure alike have something elemental in themselves . . But this implies . . that reality is further on . . Yes, a Pagan if you like. But dont forget . . there was the imperscrutable Ananke. Call it destiny, call it God, call it predestination—it comes all alike. It gives a sense to the marvelous spectacle of the world . ."
Imperscrutable is Dr. Rossi's magnificent word and Ananke is necessity or fate personified: the saeva Necessitas of Horace Odes Book I No. 35, to Fortune:
"Inexorable Necessity always marches before
thee, holding in her brazen hand huge spikes
and wedges . ." etc[11]

Intrigued by Rossi's "imperscrutable" and the general notion of a vague but potent "supreme fiction," Stevens first used the term

"Ananke" in "Like Decorations in a Nigger Cemetery" (XII) and then made it the focus of the last section of "The Greenest Continent." But the personification was too diffuse to hold the imagination, representing in fact a surrender to contemporary despair and nihilism. Stevens used it only once again, in a discarded stanza for "Examination of the Hero in a Time of War" (OP 83). In the search for a central fiction that could resist the pressure of reality, pure poetry needed more vitality to prove itself; and the influx of that vitality is already evident in *The Man with the Blue Guitar* (1937). Poem XXII, which opens with three lines that summarize a century of poetic theory, posits as the "central" not a nebulous personification but that virile interchange between reality and imagination which was to become the special concern of Stevens' poetry for the next few years.

> Poetry is the subject of the poem,
> From this the poem issues and
>
> To this returns. Between the two,
> Between issue and return, there is
>
> An absence in reality,
> Things as they are. Or so we say.
>
> But are these separate? Is it
> An absence for the poem, which acquires
>
> Its true appearances there, sun's green,
> Cloud's red, earth feeling, sky that thinks?
>
> From these it takes. Perhaps it gives,
> In the universal intercourse.   (CP 176–77)

In commenting on this poem three years later Stevens glossed it with terms that provide a ground plan for *Notes toward a Supreme Fiction*:

Poetry is the spirit, as the poem is the body. Crudely stated, poetry is the imagination. But here poetry is used as the poetic, without the slightest pejorative innuendo. I have in mind pure poetry. The purpose of writing poetry is to attain pure poetry. The validity of the poet as a figure of prestige to which he is entitled, is wholly a matter of this, that he adds to life that without which life cannot be lived, or is not worth living, or is without savor, or, in any case, would be altogether different from what it is today. . . . Imagination has no source except in reality, and ceases to have any value when it departs from reality. . . . It does not create except as it transforms. . . . Imagination gives, but gives in relation.   (L 363–64)

At the end of Stevens' comments on "The Greenest Continent," made to Hi Simons in a letter of August 1940, he refers to a recent poem, "Asides on the Oboe," as an illustration of what he was trying to achieve in the "improvisation" of Ananke. "Asides on the Oboe" is a deliberate farewell to the hesitant improvisations of the 1930s, as its opening declares:

> The prologues are over. It is a question, now,
> Of final belief. So, say that final belief
> Must be in a fiction. It is time to choose.   (CP 250)

In its dogmatic, almost pedagogical description of a central purity, "the man of glass / Who in a million diamonds sums us up," the poem focuses on that which is autonomous in the act of creation, that which poetry *adds* to life. In discussing a Chair of Poetry which would be dedicated to the study of the theory of poetry, Stevens cited a line from "Asides on the Oboe," "Thou art not August unless I make thee so," as calling to mind "the subject-matter of poetry": "It is the aspects of the world and of men and women that have been added to them by poetry" (L 377).

The cry of the glass man, "Thou art not August unless I make thee so," is a strident and purely romantic extension of the qualified romanticism found in "The Idea of Order at Key West," and it leads directly to Stevens' poetic sketch of "The Figure of the Youth as Virile Poet," delivered as a lecture in 1943 (NA 39–67). In this most obscure and most moving of Stevens' prose meditations, the idea of pure poetry and the redefinition of romanticism—the two leading themes in his poetic speculations of the 1930s—are drawn together and purified in a manner that casts light on all the later poetry and criticism. But before considering this essay we must trace Stevens' frequent and often ambiguous uses of the term "romantic" during the period 1934–42.

Stevens was much taken by Hi Simons' 1940 essay " 'The Comedian as the Letter C': Its Sense and Significance," partly because it was a perceptive reading of the poem, but partly, one suspects, because the argument outlined by Simons had immediate relevance to Stevens' poetic life. Simons found in "The Comedian as the Letter C" a cyclical development from romanticism to realism to fatalism and finally to indifferentism, and Stevens agreed that this was probably true of all minds, "unless the cycle re-commences and the thing goes from indifferentism back to romanticism all over again" (L 350). What the world always looks forward to is "a new romanticism, a new belief," and Communism may be said in this sense to be a new romanticism, although a false romantic. Stevens himself, when he returned to poetry in the early 1930s after a period of indifference, might have been expected to begin the cycle of *Harmonium* (as traced in "The Comedian") over again. But instead, as he confesses to Simons, he chose to move toward "the normal, the central."

About the time when I, personally, began to feel around for a new romanticism, I might naturally have been expected to start on a new cycle. Instead of doing so, I began to feel that I was on the edge: that I wanted to get to the center: that I was isolated, and that I wanted to share the common life.
(L 352)

Part of this search for the central or normative involved a cleansing of "the romantic," and the first "Adagia" notebook is filled with attempts at redefinition (it is significant that the term "romantic" does not appear in the second part of the "Adagia," which contains entries of a later date).

A dead romantic is a falsification.   (OP 160)

The romantic cannot be seen through: it is for the moment willingly not seen through.   (OP 160)

The imagination is the romantic.   (OP 163)

The ideal is the actual become anaemic. The romantic is often pretty much the same thing.   (OP 164)

Romanticism is to poetry what the decorative is to painting.   (OP 169)

The romantic exists in precision as well as in imprecision.   (OP 171)

The romantic is the first phase of (a non-pejorative) lunacy.   (OP 172)

These entries represent "a thought revolved," an obsessive litany designed to make the word declare its true meaning. Like "pure poetry," the term "romantic" held two major senses for Stevens, which are best expressed in an early notebook entry (c. spring 1934) that Samuel French Morse printed at the end of the "Adagia":

It should be said of poetry that it is essentially romantic as if one were recognizing the truth about poetry for the first time. Although the romantic is referred to, most often, in a pejorative sense, this sense attaches, or should attach, not to the romantic in general but to some phase of the romantic that has become stale. Just as there is always a romantic that is potent, so there is always a romantic that is impotent.[12]   (OP 180)

As with the two senses of "pure poetry," the two senses of the "romantic" are best understood through Croce. For Croce, Romanticism was an historical movement, but the "romantic" (like the "classic") was one of the permanent constituents of the artistic process, an essential element in every work of art. In *The Defence of Poetry*, at the close of the passage which Stevens quotes in "The Noble Rider and the Sound of Words," Croce pictures the man of "poetic genius" as one who takes the straight path between "romantic" and "classic," balancing the virtues and defects of both extremes. Thus the romantic, for Croce and Stevens, can be pejorative (outmoded figures and feelings) or potent (a permanent tendency of the poetic mind). This double sense helps us to understand "Autumn Refrain" ("the moon and moon") and Stevens' two prose works of 1934–35: the preface to William Carlos Williams's *Collected Poems, 1921–1931*, and the review of Marianne Moore's *Selected Poems*, "A Poet That Matters" (OP 254–57, 247–54). The Williams essay, which Williams himself deeply resented, is a critical pendant to "Like Decorations in a Nigger Cemetery," and has much more to do with Stevens' poetic obsessions than with Williams's poetry. In it the "anti-poetic," a term much used in the pure poetry debate in France, is cited as proof of Williams's vital romanticism: he has "a romantic of his own" (OP 255), and emerges from the essay as the hero-poet of "The Man on the Dump," who can discard the souvenirs of outmoded romanticism (*aptest eve . . . Invisible priest*) while transforming the anti-poetic of the contemporary.

What, then, is a romantic poet now-a-days? He happens to be one who still dwells in an ivory tower, but who insists that life would be intolerable except for the fact that one has, from the top, such an exceptional view of the public dump and the advertising signs of Snider's Catsup, Ivory Soap and Chevrolet Cars; he is the hermit who dwells alone with the sun and moon, but insists on taking a rotten newspaper.   (OP 256)

Stevens thought of Marianne Moore's poems as prime examples of the essential romantic freshened or made new, and his review of her *Selected Poems* was explicitly linked in his mind with his own poem "Sailing After Lunch" (CP 120–21), the program piece for the first (1935) edition of *Ideas of Order*.[13] When Stevens sent "Sailing After Lunch" to Ronald Latimer, publisher of the first edition, he gave the following gloss:

While it should make its own point, and while I am against explanations, the thing is an abridgment of at least a temporary theory of poetry. When people speak of the romantic, they do so in what the French commonly call a *pejorative* sense. But poetry is essentially romantic, only the romantic of poetry must be something constantly new and, therefore, just the opposite of what is spoken of as the romantic. Without this new romantic, one gets nowhere; with it, the most casual things take on transcendence, and the poet rushes brightly, and so on. What one is always doing is keeping the romantic pure: eliminating from it what people speak of as the romantic.

(L 277)

This theory of the two romantics was elaborated in the Marianne Moore essay, where her striking image "moon vines trained on fishing-twine" gives Stevens his excuse for theorizing:

Moon-vines are moon-vines and tedious. But moon-vines trained on fishing-twine are something else and they are as perfectly as it is possible for anything to be what interests Miss Moore. They are an intermingling. The imagination grasps at such things and sates itself, instantaneously in them. Yet clearly they are romantic. At this point one very well might stop for definitions. It is clear enough, without all that, to say that the romantic in the pejorative sense merely connotes obsolescence, but that the word has, or should have, another sense. Thus, when A. E. Powell in *The Romantic Theory of Poetry* writes of the romantic poet

He seeks to reproduce for us the feeling as it lives within himself; and for the sake of a feeling which he thinks interesting or important he will insert passages which contribute nothing to the effect of the work as a whole,

she is surely not thinking of the romantic in a derogatory sense. True, when Professor Babbitt speaks of the romantic, he means the romantic. . . .
Yes, but for the romantic in its other sense, meaning always the living and at the same time the imaginative, the youthful, the delicate and a variety of things which it is not necessary to try to particularize at the moment, constitutes the vital element in poetry. It is absurd to wince at being called a romantic poet. Unless one is that, one is not a poet at all.

(OP 251–52)

Irving Babbitt's mechanical humanism ("The civil fiction, the calico idea, / The Johnsonian composition, abstract man"[14]) is firmly rejected in favor of Croce. A. E. Powell's *The Romantic Theory of Poetry*, published in 1926, is an explicitly Crocean document (the first chapter, "The Romantic Ideal," is followed by a chapter on "Croce's Theory of Aesthetic"), and it provides the frame of reference for Stevens' internal dialogue on the two romantics. "Sailing After Lunch" may have preceded the prose discussions, but it opens in the middle of an argument, and demands a prose context. This may explain why Stevens displaced it in favor of the rhetorical

"Farewell to Florida" in the second edition of *Ideas of Order*. "Sailing After Lunch" had meant more to him than it should because it touched his deepest personal and poetic lives.

> It is the word *pejorative* that hurts.
> My old boat goes round on a crutch
> And doesn't get under way.
> It's the time of the year
> And the time of the day.
>
> Perhaps it's the lunch that we had
> Or the lunch that we should have had.
> But I am, in any case,
> A most inappropriate man
> In a most unpropitious place.
>
> Mon Dieu, hear the poet's prayer.
> The romantic should be here.
> The romantic should be there.
> It ought to be everywhere.
> But the romantic must never remain,
>
> Mon Dieu, and must never again return.
> This heavy historical sail
> Through the mustiest blue of the lake
> In a really vertiginous boat
> Is wholly the vapidest fake. . . .
>
> It is least what one ever sees.
> It is only the way one feels, to say
> Where my spirit is I am,
> To say the light wind worries the sail,
> To say the water is swift today,
>
> To expunge all people and be a pupil
> Of the gorgeous wheel and so to give
> That slight transcendence to the dirty sail,
> By light, the way one feels, sharp white,
> And then rush brightly through the summer air. (CP 120–21)

If "Sailing After Lunch" represents that slight transcendence which is all the Stevens of the 1930s will allow the poet of quotidian reality, and "Mr. Burnshaw and the Statue" (part two of *Owl's Clover*) represents the threats to this slight transcendence, "The Idea of Order at Key West" stands for those unusual transformations which can occur when time and place are wholly favorable to the imagination. In the fifth section of "Mr. Burnshaw and the Statue" (OP 49–50) the poet is trapped between the modern equivalent of

Keats's Grecian urn, "A trash can at the end of the world," and the "gigantic, solitary urn" of the future, which may one day yield not souvenirs but new lustres, so that "For a little time, again, rose-breasted birds / Sing rose-beliefs." But in "The Idea of Order at Key West" the exotic setting makes it possible for the poet to transact the true romantic: at the close of the poem the word "portals" transports us into a world where the language of the old romanticism can be made our own.

> Oh! Blessed rage for order, pale Ramon,
> The maker's rage to order words of the sea,
> Words of the fragrant portals, dimly-starred,
> And of ourselves and of our origins,
> In ghostlier demarcations, keener sounds.   (CP 130)

As the 1930s wore to a close Stevens' confidence in the new romantic increased. Two poems which sum up his progress in the decade, "Asides on the Oboe" and "Mrs. Alfred Uruguay" (first published in the *Harvard Advocate* for December 1940), figure an escape from "reality" into a deeper sense of reality; and in "The Noble Rider and the Sound of Words" we find Stevens in full command of the present. Escapism, like the romantic, has two senses, pejorative and vital, depending on whether or not the poet is "attached to reality." Citing a passage from C. E. M. Joad, Stevens pictures a blank, impoverished, shadowless present (like that of *The Man with the Blue Guitar*, Poem V) and then imagines a transformation as in Wordsworth's sonnet "Composed Upon Westminster Bridge":

If we say that the space is blank space, nowhere, without color, and that the objects, though solid, have no shadows and, though static, exert a mournful power, and, without elaborating this complete poverty, if suddenly we hear a different and familiar description of the place:

> This City now doth, like a garment, wear
> The beauty of the morning, silent, bare,
> Ships, towers, domes, theatres, and temples lie
> Open unto the fields, and to the sky;
> All bright and glittering in the smokeless air;

if we have this experience, we know how poets help people to live their lives. This illustration must serve for all the rest. There is, in fact, a world of poetry indistinguishable from the world in which we live, or, I ought to say, no doubt, from the world in which we shall come to live, since what makes the poet the potent figure that he is, or was, or ought to be, is that he creates the world to which we turn incessantly and without knowing it

and that he gives to life the supreme fictions without which we are unable
to conceive of it.   (NA 31)

Here the romantic is not an escape from reality, but an enlargement
which affirms our ideas of nobility.

In the major essays that followed "The Noble Rider and the
Sound of Words" Stevens' notions of pure poetry and the new
romantic were completely assimilated. "The Figure of the Youth as
Virile Poet" (1943), which is concerned with the Longinian aspects
of "elevation and elation on the part of the poet" (NA 60), is a rite
of purification that traces the progress of the ephebe toward and
through the "portals" of the future. As he approaches the "central
purity" he finds above the portal this warning against the false
romantic:

No longer do I believe that there is a mystic muse, sister of the Minotaur.
This is another of the monsters I had for nurse, whom I have wasted. I am
myself a part of what is real, and it is my own speech and the strength of it,
this only, that I hear or ever shall.   (NA 60)

But at the end of the rite the terms of the motto have subtly
changed, and "La fille de Minos et de Pasiphaé" is no longer the
muse of "pure poetry" and "the romantic" in their pejorative
senses, but the true muse of the mastering imagination.

Inexplicable sister of the Minotaur, enigma and mask, although I am part of
what is real, hear me and recognize me as part of the unreal. I am the truth
but the truth of that imagination of life in which with unfamiliar motion
and manner you guide me in those exchanges of speech in which your
words are mine, mine yours.   (NA 67)

When these permutations of "pure poetry" and "the romantic"
are held in mind, most of the obscurities in Stevens' final essays fall
away. In "Effects of Analogy," for example, the distinction between
two theories of the imagination becomes immediately comprehensi-
ble. Those who believe that the imagination is not wholly one's
own but that "it may be part of a much larger, much more potent
imagination," can never attain a central poetry. The poet of this
persuasion "pushes on and lives, or tries to live, as Paul Valéry did,
on the verge of consciousness. This often results in poetry that is
marginal, subliminal."

The second theory relates to the imagination as a power within him [the
poet] to have such insights into reality as will make it possible for him to

ent as a poet in the very center of consciousness. . . . The adher-
 imagination are mystics to begin with and pass from one mysti-
 other. The adherents of the central are also mystics to begin with.
 their desire and all their ambition is to press away from mysticism
toward that ultimate good sense which we term civilization.   (NA 115–16)

The poets of the central, who live in the here and now, a world of analogy, have through their words "made a world that transcends the world and a life livable in that transcendence."

It is a transcendence achieved by means of the minor effects of figurations and the major effects of the poet's sense of the world and of the motive music of his poems and it is the imaginative dynamism of all these analogies together. Thus poetry becomes and is a transcendent analogue composed of the particulars of reality, created by the poet's sense of the world, that is to say, his attitude, as he intervenes and interposes the appearances of that sense.   (NA 130)

Here the reiterated "transcendence" goes far beyond the "slight transcendence" of "Sailing After Lunch," claiming a central position for poetry while rejecting the mystical transcendence of the old romantic (which is the pejorative sense of "the romantic" in "Imagination as Value," where Stevens insists that the imagination must be cleansed of "the taint of the romantic" [NA 138–39]). In these two essays of the same year, Stevens delights in the difficult—but ultimately revealing—ambiguities of his terms.

In Stevens' last major essay, "Two or Three Ideas" (1951), written at the same time as the poems of *The Rock*, there is a long passage in which the word "romantic" is repeated thirteen times, each time in a slightly different sense. These repetitions are interwoven with his final defense of pure poetry, a poetry in which the conventional *l'art pour l'art* proposition that "the style of a poem and the poem itself are one" is transmuted into the deeply personal belief that "the style of man is man himself." When read in isolation this passage can support the common view of Stevens as a practitioner of willful preciosity, but when read against the background of his carefully developed theories it becomes, like the late poems, a text of transparent truth.

One of the irrelevancies is the romantic. It looks like something completely contemptible in the light of literary intellectualism and cynicism. The romantic, however, has a way of renewing itself. It can be said of the romantic, just as it can be said of the imagination, that it can never effectively touch the same thing twice in the same way. It is partly because the romantic will not be what has been romantic in the past that it is preposterous to think of confining poetry hereafter to the revelation of reality. The whole effort of the imagination is toward the production of the romantic. When, therefore, the romantic is in abeyance, when it is discredited, it remains true that there is always an unknown romantic and that the imagination will not be forever denied. There is something a little romantic about the idea that the style of a poem and the poem itself are one. It seems to be a much more broadly romantic thing to say that the style of the gods and the gods themselves are one. It is completely romantic to say that the style of men and men themselves are one. To collect and collate these ideas of disparate things may seem to pass beyond the romantic to the fantastic. I hope, however, that you will agree that if each one of these ideas is valid separately, or more or less valid, it is permissible to have brought them together as a collective source of suppositions. What is romantic in all of them is the idea of style which I have not defined in any sense uniformly common to all three. A poem is a restricted creation of the imagination. The gods are the creation of the imagination at its utmost. Men are a part of reality. The gradations of romance noticeable as the sense of style is used with reference to these three, one by one, are relevant to the difficulties of the imagination in a truth-loving time. These difficulties exist only as one foresees them. They may never exist at all. An age in which the imagination might be expected to become part of time's *rejectamenta* may behold it established and protected and enthroned on one of the few ever-surviving thrones; and, to our surprise, we may find posted in the portico of its eternal dwelling, on the chief portal, among the morning's ordinances, three regulations which if they were once rules of art will then have become rules of conduct. By that time the one that will matter most is likely to be the last, that the style of man is man himself, which is about what we have been saying. (OP 215–16)

NOTES

1. For a general account of Stevens' poetic career in the 1920s and 1930s see my own *Introspective Voyager: The Poetic Development of Wallace Stevens* (New York: Oxford University Press, 1972), pp.141–228.

2. From "Sailing After Lunch," *The Collected Poems of Wallace Stevens* (New York: Alfred A. Knopf, 1955), p. 120, hereafter cited in the text as CP. Other abbreviations used are L: *Letters of Wallace Stevens*, ed. Holly Stevens (New York: Alfred A. Knopf, 1966); NA: *The Necessary Angel: Essays on Reality and the Imagination* (New York: Alfred A. Knopf, 1951); and OP: *Opus Posthumous*, ed. Samuel French Morse (New York: Alfred A. Knopf, 1957).

3. *Poetry*, October 1921. The two poems were separated in the final order of *Harmonium*.

4. The "Adagia" printed in *Opus Posthumous* are taken (with some omissions) from two manuscript notebooks labeled "Adagia I" and "Adagia II": the first note-

book ends with the ninth entry on OP 172. Stevens appears to have recorded the entries in chronological order, ranging from about 1934 into the 1940s. However, the last six entries (OP 179–80) were taken by Morse from the commonplace notebook "Sur Plusieurs Beaux Sujects [*sic*] I, " and date from the 1930s. These notebooks are in the Huntington Library.

5. The history of this debate is traced in great detail by Henry W. Decker, *Pure Poetry, 1925–1930: Theory and Debate in France* (Berkeley and Los Angeles: University of California Press, 1962).

6. *The Criterion*, 8 (1928), 740–45.

7. Robert Penn Warren, "Pure and Impure Poetry," *The Kenyon Review*, 5 (1943), 228–54; T. S. Eliot, "From Poe to Valéry," in *To Criticize the Critic* (New York: Farrar, Straus & Giroux, 1965), pp. 27–42.

8. "From Poe to Valéry," p. 39.

9. Michel Benamou, *Wallace Stevens and the Symbolist Imagination* (Princeton: Princeton University Press, 1972), pp. 67–86.

10. Benedetto Croce, *The Defence of Poetry*, in *The Great Critics*, ed. J. H. Smith and E. W. Parks, 3rd ed. (New York: W. W. Norton and Co., 1951), p. 697. Citations of the essay in the text refer to this edition. *The Defence of Poetry* was first published by the Oxford University Press in 1933.

11. "Sur Plusieurs Beaux Sujects, I," p. 8.

12. "Sur Plusieurs Beaux Sujects, I," p. 6.

13. See L 282: "Both the poem SAILING AFTER LUNCH, and the note on SE-LECTED POEMS are expressions of the same thing. The poem preceded the note."

14. From "A Duck for Dinner," OP 65.

HERBERT N. SCHNEIDAU

Pound and Wordsworth
on Poetry and Prose

In certain recent works of criticism, Wordsworth is raised as a ghost whose warning that poetry must be the speech of "a man speaking to men" corrects the excesses of that interesting aberration, Modernism. To liken Ezra Pound to Wordsworth would then seem ironic if not perverse, for Pound would surely be the figure of choice to exemplify precisely the intransigent aspect of Modernism that makes it deficient in "communication." Who could be more resistant to the demand that he come down and talk to us on our own level than this confirmed exotic, known far and wide for baffling the reader with foreign quotations and other recalcitrant devices? Yet we know that Pound in fact led a movement similar to Wordsworth's in demanding the use of real speech in poetry: "nothing—nothing that you couldn't, in some circumstance, in the stress of some emotion, actually say."[1] In fact the careers of these two great reactionary revolutionists ran in curiously parallel courses. Pound at Eliot's funeral, steeped in significant silence, was in much the same position as Wordsworth when the latter's poetic powers briefly revived at the time of the death of James Hogg. Both old poets looked back at generations they had themselves brought together; yet at the end of their respective "movements" here they were, out of favor, charged (sometimes by former admirers) with political apostasy and poetic obscurantism too. Who could have predicted, earlier on, that each would look back with so many misgivings at what they and their eras had come to?

The irony of these retrospects is compounded when we return to Pound's stylistic crusade in favor of the spoken idiom as the norm for poetry, for at its inception Pound had been concerned that his own efforts might be construed as identical to Wordsworth's. He felt obliged to claim Flaubert, via Ford Madox Ford, as his true ancestor: "The common word is not the same thing as the *mot juste*, not by a long way."[2] Perhaps his discomfort was that of the reformer who finds that his cause was once urged by those he now considers opponents; but in any case the aspiring Imagist was told to "read as much of Wordsworth as does not seem too unutterably dull."[3] Pound certainly knew that Wordsworth, like himself, had sought to purge and upraise the style, and hence the *morale,* of his times. Wordsworth's rancor against "sickly and stupid" or "idle and extravagant" works pandering to a "degrading thirst after outrageous stimulation" corresponds to the vigor with which Pound denounced "public stupidity in the arts." For both poets were heirs of the Puritans: in the issue of style they saw the fate of the culture being decided. Wordsworth's belief, expressed in the Preface, that "language and the human mind act and re-act on each other," so that a stylistic issue forecasts "the revolutions not of literature alone, but likewise of society itself," could fit without alteration into Pound's "How to Read." Pound was capable of stating his version of this belief in startlingly literal terms. In 1917, in the process of praising Joyce's French-bred prose style, he commented:

The hell of contemporary Europe is caused by the lack of representative government in Germany, *and* by the non-existence of decent prose in the German language. Clear thought and sanity depend on clear prose. . . . The mush of the German sentence, the straddling of the verb out to the end, are just as much a part of the befoozlement of Kultur and the consequent hell, as was the rhetoric of later Rome the seed and the symptom of the Roman Empire's decadence and extinction.[4]

Pound's reiterated dismissals of Wordsworth as a "silly old sheep" still grudgingly ascribed to him "a genius, an unquestionable genius, for imagisme, for a presentation of natural detail."[5] And Pound would have found still more points of sympathy had he not been so obviously defensive about the comparison; for instance, in a curious extension of their parallel attacks on "poetic diction," each offered prose as a model for good poetry. Wordsworth's position is well known: in the Preface of 1800 he maintained that "there neither is, nor can be, any *essential* difference between the language of prose and metrical composition." Using a sonnet by Gray for demonstration, he asserted as "obvious" the conclusion that the only good lines were those in which "the language . . . does in no respect differ from that of prose." In general, "some of the most interesting parts of the best poems will be found to be strictly the language of prose when prose is well written." He went so far as to anticipate critics asking him why, holding these views, he wrote in verse at all.

With this we may compare Pound's belief in the "prose tradition in verse," his dictum that poetry must be "as well written as prose," and so on. Forrest Read persuasively contends that the major influences on Pound's formative years, especially for the *Cantos*, were prose writers rather than poets.

Ford Madox Ford had impressed on Pound as early as 1911 the importance of 19th century prose, especially the style of Flaubert, [and Pound's] awareness of the range and uses of prose techniques and subjects underwent continuing development during his London years. . . . In 1922, however, Pound gained a new awareness of the prose tradition as a development from the epic tradition. . . . With Stendhal vital literary expression—at least work of epic scope—had "gone over to prose." Since Stendhal the main line had developed out of Flaubert, passed through the Goncourts, Dostoievsky, and James, and come to a final fruition in Joyce.[6]

Thus, as Hugh Kenner puts it, when Pound finally was enabled to read *Ulysses* as a whole in 1922, he "determined what he was doing in the *Cantos*."[7]

If pressed to justify their views on prose, both Pound and Wordsworth would probably have responded with elaborations of the belief that prose embodies real speech. Wordsworth insisted that prose, not painting, was the "sister art" of poetry, for "they both speak by and to the same organs. . . . Poetry sheds no tears 'such as angels weep,' but natural and human tears; she can boast of no celestial ichor that distinguishes her vital juices from those of prose; the same human blood circulates through the veins of them both." Hence prose is an antidote for poetry's recurrent disease of artificiality, and a demythologization of its celestial pretensions. Like other iconoclasms, this train of thought has the problem of erecting a new idol in the process of destroying the old: that metaphorical "same human blood," like the Romantic "Nature," has long since acquired a train of worshippers. Besides, the chthonic vigor of speech does not fully explain Pound's exaggerated respect for prose writers: he once tried to model his style on that of Tacitus.[8] Read's "epic tradition" is not exclusively a vernacular one; and in any case we know, in spite of M. Jourdain, that prose is not simply a transcription of speech (see the White House tapes), that in fact they probably have distinct "grammars."[9] Furthermore, the best work of both poets shows significant departures from the norm of conversational speech: no talker could have uttered the Immortality Ode, any more than he could have produced Canto I. In short, this explanation raises as many problems as answers.

Let us try another cross light, with a newer view of the prose-poetry question founded on Roman Jakobson's thesis that the "poles" of language in use can be called metaphoric and metonymic, and that each is the "line of least resistance" for poetry and prose respectively.

The development of a discourse may take place along two different semantic lines: one topic may lead to another either through their similarity or through their contiguity. The METAPHORIC way would be the most appropriate term for the first case and the METONYMIC way for the second, since they find their most condensed expression in metaphor and metonymy respectively. . . . In normal verbal behavior both processes are continually operative, but careful observation will reveal that under the influence of a cultural pattern, personality, and verbal style, preference is given to one of the two processes over the other.[10]

Jakobson's thesis appears more and more frequently in contemporary criticism, though not all projects incorporating it have borne particularly rich fruit. We who have waited like so many Simeons for the appearance of a new word from the discipline of linguistics that will, if not exactly save us, at least put all our work on a sound footing, have had our faith tested: some are beginning to wonder if any good thing can come out of that precinct. Indeed, in the citadels of the genteel tradition one may find Jakobson referred to as "an insensitive engineer who should never have been allowed access to the poetry bank."[11]

Much of the value of Jakobson's thesis, however, is in its poetic, suggestive, even visionary quality, rather than in its status among linguistic theorists. For instance, he points to the metaphor-metonymy contrast not only in poetry and prose generally, but also in romantic and symbolist styles as opposed to realist ones. The enticing prospect arises of aligning literary history with linguistic clues. But also this typology may help us with some of the contradictions in Pound's and Wordsworth's views. As Jakobson points out, poetry is essentially an affair of similarity functions: its traditional marking devices (rhyme, meter, alliteration, and metaphor) tend to establish relationships of equivalence. Further, in poetry these relationships sometimes govern functions otherwise in the domain of contiguity: *"The poetic function projects the principle of equivalence from the axis of selection into the axis of combination."*[12] Rhyme is the most obvious instance; its needs may govern the selection of a word that in prose would only have to fulfill syntactic and semantic requirements. "In metalanguage [such as *'mare* is *the female of the horse'*] the sequence is used to build an equation, whereas in poetry the equation is used to build a sequence."[13] We may find Pound and Wordsworth rebelling against this way of proceeding. But, in

Jakobson's terms, the metaphorical style dominates poetry to such an extent that it has come to be identified as the basic constitutive element: we sometimes use "metaphor" as a catchall term, a synecdoche in fact, for poetic devices and effects in general.

The dangers here are obvious. In poetry that takes itself too unreservedly as "poetry," where the display of the armory of functions and devices seems to be the rationale for writing, the effect can be stasis: endless periphrastic variation of equivalences and correspondences, signifying nothing, often effusing into a rarefied and stilted "poetic diction." Whatever looks like common language may come to be denounced as prosaism: exactly the situation Wordsworth complained of. This diction, "reddening Phoebus lifts his golden fire" replacing "the sun rises," was itself the "celestial ichor" he derided.

In Jakobson's analysis, the old Lockean terminology of "similarity and contiguity" is usefully transformed into other polarities, especially "substitutive and predicative." He illustrates these latter terms with typical answers to free-association tests. If to the stimulus "hut" one answers with synonym or antonym ("hovel," "palace") that is substitutive; if one answers "burnt out," that is a predicative reaction (p. 91). Most responses mix the functions, again, but we may see how the first tendency would idiomatically dominate a poetry of periphrasis ("finny tribe"), leading to a feeling of circularity and pointlessness. Wordsworth indicted "what is usually called POETIC DICTION" for being "arbitrary, and subject to infinite caprices." A dose of prose might help to restore pointedness through predication. Josephine Miles calls "the chief English prose style, the predicative," distinguishing it from the "connective-subordinative" and "adjectival" styles.[14] Perhaps it was this characteristic that appealed most to Pound and Wordsworth. Future critics might well test the proposition that Wordsworth's poetic structures have a predicative interest that differentiates them from preceding styles. Certainly the corollary appears true for Pound; his inclination toward predication marks his poetics. We may see it, for instance, in his excitement on reading Fenollosa's essay on the Chinese written character. To Iris Barry he wrote: "You should have a chance to see Fenollosa's big essay on verbs, mostly on verbs. Heaven knows when I shall get it printed. He inveighs against 'IS,' wants transitive verbs. 'Become' is as weak as 'is.' Let the grime *do* something to the leaves. 'All nouns come from verbs.' To primitive man, a thing only IS what it *does*. That is Fenollosa, but I think the theory is a very good one for poets to go by."[15]

Some critics neglect this aspect of Pound, and of Fenollosa, by failing to look beyond the ideas as literal prescriptions: they would presumably pounce on any use of the word "is" in Pound's writing (as in the letter). But more insight may be gained from a fact that puzzles Forrest Read, that Pound added Fenollosa's name in listing the canon of prose writers who form an "epic tradition." "After Joyce, what? Pound appends enigmatically 'Fenollosa on the Chinese Ideograph.' "[16] Perhaps Read's enigma is not so puzzling after all. Fenollosa represented for Pound, I have argued elsewhere, a poetic of "letting things say themselves," and of recognizing and illuminating the verbal element underlying, according to Fenollosa's analysis, not only nouns but all parts of speech.[17] It seems that by 1922 Pound may have thought of "the prose tradition," and of the clarity that had "gone over to prose" with Stendhal, as Fenollosan *avant la lettre*. It would follow that a poet might usefully interbreed his verse techniques with those of a spare and vigorous prose. As T. S. Eliot remarked in a related connection: "Verse stands in constant need of what Samuel Butler calls a 'cross.' "[18]

Where metaphor becomes a merely substitutive device, it stands at the opposite pole to the predicative function. Although Fenollosa praised metaphor, he seems to have thought of it as predicative rather than substitutive (or comparative). For example, in explicating the ideograph "*ming* or *mei*," the sign of sun and moon together, Fenollosa insisted that "it serves as verb, noun, adjective. Thus you write literally, 'the sun and moon of the cup' for the 'the cup's brightness.' Placed as a verb, you write 'the cup sun-and-moons,' actually 'cup sun-and-moon,' or in a weakened thought, 'is like sun,' i.e. shines."[19] Pound, who was impatient of analogy, is not likely to have missed the connotations of the phrase "weakened thought." If the ideograph is thought of as basically and primarily verbal, the force is predicative; if it is merely a comparison of two forms of brightness, force is lost and the device is merely substitutive. Here it may be well to remember that Wordsworth too was somewhat wary and hesitant about metaphor, a topic conspicuously absent from the Preface. He might well have associated it with the practitioners of poetic diction, thus in a way anticipating Jakobson's alignment of it with a poetry of devices. Whether either poet actually achieved a "metonymic" style is another question, but their attitudes toward prose might hint at such an aspiration.

Certainly Pound strove to make his poetry predicative, and to adopt Fenollosa's principle that true poetry imbues all parts of speech with verbal force. Canto II provides vivid samples:

> Seal sports in the spray-whited circles of cliff-wash . . . [20]

Note that the two compound words, though appearing as adjective and noun, possess verbal aspects: "cliff-wash," unlike "dish-wash," suggests a process or action, not a liquid. "Sports" can be read as a noun, but the context strongly implies that it is a verb. Compare:

> And the blue-gray glass of the wave tents them   (C 6)

or

> The gulls broad out their wings . . .   (C 6)

Even in lines where no overt verb appears, powerful predicative force may emerge:

> Sniff and pad-foot of beasts,
>   eye-glitter out of black air.   (C 8)

This Canto is especially appropriate because of its Ovidian theme of metamorphosis: not random change but a revealing transformation, a full actualization—in short a predication. However, similar processes can be noted throughout the *Cantos*. Turning to Canto III:

> Light: and the first light, before ever dew was fallen.   (C 11)

The colon acts to transform the nominal element, to give it the sense of a verb, a shining-forth.

"Defeat of expectation" is a phrase commonly resorted to in discourse on stylistics. In Pound's development of Fenollosan principles we can see revolutionary potentiality, renewal, awakening, re-energizing, perhaps because the norms of poetry and prose, of metaphor and metonymy, of substitution and predication, have been usefully crossed. Merely "metaphoric" expectations about poetry are recurrently defeated.

> And then went down to the ship
> Set keel to breakers . . .   (C 3)

The first figure in the *Cantos* as they now exist, tone-setting to an extent, is a synecdoche, which for Jakobson is a species of metonymy. Note that verbal force so dominates that the usual pro-

nominal subject disappears. Even the famous connectives in the
Cantos ("And," "so that") are essentially predicative, metonymic in
the sense of forwarding discourse by contiguity. Hugh Kenner, in
The Pound Era, offers many invaluable comments on Pound's use of
creative, nonnormative syntax, emphasizing mostly the verbal energy in Pound's work and ideas. For Pound, we might say, the
devices of equivalence and selection (another face of substitution)
are overshadowed by those of relation and sequence. Now relation
is primarily not similarity (or opposition), but rather difference,
which must be predicated. (As in Fenollosa's example of the ideograph for *east:* "Sun in tree branches." The sun is neither like nor
unlike the tree branches, but is in a relation of contiguity to them.)
Pound does not eschew all similarity devices, of course; for instance
he uses subject-rhyme, sudden juxtapositions of different events
revealing hidden similarities. Yet it has been said, by D. S. Carne-
Ross, that the striking characteristic of Pound's poetry is that it is
"not polysemous," does not set up reverberations (which are har-
monic or equivalence structures) on different semantic levels:
"There is no murmurous echo chamber where deeps supposedly
answer to deeps."[21] Kenner has said much the same thing. This
quality, which has made Pound so "unreadable" by traditional
techniques, would seem to correspond to a diminution of metaphor
and similarity structures in favor of predicative, differential ones.
Jakobson might call it "superinducing contiguity upon similarity,"
since, he says, poetry has traditionally done the opposite, "used the
equation to build a sequence."[22] Charles Olson, in "Projective
Verse," contends that "right form, in any given poem, is the only
and exclusively possible *extension of content* under hand." *Extension
of content* is metonymy in action, the principle of contiguity. Olson's tract proclaims its derivation from Fenollosa and Pound: now
it may be seen in relation to Jakobson. Indeed, another of its prescriptions seems to characterize Pound's practice even though Olson says he got it from Edward Dahlberg: "ONE PERCEPTION
MUST IMMEDIATELY AND DIRECTLY LEAD TO A FURTHER
PERCEPTION."[23]

If we consider one final "visionary" aspect of Jakobson's work,
however, we may find that this whole topic has some unsettling
aspects, which may bring us back to Pound's and Wordsworth's
sense of failure. The remarkable etiology of Jakobson's theory of the
metaphoric and metonymic poles, which most of his disciples in
linguistics have ignored, provides us with a new context: aphasia.
The theory is based on observations compiled from studies of
speech blockage. Is it not striking that language should reveal itself

precisely in its failure? Only when it breaks down do we see its underlying constitution. What Jakobson found, sifting through the case studies, was that aphasics fall into two polar types: in one, the faculty for "selection and substitution" is impaired, but "combination and contexture" are intact; in the other type, this pattern is reversed.

The first type is more interesting to us. His symptoms include intolerance of redundancy in any form:

The aphasic with a defect in substitution will not supplement the pointing or handling gesture of the examiner with the name of the object pointed to. Instead of saying "this is [called] a pencil," he will merely add an elliptical note about its use: "to write." . . . Even simple repetition of a word uttered by the examiner seems to the patient unnecessarily redundant, and despite instructions received he is unable to repeat it. Told to repeat the word "no," Head's patient replied "No, I don't know how to do it."   (P. 80)

This patient had not lost the word; he could produce it in verbal context, but not as a freestanding form by "autonomous selection." He cannot utter ordinary types of metalinguistic definitions ("a bachelor is an unmarried man"), though he could use either term in a sentence if only the conversation would give him a context for it. His speech is reflex, reactive, purely combinatory; once the examiner or other stimulus starts a sentence, he can finish it, but has difficulty beginning one himself, and tends to omit the subject. Because similarity is alien to him, he cannot grasp metaphors, but spontaneously produces metonymies, combinatory forms. "*Fork* is substituted for *knife, table* for *lamp, smoke* for *pipe, eat* for *toaster*. . . . The escape from sameness to contiguity is particularly striking in such cases as Goldstein's patient who would answer with a metonymy when asked to repeat a given word and, for instance, would say *glass* for *window* and *heaven* for *God*." In contrast, the second type of aphasic (contexture-deficient) "deals with similarities, and his approximate identifications are of a metaphoric nature." His speech is ruled by a principle: "To say what a thing is, is to say what it is like" (pp. 83–84, 86).

Mildly amused by such spectacles, as of the poor soul who cannot repeat "God" and says "heaven" instead, we congratulate ourselves on our articulateness; and of course we rank the poet as the sheer antipode of the aphasic, literature consisting after all of a heightened rather than impaired ability to think of words or put them together. But how do we know the labor of a poet, faced with that aphasic situation, the blank page? His worksheets may show him almost stuttering on paper. And it is rather obvious that Jakobson's characterization of the first type of aphasic, similarity-deficient, conveys a haunting likeness to the compositional habits of Ezra Pound—and other writers too. He even has the tendency to omit the subject.

Are we not all aphasics? The difference is in the regularity. We "forget" words, block them, produce metonymies and metaphors for them in struggling to remember. And which of us has not had the experience of the patient, suffering from similarity disorder, whose understanding was limited to utterances in his own "idiolect" or particular verbal style? To all other utterances he replied, " 'I can hear you dead plain but I cannot get what you say. . . . I hear your voice but not the words. . . . It does not pronounce itself.' " Confronted with a page of anything that is for us "technical," whether philosophy or mechanics, we, like the patient, consider it "either gibberish or at least in an unknown language" (pp. 82–83).[24] Whole dialects and argots (of the ghetto, of adolescents, of criminals) are designedly "idiolects" outside of ours; we can hear what is being said but can't understand it.

Of course this irresistibly reminds us of Wordsworth's experience with the Leech-Gatherer (or the Solitary Reaper for that matter). But the problem was not simply that the old man spoke an argot; the real "defect" was the poet's. The first stanzas of the poem lead up to an image of carefree indifference to oral stimuli ("I heard the woods and distant waters roar / Or heard them not . . ."), but this is superseded by a blockage ("blind thoughts I knew not, nor could name"). The old man's contiguity-governed words ("each in solemn order followed each") sink, for a poet wrestling with unsatisfactory metaphors of "sea-beasts" and with fears about poetry and poets, into an alien discourse: "But now his voice to me was like a stream / Scarce heard; nor word from word could I divide."

The poet is rescued from despondency by the "grave" and "stately" prose of the old man. The "cross" verse needs has worked; not what the old man says, but the fact that his speech exists brings a triumph over loneliness and self-concern. The poem is a parable: the poet must not only cease to worry about "mighty poets in their misery dead"; he must open his poetry to admit prose. "The fear that kills," though it haunts Wordsworth in the guise of worries about financial security, about the death or absence of loved ones, about the fading of youthful powers and sympathies (these throughout all his poems, of course), is at bottom the fear of losing the power of speech. Linguistic nervous breakdown is the specter of our times, at least of our writers; our analyst is not Freud but Jacques Lacan.

The poem itself is a temporary victory, a timely utterance to give the thought relief, just as "Dejection: An Ode" belies its subject. But these momentary stays against confusion raise an all-devouring question, one that hovers round the fringes of all Wordsworth's poems: might it not be true that to succeed as a poet is to fail? What unites Romanticism to Modernism is a certain quivering before that question. The silence of Mallarmé or Melville, the reticence of Kafka, these have long since suggested that literature for us is somehow inextricably tied up with its own failure. Even mediocre talents have taken refuge and paradoxical comfort in the idea of failure. Pound and Wordsworth were not so fainthearted: they find ways, prose infusions being one, to get started again. Yet even the prose remedy raises the same question. In spite of Wordsworth's spirited assertions to the contrary, prose can still be considered— not as simply as in Arnold's patronizing phrase about Pope and Dryden—a failure of poetry. We are not like the critics Wordsworth imagined, who on looking at the opening lines of "Michael" would say "Aha! These might perfectly well be printed as prose"; we know that Mallarmé wrote prose poems, and that others, like Joyce, have written poetic prose; but we may see even in the fruits of successful interbreeding of norms of discourse an acknowledgment of what might be called (and has been) the poetics of failure. For the prose infusion, as in Wordsworth's parable, may give rise to the illusion that a "truer" language has been reached with its aid; and such illusions are bound to collapse. Silence is the result.

For Chaucer it was a comic device, that his persona in the *Tales* should fail at poetry and succeed only in prose; for Pope, fascination lay in the possibilities of meretriciousness in language, as when pompous poetry revealed itself as abject prose; for us the fascination is in the failure of language to be "true." Unfinished poems, careers looked back on regretfully—these were somehow fated for Pound and Wordsworth. The *Canterbury Tales* is unfinished as is a cathedral; but the *Cantos,* and even more Wordsworth's projects, are something else.

Pound is the more defiant, if also the more regretful. His method produced not only momentary victories, but a poetics that incorporates language as failure to produce a poetry of ellipsis. Like the similarity-deficient aphasic he resembles, Pound tends to produce "an elliptical note about its use"—a predication—instead of naming an object ("a thing only IS what it *does*"). For the aphasic, "sentences are conceived as elliptical sequels to be supplied from antecedent sentences uttered, if not imagined" by the speaker or by an actual or imaginary "partner in the colloquy" (p. 78). That again parallels some of the practices in the *Cantos*. Ellipsis is a running of the risks of incoherence in order to preclude redundancy as far as possible; all readers of the *Cantos* see this pattern immediately. "Pound omits, omits," as Hugh Kenner puts it: he forces us to look for connections, yet he is not a *pointilliste;* nor is he a *Symboliste,* for the ellipses are rather implicatory than evocative.[25] Ellipsis forwards predication, and contexture: jagged details stand out, reach toward each other everywhere, stripped of redundant linguistic padding. As Kenner would say, in the *Cantos* everything is the context of everything else. What Yeats, who "had come to identify Pound with ellipsis," thought he saw in the poem is instructive: "at moments more style, more deliberate nobility and the means to convey it than in any contemporary poet known to me, but it is constantly interrupted, broken, twisted into nothing by its direct opposite, nervous obsession, nightmare, stammering confusion."[26] Yeats, with his rhetorical impulse, did not always remember that the painter's brush consumes his dreams; he strove till the end for a final summary statement, oblivious of its inevitable self-contradiction: "Man can embody truth but he cannot know it," he says, knowing it. Pound, on the other hand, did not seek to have the last word with language. His distrust of the ideal of eloquence ("Italy went to rot, destroyed by rhetoric, destroyed by the periodic sentence and by the flowing paragraph")[27] carried him finally beyond any idea of language but the problematic. His paratactic flattening-out of elements onto one plane, dispensing with the "tone of time" and the reverberations of the "polysemous," sets things into the manifold contiguities (differences) of relation, not the limited ones of statement.

An elliptical poetics might take as its motto that one in the poem, transplanted from Malatesta to Jefferson: *Tempus loquendi, tempus tacendi.* Or as Kenner puts it: "His silent old age was didactic still."[28] Like language revealing itself in aphasia, some poetry may be better heard in the poet's silence, even in his failure.

NOTES

1. *The Letters of Ezra Pound, 1907–1941,* ed. D. D. Paige (New York: Harcourt, Brace, 1950), p. 49.

2. "Affirmations" (1915), in *Gaudier-Brzeska: A Memoir* (New York: New Directions, 1960), p. 115.

3. "A Few Don'ts" (1913), in *Literary Essays of Ezra Pound,* ed. T. S. Eliot (New York: New Directions, 1954), p. 7.

4. Reprinted in *Pound/Joyce,* ed. Forrest Read (New York: New Directions, 1967), p. 90.

5. "The Rev. G. Crabbe, Ll. B." (1917), in *Literary Essays,* p. 277.

6. "Pound, Joyce, and Flaubert: The Odysseans," in *New Approaches to Ezra Pound,* ed. Eva Hesse (Berkeley and Los Angeles: University of California, 1969), pp. 127–29.

7. *The Pound Era* (Berkeley and Los Angeles: University of California, 1971), p. 381.

8. See *Letters,* pp. 87–88, and *Literary Essays,* p. 50.

9. See *Literary Style: A Symposium,* ed. Seymour Chatman (London: Oxford University Press, 1971), pp. 7, 13.

10. "Two Aspects of Language and Two Types of Aphasic Disturbances," in *Fundamentals of Language,* by Roman Jakobson and Morris Halle, 2nd. ed. (The Hague: Mouton, 1971), p. 90. Hereafter cited in the text.

11. Dudley Young, in the *New York Times Book Review,* 79, No. 21 (1974), p. 16.

12. "Linguistics and Poetics," in *Style in Language,* ed. Thomas A. Sebeok (Cambridge, Mass.: M.I.T. Press, 1960), p. 358.

13. Ibid.

14. *Style and Proportion* (Boston: Little, Brown, 1967), pp. 97, 4.

15. *Letters,* p. 82.

16. "Pound, Joyce, and Flaubert," p. 129.

17. In *Ezra Pound: The Image and the Real* (Baton Rouge: Louisiana State University Press, 1969), pp. 56–73; cf. Eva Hesse, "Introduction," in *New Approaches,* pp. 23, 47.

18. "Verse Pleasant and Unpleasant" [signed "Apteryx"], *The Egoist,* 5 (March, 1918), 43.

19. "The Chinese Written Character as a Medium for Poetry," reprinted in *Prose Keys to Modern Poetry,* ed. Karl Shapiro (New York: Harper, 1962), p. 146.

20. *The Cantos of Ezra Pound* (New York: New Directions, 1970), p. 6. Hereafter cited as C.

21. "The Music of a Lost Dynasty," *Boston University Journal,* 21 (Winter, 1973), 38.

22. See "Linguistics and Poetics," p. 370.

23. See *Selected Writings of Charles Olson,* ed. Robert Creeley (New York: New Directions, 1966) pp. 16–17, 18, 21.

24. Of course our processes are blocked not by lesions but by other processes, the swarming of verbal associations. The self-cancelling properties of language should be studied.

25. *The Pound Era,* p. 133.

26. Preface to the *Oxford Book of Modern Verse;* quoted by Richard Ellmann, "Ez and Old Billyum," in *New Approaches,* p. 82; cf. p. 83.

27. *Gaudier-Brzeska,* p. 113.

28. *The Pound Era,* p. 266.

Walter Savage Landor and Ezra Pound

"Wordsworth is an essential part of history; Landor only a magnificent by-product." So wrote T. S. Eliot in 1933, expressing a consensus of twentieth-century opinion.[1] But for Ezra Pound, Wordsworth was "a silly old sheep with a genius, an unquestionable genius, for imagisme"; whereas Landor was the central and seminal figure among the English Romantics, the most important writer in English between Pope and Browning.[2] This essay will explore Pound's heterodox view of Landor and the other English Romantics, and his sense of the literary traditions which lead to and from Romanticism. As Donald Davie has noted, "there is need of an essay or monograph that would map a way into the poetic universe of Pound by the firmly interlinked stages of an English route that runs from Landor to Hardy through Browning."[3] This essay seeks to chart some of those stages, in the belief that its relation to Romanticism is a defining characteristic of Modernism.

Pound's denigration of Wordsworth and "dippy William" Blake belongs to the neoclassical reaction against Romanticism of which Irving Babbitt, T. E. Hulme, and (in part) Matthew Arnold are the most prominent spokesmen (LE 72).[4] Pound reacted specifically to a late Victorian reading of the Romantics which enshrined Wordsworth and Keats with Milton and Tennyson in a pantheon of stylistic and social respectability. This "cult of the innocuous" impeded the acceptance of the modern poetry which Pound's circle was creating. "The cult of the innocuous has debouched into the adoration of Wordsworth. . . . he has been deemed so innocuous that he has become, if not the backbone, at least one of the ribs of British kultur" (LE 277). Pound's reaction was the stronger because a late Victorian passion for Keatsian Romanticism had figured in his own early development. At the start of his career he, like William Carlos Williams, admired and imitated Keats.[5] So Pound's rejection of the Romantics was in part a rejection of his earlier self, attended by an appropriate ambivalence.

In fact Pound admired many aspects of the English Romantic achievement. Although he parodied Blake's poetry ("Tiger, Tiger, catch 'em quick! / All the little lambs are sick") and declared Blake's visual art inferior to Whistler's, Pound nevertheless assigned Blake an honorific place in Canto 16, where he appears in purgatory in the company of Saint Augustine, Sordello, and Dante himself, all of whom have experienced visions of hell and of the ideal city.[6] Of Coleridge's work Pound never mentions the poetry but fondly quotes phrases from the criticism throughout his own critical writings.[7] He admired the last act of Shelley's *Cenci*, but did not care for "The Sensitive Plant" or "Ode to the West Wind" (LE 305, 292). "Bad Keats" he defined as "pseudo-Elizabethanism" (LE 287); yet he called Keats at his best "subtle" and "crafty" (SP 35), and he appreciated Keats's influence upon the aesthetic movement (LE 292). Sensitive to many of their virtues, Pound was turning not against the Romantics themselves so much as against their latter-day imitators and idolators. If Wordsworth, Keats, and Tennyson had been made respectable establishment figures whose influence was grown oppressive, then they had to be undermined and blasted to make way for the new poetry.

Pound's strategy was to offer a deliberately subversive reading of literary history intended to shock received opinion. He set up a counter-tradition, proclaiming that the most important poets in English between the death of Pope and the early work of Browning were Crabbe, Landor, the later Byron, and Beddoes.[8] In the anthology section of his *ABC of Reading*, Pound devotes four pages to Crabbe, nine to Landor, and none to Blake, Wordsworth, Coleridge, Byron, Shelley, or Keats. This emphasis is no mere Browningesque obsession with the *scriptores ignoti*, the unknown secondary artists of the period. It is a revolutionary effort to establish a heritage for a literary counter-culture. The poetry to which Pound calls attention is social, political, and satiric rather than psychological, visionary, and confessional.[9] Except for Beddoes, the poets Pound chose reacted conservatively themselves to Romanticism, carrying many values of eighteenth-century culture over into the nineteenth century. The Byron he admired was not the Romanticist of *Childe Harold* and *The Corsair*, but the satirist of *Beppo* and *Don Juan*.[10] The poets of Pound's counter-tradition paid for their dissent with a loss of reputation later in the nineteenth century. The fact that they were neglected or unpopular in Victorian eyes connected them to the poets of Pound's own generation, providing the latter with martyrs as well as saints. In Landor and Byron, Pound admired the literary stance of the civilized man of letters who has inherited a rich tradition from the European past, and who is determined to preserve and transmit it to future generations, even at the cost of ostracism and exile.

Pound's sense of Landor's isolation was no doubt enhanced by the circumstances in which he first read Landor. In the war winter of 1915–16, he and Yeats studied C. G. Crump's ten-volume edition of *Selected Works of Walter Savage Landor* at Yeats's cottage in Coleman's Hatch, Sussex.[11] "Yeats and I spent our last winter's months on Landor," Pound told Iris Barry in July 1916. "There is a whole culture" (L 89). About the same time he advised William Carlos Williams to "reread 'Sordello' and then get the ten vols of Walter Savage Landor. Converse with no one until you have read all save a few of the dialogues on politics and orthography. He is the best mind in English literature. Don't hand this on to the mob yet."[12] Pound's first enthusiasm for Landor remained keen throughout 1916 and 1917. In these months Pound wrote an essay on Landor and an imaginary conversation of his own; he also translated twelve of Fontenelle's dialogues of the dead.[13] A second phase of interest in Landor came between 1929 and 1938, when Pound was formulating an educational curriculum and found in Landor's works a veritable college course.[14] By then, apparently, Pound was ready to hand Landor "on to the mob."

Landor was handed on to Pound by his two favorite Victorian poets, Browning and Swinburne. Their allegiance to Landor must have confirmed Pound's sense of a counter-tradition. Browning met Landor in 1836 and was gratified later that year by the older man's praise of *Paracelsus*. Browning honored Landor in a passage of Pound's favorite Victorian poem, *Sordello*, and was in turn complimented by Landor in a handsome eulogy which Pound used in the *ABC of Reading*. For a time during Landor's last years in Florence, the Brownings looked after all his affairs, and Landor is buried in the same Florentine cemetery as Elizabeth Barrett Browning.[15] According to Mrs. Browning, "Robert always said that he owed more as a writer to Landor than to any contemporary."[16] Both she and later critics have noted connections between Landor's verse drama and Browning's.[17] But Pound, as we shall see, perceived other similarities between the works of the two men.

In the year of his death Landor was visited by Swinburne. "There is no other man living," wrote the young pilgrim, "from whom I should so much have prized any expression of acceptance or goodwill in return for my homage."[18] Landor, Hugo, and Mazzini were Swinburne's greatest heroes. He dedicated several poems to Landor and mentioned him often in essays.[19] In Swinburne's ardent "homage" Pound recognized the feeling of "Apostolic Succession" that informed his own literary allegiances.[20] He always regretted not having met Swinburne, who died a few months after Pound reached London: "Swinburne my only miss / and I didn't know he'd been to see Landor" (C 523). Swinburne and Browning, then, made Landor a living presence in Pound's own immediate heritage.

The two Victorians mediated different aspects of Landor to Pound. Pound's sense of Landor's work is indebted to Browning, whereas his sense of Landor's life owes much to Swinburne. The balance of this essay will explore both facets of Landor: first, his importance to Pound as a Browningesque voice, transmitting the culture of the past; and second, his significance as an artist in isolation, whose career established a symbolic pattern of unpopularity and expatriation.[21] The first of these interests may be called neoclassical; the second, romantic.

According to the *Guide to Kulchur*, "Browning carried on from Landor."[22] He carried on Landor's endeavor to voice the culture of the past. Pound saw, or rather heard, a connection between Browning's dramatic monologues and Landor's imaginary conversations. Both forms require a cultural ventriloquism that fascinated the author of *Personae*. As he said in the *ABC of Reading*, Landor's *Imaginary Conversations* present a culture "full of human life ventilated, given a human body, not merely indexed" (ABC 186). Pound first read Landor just as his own work was returning, after Imagism and Vorticism, to the personae which had occupied him at the start of his career. In 1916–17 he was engaged with the *Homage to Sextus Propertius* and with the various masks in the early versions of *The Cantos*. If *Propertius* demonstrates the permanent relevance of the values and tones of the classical past, Pound no doubt saw a similar enterprise in Landor's *Imaginary Conversations.*

Likewise Pound was intrigued around 1917 by dialogues of the dead. Lucianic in origin, this popular seventeenth- and eighteenth-century genre presents a conversation of famous shades, often from different historical eras, set in Hades or Elysium. Together with the philosophical dialogue, the dialogue of the dead was a major influence upon Landor's imaginary conversations.[23] In 1916–17, as if practicing for *Propertius*, Pound translated twelve of Fontenelle's *Nouveaux Dialogues des morts* (1683). The genre must have struck Pound as an interesting formal problem in "homage." Its most recent student observes that "such a dialogue depends upon the successful artistic equivalent of resuscitation."[24] Like the persona, like the dramatic monologue, and like the imaginary conversation, the dialogue of the dead interested Pound as a form that could provide "blood for the ghosts."[25]

Not only the form but also the content of Landor's conversations had a cultural significance in Pound's mind. He found in Landor's dialogues a systematic digest of European civilization. "As to earlier guides to Kulchur or Culture?" asked Pound. "Fontenelle and Landor tried consciously, I think, to make summaries" (GK 207). Pound saw in Landor an inheritor of the French philosophes of the eighteenth-century Enlightenment. Not only was Landor an anticlerical rationalist and republican, but his learning seemed as comprehensive as that of the French encyclopedists. "You can go to Landor for an epitome; all culture of the encyclopedists reduced to manageable size, in the *Imaginary Conversations*. . . . Landor comes after the work is done, Rabelais, Peter Bayle, Voltaire, Diderot, Holbach . . . and if you want a handy introduction you have it in his *Conversations*" (ABC 186).

This encyclopedic dimension of Landor's work was especially important to Pound in the 1930s, when he himself was engaged more deeply than ever before in formulating an educational curriculum. He spoke in the *ABC of Reading* of "a culture as thorough as Landor's" (ABC 185), and in an earlier essay on Remy de Gourmont he said flatly: "A set of Landor's collected works will go further toward civilizing a man than any university education now on the market" (LE 344). Pound associated Landor with De Gourmont and Fontenelle in the French tradition of the *homme des lettres,* and he told British readers that Landor was "perhaps the only complete and serious man of letters ever born in these islands" (LE 33).[26] It would not surprise Pound to know that his view of the *Imaginary Conversations* differs from that of recent university critics, who see the conversations not as a systematic syllabus of culture but as a form of personal essay, occasional in inspiration, topical in reference, and unsystematic in accretion.[27] Pound would say that this reading is typical of a general academic conspiracy against Landor: "He, Landor, still plays an inconspicuous role in university courses. The amount of light which he would shed on the undergraduate mind would make students inconvenient to the average run of professors."[28]

Pound heard the voice of the civilized past in Landor's poetry as well as in the *Imaginary Conversations.* In recent study of that poetry, Robert Pinsky argues that its distinguishing quality is an urbane awareness of established rhetorical and stylistic traditions, a "suggestion, to a varying and controlled extent, of a voice more resonant than that of any particular moment of history." This is less a matter of form or content than a question of style and tone. Pinsky rightly notes that "the civilizing assertion of the tone" in Landor's poetry was enormously attractive to Pound.[29] It is audible in the two poems by Landor that Pound loved best and quoted most often. Both deal, appropriately enough, with classical shades:

TO IANTHE

Past ruin'd Ilion Helen lives,
   Alcestis rises from the shades;
Verse calls them forth; 'tis verse that gives
   Immortal youth to mortal maids.

Soon shall Oblivion's deepening veil
   Hide all the peopled hills you see,
The gay, the proud, while lovers hail
   In distant ages you and me.

The tear for fading beauty check
   For passing glory cease to sigh;
One form shall rise above the wreck,
   One name, Ianthe, shall not die.

DIRCE

Stand close around, ye Stygian set,
   With Dirce in one bark conveyed!
Or Charon, seeing, may forget
   That he is old and she a shade.[30]

Tones like these, at once impersonal and personal, ancient and contemporary, were among the effects Pound aimed for in *Propertius*
and the "Envoi" of *Hugh Selwyn Mauberley*. As Pinsky says,
"Pound's or Landor's knowledge of a certain body of excellent writing, historically arranged, lends depth and serious elegance to the
poet's style."[31]

"To Ianthe" and "Dirce" testify to Landor's interest in the Greek
epigram. Pound admired the two poems partly because, in his Imagist days, he too had imitated the form. "Pound, like Landor,"
writes Vivian Mercier, "was trying to revive the Greek tradition of
epigram found in the *Palatine Anthology*, better known as the Greek
Anthology."[32] And the epigram was really the only aspect of Landor's Hellenism that *did* interest Pound.[33] He never praised Landor's *Hellenics*, the favorite poems of both Swinburne and Richard
Aldington.[34] The idyls in which Landor re-creates Greek myths and
legends have no direct influence upon the comparable sections of
Pound's *Cantos*. And certainly Pound did not share Landor's taste
for Pindar. For Pound, Landor's Rome is more important than Landor's Greece. The two men hold similar views of Ovid and Horace;
and although Landor did not particularly admire Propertius,
Pound's sense of Rome in the *Homage to Sextus Propertius* was deepened by his reading of Landor. The literary temperaments of Pound

and Landor have perhaps their deepest affinity in a mutual admiration of Catullus which is connected to their interest in the classical epigram. Pound often cites Landor's essay on "The Poems of Catullus" (1842) as a model of practical criticism, and he uses a translation of Catullus by Landor in the *ABC of Reading*.[35] Moreover, there are strong Catullan elements in the verse of Landor that Pound liked best: the short, epigrammatic, occasional poems. As Vivian Mercier observes, "Catullus, even more than Horace, was the crucial Latin influence upon Landor's shorter poems."[36] Both the Greek Anthology and the epigrams of Catullus were important sources for the Imagists in 1913–14, so it must have pleased Pound to rediscover both interests in Landor in 1916–17.[37]

In Pound's view the tradition of the epigram leads to a nineteenth-century stylistic heritage called the "hard" or "prose" tradition. Because Landor wrote both prose and epigrammatic poetry well, Pound placed him in this tradition. Pound saw hard style descending from Stendhal to Flaubert to Joyce in fiction, and from Gautier to the Parnassians to Imagism in poetry. The opposite of hard style is "the swash of Hugo, De Musset & Co."—in other words, the style of Romanticism (LE 286). In Pound's view hardness in the nineteenth century is primarily a French affair, and Landor is the only English poet of the period who attained it. "We have however some hardness in English, and in Landor we have a hardness which is not of necessity 'rugged'; as in 'Past ruin'd Ilion Helen lives.' Indeed Gautier might well be the logical successor to Landor, were he not in all probability the logical co-heir with Landor of certain traditions" (LE 286). John J. Espey has shown how Pound and Eliot turned, around 1918, to the rhymed quatrains of Gautier's *Emaux et camées* to restore hardness to an Imagist free verse gone soft.[38] Pound's coincidental discovery of Landor's epigrams, many of them written in a "lapidary style" and "manifestly inscribed," must have confirmed his renewed taste for a sculptural poetry (ABC 185). In his 1917 essay on Landor, Pound asserted that "Gautier himself has never given to the world a more chiselled marmorean quatrain than Landor's

> Past ruin'd Ilion Helen lives,
> Alcestis rises from the shades;
> Verse calls them forth; 'tis verse that gives
> Immortal youth to mortal maids." (SP 385)

Since Landor himself spoke in sculptural terms of "those carvings as it were on ivory or on gems, which are modestly called epigrams by the Greeks," Pound could reasonably claim him for a Parnassian tradition of "the 'sculpture' of rhyme."[39] Landor's most distinguished French critic, Pierre Vitoux, makes the same claim independently of Pound: "the true place of Landor is outside his country, on the straight road which leads from André Chenier . . . to Parnassus. . . ."[40]

All these voices—Greek, Roman, and French—Pound heard in the tones of Landor's shorter poems. But his bias toward the sculpted epigram made him deaf to the resonances of Landor's longer poems. Pound recognized, as every reader must, that "Landor is, from poem to poem, extremely uneven" (LE 286). And because of this unevenness, he did not recommend Landor as a model for beginning poets (L 89). But Pound went further, arguing that "Landor never learned to write a long passage of verse without in some way clogging and blocking the reader's attention" (SP 387).[41] He contended that "a great part of Landor's longer poems are still inaccessible because the language is so far removed from any speech ever used anywhere" (ABC 185). Pound therefore had no use for the *Hellenics* or the *Heroic Idyls*, and none for Landor's early poems in the heroic tradition: *Gebir*, *Crysaor*, and *The Phocaeans*. Pound spoke of the "particularisation which makes Landor's later work so much better than his early poems" (SP 388). He seems never to have noticed the thematic resemblances between his own *Cantos* and Landor's early work.[42] Pound thought of Landor's poetry too exclusively as fragments of carved stone broken from a ruined structure. Once, after quoting a strophe of eight lines, Pound observed: "How fine we should think him if we had found the three and a half opening lines cut in a fragment of stone. How utterly it goes to pieces when we come upon [the closing lines] !" (SP 387). This taste for classical fragments of Landor is the opposite of Richard Aldington's, who admired "the architectural qualities" of Landor's poetry, and found it difficult to locate "witty or pointed couplets or lovely suave phrases" that are "easily quotable." Aldington nonetheless agreed with Pound that Landor's classicism is counter-Romantic and thereby akin to Modernism.[43]

The specificity of Landor's classicism carried over into his literary criticism, where it also drew Pound's praise. "Almost no Englishman save Landor has ever written a line of real criticism," Pound groused.[44] By "real" criticism he meant what Landor called "verbal" and we might call "practical" criticism. Landor was, said Pound, "the first useful critic, or the first analytical critic in English; the first man to go through an English poem line by line marking what was good, what was poor, what was excessive; the first seriously to consider and write down this, almost the only sort of criticism that can profit a later writer" (SP 388). Criticism of this kind is familiar to any reader of Pound's letters to fellow poets. Landor declared his preference for it in the conversation between Alfieri and Salomon the Florentine Jew: "All good criticism hath its foundation on verbal. . . . A perfect piece of criticism must exhibit *where* a work is good or bad, *why* it is good or bad; in what degree it is good or bad."[45]

Pound's favorite example of verbal criticism in Landor is the essay on "The Poems of Catullus," which one commentator describes as "a transference of the scholia of classical criticism to English literature."[46] Pound also admired Landor's detailed criticism of Dante in *The Pentameron*, and thought often of Landor when consulting with Laurence Binyon in 1938 on Binyon's translation of Dante (LE 203). On one occasion, after offering several pages of specific verbal comments on Binyon's work, Pound observed: "Nobody has had such a good time of this kind since Landor did his notes on Catullus" (L 318). By making the classics "useful" to later writers, Landor affirmed their permanent relevance. He "judged Pindar and Wordsworth each *per se:* one would think he was a contemporary of both," writes Stanley T. Williams.[47] Pound's critical stance was the same: "All ages are contemporaneous," he wrote. "What we need is a literary scholarship which will weigh Theocritus and Yeats with one balance."[48] Landor's literary criticism appealed to Pound because it seemed to share many of his own assumptions.

Transmission of the culture of the past—this is the unifying focus of Pound's remarks on the imaginary conversations, the poetry, and the literary criticism of Landor. We have called this concern neoclassical because of its emphasis upon Greece, Rome, and eighteenth-century France, and also because of its stress upon certain "sculptural" qualities of literary style. It may also be called Browningesque because of its fascination with the dramatic re-creation of the voices and tones of the past. But for both Pound and Yeats there was a discrepancy between the classicism of Landor's work and the romanticism of his life. "Savage Landor topped us all in calm nobility when the pen was in his hand, as in the daily violence of his passion when he laid it down," Yeats wrote shortly after reading Landor with Pound at Stone Cottage.[49] This discrepancy seemed to confirm Yeats's theory of the anti-self, or mask. In *A Vision* (1938) he described Landor as a "daimonic" man who strives in his work for "simplification through intensity," his true mask. "The most violent of men, he uses his intellect to disengage a visionary image of perfect sanity . . . seen always in the most serene and classic art imaginable."[50] Though less systematically than Yeats, Pound also perceived a discrepancy between Landor's works and his agitated life. Pound was particularly interested in the significance of Landor's career as a man of letters in relation to his society. This concern may be called romantic because of its emphasis upon the artist's unpopularity, isolation, and expatriation. We shall also call it Swinburnian because of its sense of personal contact and hero worship.

"Swinburne and Landor," writes W. B. D. Henderson, " . . . are not, and never were or can be popular."[51] Pound too emphasized that "Landor has not been a popular author" (SP 384). Landor's political and religious convictions, Pound believed, were too "heretical" to suit Victorian tastes: "Landor, a republican, at a time when such politics were more suspect than syndicalism is at present, was carefully edged out of the way. In his dialogue on the Chinese Emperor, the little children of the palace oppose their simple arithmetic to the western doctrine of the Trinity" (SP 384). The extirpation of Landor's heresies took subtle forms. "Even Landor was almost suppressed, not officially and by edict, but left unobtainable, or 'selected' by Colvin" (SP 200). It seemed to Pound that Landor faced the same mindless censorship that the men of 1914 knew only too well. Pound compared the difficulties Landor encountered in placing the manuscript of the *Imaginary Conversations* to the difficulties Joyce encountered in placing the manuscript of *A Portrait of the Artist as a Young Man.*[52] The fact that Landor is not available in good editions and is not taught at most universities also seemed part of the establishment's conspiracy against him. Before dismissing all this as a paranoid projection of Pound's own battles, we should ask ourselves whether the facts of Landor's career do not support Pound's interpretation.[53]

Gross public incomprehension was another obstacle that Landor shared with Pound. Readers have always been quick to level the charge of obscurity against both authors. The terms of the accusation are sometimes almost identical. Only the flavor of the phrasing shows that the following remark was made about *Gebir* rather than *The Cantos:* "It wants common sense: there are exquisitely fine passages; but they succeed each other by such flea-skips of association, that I am unable to track the path of the author's mind, and verily suspect him of insanity."[54] Of which poet were the following Johnsonian observations made? "He is so anxious to avoid saying what is superfluous that he does not always say what is necessary. As soon as he has given adequate expression to any idea, he leaves it and passes on to the next, forgetting sometimes to make clear to the reader the connexion of his ideas with one another."[55] This also describes Landor but might well be about Pound. The reputation of being learned, difficult, obscure, and eccentric attached itself so firmly to Landor and Browning that it must have seemed to Pound an almost infallible sign of merit and of brotherhood in the nineteenth-century counter-tradition. In certain moods Pound was proud of carrying the same reputation and damned the public as lustily as Landor ever did.[56]

In Pound's view this public, uncomprehending and hostile, came into being during Landor's lifetime and has remained essentially unchanged since then. Landor's departure for Italy in 1814 is for Pound a richly symbolic moment in literary history because it signifies the final ascendancy of the modern bourgeois audience and tells the exact moment when England became uninhabitable for its artists. "The decline of England began on the day when Landor packed his trunks and departed to Tuscany. Up till then England had been able to contain her best authors; after that we see Shelley, Keats, Byron, Beddoes on the Continent, and still later observe the edifying spectacle of Browning in Italy and Tennyson in Buckingham Palace" (LE 32). Once again Landor's career seemed to anticipate that of Pound's own generation. Pound himself followed the Romantic paradigm of expatriation, leaving first America, then England to make his home in Italy. The parallel between his career and Landor's is explored wittily and unromantically by Donald Davie in his "Fourth Epistle to Eva Hesse":

> Savage Landor—there's a poet
> Spurned England, and took pains to show it.
> . . . .
>
> No surprise, then, if he's found
> In the pantheon of Pound
> Who, similarly unabashed,
> Was the very thing he lashed
> . . . .
>
> Both poets, relishing the state
> Of mortified expatriate,
> Through blunder after patent blunder,
> Scrape after scrape, found face to thunder
> At home-grown mischiefs, and expose
> Fools or knaves, in verse and prose.
>   Such doubleness is on the cards
> Too plainly, for self-banished bards
> Who never lack for occupation,
> Each hectoring his relinquished nation
> Even as they exemplify
> The prepossessions they decry.[57]

As his rhymed couplets suggest, Davie is speaking in the tradition
of Neoclassical satire against Romanticism. He treats the expatriation of Landor and Pound as a vagary of the individuals involved
rather than an indictment of their society. Indeed Davie's shrewd
persona implicitly defends that society.

Pound, by contrast, inferred from Landor's expatriation a decline
in the quality of English national life. He was struck by the fact that
so much of Landor's work takes its material from the past, and he
saw in this a commentary on the England of Landor's day. In the
ABC of Reading he notes that Landor's work is "80 per cent retro-
spective," whereas the comparable percentage of Chaucer's work is
much lower (ABC 187). In other words the England of Chaucer's
time provided subjects for poetry, but the subsequent cultural decline has forced poets to take more and more of their material from
the past. Pound was fond of saying that Landor wrote the *Imaginary
Conversations* because there was no one for him to talk to. "*Landor
finding no good conversation had to pretend it had sometimes existed*"
(GK 84). In *The Pisan Cantos* Pound restates this idea with reference
to his own Italian isolation in the Detention Training Center: "or to
write dialog because there is / no one to converse with" (C 499).

Landor figures prominently in *The Pisan Cantos,* where he is part
of the vanished culture which the poem mourns. He is associated
with traditions of fine conversation, especially with vivid anecdotes
of famous writers. The personal contacts in the following passage
run from Landor to Swinburne to Elkin Mathews, Pound's early
London publisher. Mathews once carried Swinburne's suitcase and
later took tea at Putney with Swinburne and Theodore Watts-Dunton.

> Swinburne my only miss
> and I didn't know he'd been to see Landor
>   *and* they told me that an' tother
> and when old Matthews went he saw the three teacups
>   two for Watts Dunton who liked to let his tea cool,
> So old Elkin had only one glory
>   He did carry Algernon's suitcase *once*
> when he, Elkin, first came to London.
>   But given what I know now I'd have
>   got through it somehow . . . Dirce's shade
>   or a blackjack.
>   (C 523)

The allusion to Landor's "Dirce" suggests the passing away of these
men and the culture they embodied. The "blackjack" perhaps represents the oblivion that threatens the poet in the wreckage of two
world wars. Later in the same canto (82) Pound alludes again to

"Dirce," drawing upon its elegiac connotations to mourn the passing of Yeats and Ford Madox Ford and their conversation:

> and for all that old Ford's conversation was better,
> consisting in *res* non *verba*,
>   despite William's anecdotes, in that Fordie
> never dented an idea for a phrase's sake.
>
> and had more humanitas 仁 jen
>
> (Cythera   Cythera)
> With Dirce in one bark convey'd   (C 525)

The Greek and Latin nouns in the passage suggest the classical base of the culture that Landor, Ford, and Yeats tried to preserve and transmit. Their conversation, and the social order to which it belonged, now remain only in the passionate memory of the elegist. Nowhere is Pound's personal identification with Landor expressed more poignantly than in Canto 82.

Pound's Landor is a highly personalized and selective creation. He mirrors some of the most abiding interests of his creator: the revival of history through dramatis personae, the prose guide to kulchur, the classical epigram, the "hardness" of French style, practical criticism, difficulties with publishers and the reading public, and expatriation. Perhaps this Landor illustrates Harold Bloom's idea that literary influence necessarily involves a creative distortion of one author by another. And perhaps the psychology of influence sketched by Bloom explains Pound's shutting out of the major Romantics, by whose stylistic heritage he felt threatened.[58] Yet Pound's Landor hardly seems the result of a serious misreading or, in Bloom's parlance, "misprision." Any reader of Landor can recognize Pound's hero, and other critics, as we have seen, point out many of the same characteristics that Pound emphasizes. Pound's Landor has substance and vitality, and he is a standing challenge to the conventional valuation of the literary traditions of the Romantic period.

NOTES

1. T. S. Eliot, *The Use of Poetry and the Use of Criticism* (London: Faber and Faber, 1933), p. 88. Eliot places Landor among the minor poets in "What Is Minor Poetry?" (1944), reprinted in *On Poetry and Poets* (New York: Noonday Press, 1964), p. 39.

2. Ezra Pound, "The Rev. G. Crabbe, LL.B." (1917), in *Literary Essays of Ezra Pound*, ed. T. S. Eliot (London: Faber and Faber, 1954), p. 277. Hereafter cited as LE.

3. Donald Davie, *Thomas Hardy and British Poetry* (New York: Oxford University Press, 1972), p. 3.

4. In this essay, as in this sentence, I shall capitalize Neoclassicism, Romanticism, Modernism, and their cognates to denote specific historical movements of, respectively, the seventeenth and eighteenth, the nineteenth, and the twentieth centuries. Uncapitalized, the terms will denote literary sensibilities, not restricted to the same periods as the movements.

5. See "M. Antonius Flamininus and John Keats, a Kinship in Genius," *Book News Monthly*, 26 (1908), 445–47, and "Sonnet of the August Calm," in *A Lume Spento and Other Early Poems* (New York: New Directions, 1965), p. 118. The sestet of this sonnet is imitated from Keats's "When I have fears that I may cease to be."

6. For the parody, see LE 72. On Blake and Whistler, see Ezra Pound, *Selected Prose: 1909–1965*, ed. William Cookson (New York: New Directions, 1973), p. 418. Hereafter cited as SP. On Blake and Dante, see *The Cantos of Ezra Pound* (New York: New Directions, 1970), p. 68. Hereafter cited as C.

7. See LE 373, and SP 110, 414, and 429. Coleridge's criticism is also quoted in Pound's early poem "In Durance." See *Personae: The Collected Shorter Poems of Ezra Pound* (New York: New Directions [1949]), p. 20.

8. This counter-tradition is most clearly presented in Ezra Pound, *ABC of Reading* (New York: New Directions, 1960), pp. 172–91. Hereafter cited as ABC. See also "Beddoes and Chronology," SP 378–83. Beddoes's *Death's Jest Book* was one of Pound's earliest favorites; see Noel Stock, *The Life of Ezra Pound* (New York: Pantheon Books, 1970), p. 18.

9. My description of mainstream Romanticism as psychological, visionary, and confessional is indebted to M. H. Abrams, *Natural Supernaturalism: Tradition and Revolution in Romantic Literature* (New York: W. W. Norton, 1971).

10. Pound imitated *Don Juan* in "L'Homme moyen sensuel," *The Little Review*, 4 (1917), 8–16; reprinted in *Personae*, pp. 238–46. He discusses both poems in *The Letters of Ezra Pound 1907–1941*, ed. D. D. Paige (New York: Harcourt, Brace, and World, 1950), p. 58. Hereafter cited as L. In *Confucius to Cummings: An Anthology of Poetry*, ed. Ezra Pound and Marcella Spann (New York: New Directions, 1964), pp. 201–16, Byron is represented by the "Dedication" to *Don Juan* in which he attacks the Lake Poets. On Byron and Pulci, see SP 95.

11. *Selected Works of Walter Savage Landor*, ed. C. G. Crump, 10 vols. (London: J. M. Dent & Co., 1891–93). Pound and Yeats shared views on many authors during their three winters at Stone Cottage. For another example, see George J. Bornstein and Hugh H. Witemeyer, "From *Villain* to Visionary: Pound and Yeats on Villon," *Comparative Literature*, 19 (1967), 308–20.

12. Charles Norman, *Ezra Pound* (New York: Macmillan, 1960), p. 194.

13. See "Landor (1775–1864): A Note," *The Future*, 2 (1917), 10–12; reprinted in SP 384–88. See also "An Anachronism at Chinon," *The Little Review*, 4 (1917), 14–21. The translations of Fontenelle appeared in *The Egoist* between 1 May 1916 and 4 June 1917 and were published in October as *Dialogues of Fontenelle*, trans. Ezra Pound (London: The Egoist Ltd., 1917).

14. Landor figures prominently in "How to Read" (1929), *ABC of Reading* (1934), and *Guide to Kulchur* (1938). See also "The Case of Landor," *The Observer* [London], 14 January 1934, p. 9.

15. R. H. Super, *Walter Savage Landor: A Biography* (New York: New York University Press, 1954), pp. 267, 272, 318–19, 357, 468–75.

16. Letter to Sarianna Browning of December 1859, in *The Letters of Elizabeth Barrett Browning*, ed. Frederic G. Kenyon (New York: Macmillan, 1910), II, 354. I am grateful to R. H. Super for helping me to locate the source of this quotation.

17. See *Elizabeth Barrett to Miss Mitford*, ed. Betty Miller (New Haven: Yale University Press, 1954), pp. 80–81, 154, and Donald S. Hair, *Browning's Experiments with Genre* (Toronto and Buffalo: University of Toronto Press, 1972), p. 50. Pound probably did not know Landor's verse dramas, which were omitted from Crump's edition of Landor. Another example of Landor's influence upon Browning is discussed by Boyd Litzinger in "The Prior's Niece in 'Fra Lippo Lippi,'" *Notes and Queries*, 206 (1961), 344–45.

18. Super, p. 504.

19. See W. Brooks Drayton Henderson, *Swinburne and Landor: A Study of Their Spiritual Relationship and Its Effect on Swinburne's Moral and Poetic Development* (London: Macmillan, 1918), pp. 2, 54–55, and Clyde K. Hyder, ed., *Swinburne as Critic* (London: Routledge & Kegan Paul, 1972), pp. 5, 174–79.

20. On "Apostolic Succession" see Pound, "How I Began," *T. P.'s Weekly*, 6 June 1913, p. 707. Pound's own poetic homage to Swinburne was published in 1908; see "Salve O Pontifex: To Swinburne," in *A Lume Spento and Other Early Poems*, pp. 63–66.

21. The notion of the "artist in isolation" is borrowed from Frank Kermode, *Romantic Image* (New York: Vintage Books, 1964), pp. 1–29.

22. Ezra Pound, *Guide to Kulchur* (New York: New Directions [1952]), p. 227. Hereafter cited as GK. A recent dissertation that connects Landor and Browning to Pound is John Frederick Peck's "Pound's Idylls, with Chapters on Catullus, Landor, and Browning" (Stanford, 1973); see *Dissertation Abstracts*, 34 (1973), 1290A.

23. See Pierre Vitoux, *L'Oeuvre de Walter Savage Landor* (Paris: Presses Universitaires de France, 1964), p. 172. Of course, Landor's conversations often have living speakers and contemporary settings and therein differ from traditional dialogues of the dead.

24. Frederick M. Keener, *English Dialogues of the Dead: A Critical History, an Anthology, and a Checklist* (New York: Columbia University Press, 1973), p. 9.

25. Hugh Kenner, "Blood for the Ghosts," in *New Approaches to Ezra Pound*, ed. Eva Hesse (Berkeley and Los Angeles: University of California Press, 1969), pp. 331–48.

26. Pound would probably have endorsed Ernest Dilworth's observation that Landor "made a place for himself, a peculiarly French sort of place in English literature, as a classic artist in prose." See Dilworth, *Walter Savage Landor* (New York: Twayne, 1971), p. 85.

27. See Super, p. 159, and Vitoux, p. 178.

28. Ezra Pound, "James Joyce," *The Egoist*, 4 (1917), pp. 21–22; reprinted in *Pound/Joyce*, ed. Forrest Read (New York: New Directions, 1967), p. 89.

29. Robert Pinsky, *Landor's Poetry* (Chicago: University of Chicago Press, 1968), pp. 10–11.

30. *The Complete Works of Walter Savage Landor*, ed. T. Earle Welby and Stephen Wheeler (London: Chapman and Hall, 1927–36), XV, 376, and XVI, 72. Both poems were published in 1831.

31. Pinsky, p. 10.

32. Vivian Mercier, "The Future of Landor Criticism," in *Some British Romantics: A Collection of Essays*, ed. James V. Logan, John E. Jordan, and Northrop Frye (Columbus: Ohio State University Press, 1966), p. 68.

33. Pound borrowed, for an Imagist lyric of his own, the Hellenized name "Ione" from passages that Landor wrote to celebrate a certain Miss Jones of Wales. The lyric in question is "Ione, Dead the Long Year," first published in December 1914; see *Personae*, p. 112. The derivation of the name "Ione" from Landor is noted by Hugh Kenner in *The Pound Era* (Berkeley and Los Angeles: University of California Press, 1971), p. 63.

34. On Swinburne's interest in the *Hellenics*, see Henderson, pp. 91–92, 123. On Aldington's, see "Landor's Hellenics" in Richard Aldington, *Literary Studies and Reviews* (London: George Allen and Unwin, 1924), pp. 141–54.

35. On Landor and Catullus, see L 69, 318; SP 392; and ABC 185. On Landor and Ovid, see LE 34. On Landor and Horace, see Pound, "Horace," *Arion*, 9 (1970), 178–87; first published in *The Criterion*, 9 (1929–30). See also A. La Vonne Ruoff, "Walter Savage Landor's Criticism of Horace: The Odes and Epodes," *Arion*, 9 (1970), 189. As if to indicate his preference for Landor's Rome, Pound changed the opening line of "To Ianthe" when he used part of it in Canto 9: "and in the style 'Past ruin'd Latium' " (C 41).

36. Mercier, p. 65.

37. On Imagism, see Hugh Witemeyer, *The Poetry of Ezra Pound: Forms and Renewal, 1908–1920* (Berkeley and Los Angeles: University of California Press, 1969), pp. 114–15.

38. John J. Espey, *Ezra Pound's Mauberley* (London: Faber and Faber, 1955), pp. 25–41.

39. Landor, *Works*, XV, 434. "The 'sculpture' of rhyme" is a phrase from Pound's *Hugh Selwyn Mauberley*; see *Personae*, p. 188.

40. Vitoux, p. 157: "En définitive, la vraie place de Landor est en dehors de son pays, sur la route droite qui conduit d'André Chenier . . . au Parnasse dont il est très proche á la fin de sa dernière étape."

41. Much the same view is taken by Donald Davie in "Landor's Shorter Poems," *Purity of Diction in English Verse* (New York: Schocken Books, 1967), pp. 183–96.

42. Landor's early poems feature themes of exile, voyage, conquest, colonization, and the foundation, rise, and fall of empires. *Gebir* especially is concerned with the wrong and right ways to found a civilization, as embodied in the contrasting careers of the hero and his brother, Tamar. In book 2 Gebir anticipates the heroes of Pound's *Cantos* when he is frustrated in his attempt to build a city; and in book 3 Gebir descends to an underworld that, like Pound's hell, contains contemporary political figures whom the poet blames for betraying his society.

43. Aldington, pp. 143–44 and 150–51.

44. Pound, "Horace," p. 178.

45. Landor, *Works*, III, 109–10.

46. Stanley T. Williams, "Walter Savage Landor as a Critic of Literature," *PMLA*, 38 (1923), p. 913.

47. Williams, p. 906.

48. Ezra Pound, *The Spirit of Romance* (New York: New Directions [1953]), p. 8.

49. W. B. Yeats, "Per Amica Silentia Lunae" (1918), in *Mythologies* (New York: Macmillan, 1959), p. 328.

50. Yeats, *A Vision* (New York: Macmillan, 1961), pp. 140–41, 144–45. Landor belongs to Phase 17, the phase in which Yeats placed himself, Shelley, and Dante. Landor is mentioned in two of Yeats's poems: "To a Young Beauty" and "A Nativity."

51. Henderson, p. 50.

52. *Pound/Joyce*, p. 88.

53. For two recent accounts of Landor's difficulties with publishers, see R. H. Super, *The Publication of Landor's Works*, Supplement to the Bibliographical Society's Transactions, no. 18 (London, 1954), and A. La Vonne Ruoff, "The Censorship of Landor's Imaginary Conversations," *Bulletin of the John Rylands Library*, 49 (1967), 427–63.

54. J. W. Robberds, *Memoir of . . . William Taylor of Norwich* (London, 1843), I, 357–58, quoted by Super, *Walter Savage Landor*, p. 45. The remark is Taylor's.

55. Sidney Colvin, *Landor* (New York: Harper and Brothers, n.d.), p. 3.

56. Politically, both writers were antidemocratic, anticlerical aristocrats with a contempt for the masses and the crowned heads of Europe, but with a weakness for the benevolent dictatorship of self-made great men. One commentator even finds in modern fascism the fulfillment of Landor's political ideals; see Emil Ehrich, *Southey und Landor* (Göttingen: Druck der Dieterichschen Universitàts-Buchdruckerei, 1934), pp. 156–61. Although Ehrich probably exaggerates, it is interesting to speculate about Landor's political position had he lived in the 1930s. Would he not have taken a conservative position vis-à-vis communism? Would he have gone to Spain to fight against the fascists as he went to fight against the French in 1808?

57. Donald Davie, *Collected Poems Nineteen Fifty to Nineteen Seventy* (New York: Oxford University Press, 1972), p. 267.

58. Harold Bloom, *The Anxiety of Influence: A Theory of Poetry* (New York: Oxford University Press, 1973).

GLENN O'MALLEY

Dante, Shelley, and T. S. Eliot

At the Italian Institute, London, 4 July 1950, T. S. Eliot told how forty years before he had begun "to puzzle out the Divine Comedy" with a text and a prose translation, and for years had steeped himself in Dante's poetry, memorizing especially delightful passages in the Italian, "so that . . . I was able to recite a large part of one canto or another to myself, lying in bed or on a railway journey."[1] This must evoke respectful thought of Dante's own long Virgilian study and *il grande amore*. And Eliot's sedulous way with Dante, so suggestive of subtle, pervasive, cumulative responses and associations in thought and writing, must warn against any facile assessment of the one poet's debt to the other. The talk at the Italian Institute, which starts by calling Dante's poetry "the most persistent and deepest influence upon my own verse" (p. 125), is itself a careful, instructive personal consideration of how writers commerce. It shows at least how such commerce may surprise, for surely many hearers that day and many readers since must have marveled that Eliot, while barely quoting Dante at all and, from humble deference, deliberately refraining from any Italian speech beyond *terza rima* and the wonderful verb *transumanar*, quoted no less than thirty-three lines of Shelley, three from his version of Dante's canzone "Voi ch' intendendo il terzo ciel movete," and thirty consecutive ones from *The Triumph of Life* (pp. 131–32).[2]

The passage from Shelley's *Triumph* Eliot brought into comparison with one about twice as long from *Little Gidding*. His own he described as "intended to be the nearest equivalent to a canto of the Inferno or the Purgatorio . . . that I could achieve" and said it "cost me far more time and trouble and vexation than any passage of the same length that I have ever written (pp. 128, 129). This simulacrum of a Dante canto strikes me and perhaps others as the most fascinating segment of *Four Quartets*, of Eliot's inveterate mimetic bent, and of his intense Dante cult. The Shelley passage (which mainly stages a ghostly ruin of Rousseau, prime captive in Life's triumph) Eliot's talk signalized as "some of the greatest and most Dantesque lines in English" (p. 130). Having recited them, and mindful specifically of Shelley's Dantesque aim, Eliot concluded with simple generosity: "Well, this is better than I could do" (p. 132).

Shelley and Eliot, however unlike otherwise, stand together as probably the two English poets who have outstripped all others in enhancing Dante's esteem. Any rivalry between them I have no presumption of attempting to judge. Briefly here I wish only to comment on them both as translators and imitators of the *Commedia* and to remark finally on Eliot's applause of Shelley's performance in *The Triumph of Life*, which I suppose has not altogether enchanted recent generations.

To speak of Eliot as Dante's translator may seem puzzling. I mean what I guess to be Eliot's part in those prose versions of the *Commedia* that follow Italian citations in his famous Dante "primer" of 1929, which first appeared as a small book but is best known undoubtedly in the "Dante" of *Selected Essays*.[3] These translations account for close to two hundred lines of the original. *Selected Essays*, which omits the book's preface, gives no hint of their provenance, and one wonders where many, even most, readers think they originate. The preface provides some guidance: "I have in quotations followed the *Temple Classics* edition text, and have followed pretty closely the translation in the same volumes. It is hardly necessary to say that where my version varies it nowhere pretends to greater accuracy than that excellent translation."[4] What "my version" may signify beckons investigation.

In the "Dante" essay I count some thirty separate translations and, considering them along with *Temple Classics* counterparts, have reached only tentative conclusions about Eliot's variations. Though Eliot's first five versions (all short, all of *Inferno*) might suggest that C. E. Norton rather than *Temple Classics* was his nearest model, one can agree that his general tendency is indeed to follow the latter "pretty closely."[5]

Eliot's principal changes (perhaps broadly influenced by Norton), by simplifying diction and phrasing, by avoiding archaisms and inversions, and by other means, aim at greater clarity, succinctness, and emphasis. This may be illustrated, at least partially, by giving the *Temple Classics* translation of *Purgatorio* 16.85–96 with Eliot's revision interspersed in enclosed italics. Dante's Marco Lombardo speaks of the soul:

From his hands who fondly loves her ere she is in being (*From the hands of Him who loves her before she is*), there issues, after the fashion of a little child that sports, now weeping, now laughing (*there issues like a little child that plays, with weeping and laughter*), the simple, tender soul (*the simple soul*), who knoweth naught save that (*that knows nothing except that*), sprung from a joyous maker (*come from the hands of a glad creator*), willingly she turneth to that which delights her (*she turns willingly to everything that delights her*). First she tastes the savour of a trifling good (*First she tastes the flavour of a trifling good*); there she is beguiled and runneth after it, if guide or curb turn not her love aside (*then is beguiled, and pursues it, if neither guide nor check withhold her*). Wherefore 'twas needful to put law as a curb (*Therefore laws were needed as a curb*), needful to have a ruler who might discern at least the tower of the true city (*a ruler was needed, who should at least see afar the tower of the true City*).[6]

Such revision, modestly aesthetic, is welcome, even if one concedes that the *Temple Classics* version remains, after all, a better "crib," and Eliot produces small unshadowed glories, as in converting "Like to the lark who soareth" into "Like the lark which soars."[7] A few changes suggest a rather personal poetic impulse. For example, one wonders about the repeated "wailing" and the tone of "striving" when Eliot alters "I saw the shadows come, uttering wails, borne by that strife of winds" to "I saw the wailing shadows come, wailing, carried on the striving wind."[8] Again, some element of dryness seems added when La Pia refers to "him who *after due engagement* wedded me with his ring."[9] But possibly the most interesting of such minor notes sounds toward the end of the Ulysses episode, when the storm from Purgatory sinks his ship. *Temple Classics* reads: "Three times it made her whirl round with all the waters; at the fourth, made the poop rise up and prow go down, as pleased Another, till the sea was closed above us." Eliot: "Three times it whirled her round with all the waters; the fourth time it heaved up the stern and drove her down at the head, as pleased Another; until the sea closed over us."[10] This has the effect of vigorous poetic intrusion, as though Eliot could not refrain from underscoring his imaginative response to this episode and to the sea and sailing.

Eliot's intent in some changes, like his occasional parenthetical explications,[11] seems didactic rather than aesthetic. One instance fairly shouts. At *Purgatorio* 26.148, Dante says of Arnaut Daniel, "Poi s'ascose nel foco che gli affina" ("Then he hid him in the fire which refines them").[12] Eliot prints the Italian in small roman capitals and translates, "Then dived he back into that fire which refines them,"[13] thus giving marked kinetic, demonstrative emphasis to Arnaut's purgatorial ardor. Earlier in the same canto, penitents are "ever on their guard not to come forth where they would not be burned"; Eliot alters the faithful wording "not be burned" to "not be in the fire" and changes print from his usual italic to roman.[14] Such lectern raps divert attention from the material to one particular teacher but need not occasion the invidious generalization that Eliot's essay better serves our reading of his own poetry than of Dante's. They may rather help characterize the "Dante" versions as primarily heuristic, meant chiefly to stimulate and guide, without anxiety about deprecation or even oblivion, tutorial fates.

Eliot's prose in these versions occasionally slips (would the poet himself say *deteriorates?*) into blank verse. Sometimes of course he simply follows *Temple Classics,* as in

> He rose upright with breast and countenance,
> as though he entertained great scorn of Hell,

where *though* alone changes (from *if*).[15] But he can apparently seek blank verse, as when "Brother, do not so, for thou art a shade" becomes

> "Brother! refrain, for you are but a shadow."[16]

And the great traditional cadence appears borrowed to impart a fine conclusive effect to Dante's recognition of Beatrice in *Purgatorio* 30.48 ("conosco i segni dell' antica fiamma"):

> I know the tokens of the ancient flame.[17]

This line Singleton adopts in his magisterial prose *Divine Comedy,*[18] which otherwise shows little sign of particular influence from Eliot's version. Singleton provides a kind of culminant Authorized Version among English prose translations: "Let me clearly acknowledge . . . that I have constantly kept before me a considerable number of other English prose translations, and that I have let these efforts of others serve as my silent 'reader,' . . . who constantly suggested to me ways of improving my own."[19] Eliot, with his gifts of language and rhythm, might have bequeathed prose translators a model for a "definitive" modern version. I do not believe he aspired at all to that or perhaps even took as much pains with Dante as with St.-John Perse's *Anabasis* (1930); and Cunningham's valuable survey of twentieth-century English translations of the *Commedia* passes over Eliot's contribution.[20] Not that the eagle did not stir his wings, only perhaps that the aquiline Eliot here somewhat bewilderingly recalls lark and owl.

For his *Little Gidding* imitation, Eliot in his talk said, "My first problem was to find an approximation to the *terza rima* without rhyming" (p. 128), for he rejected as variously unsatisfactory both *terza rima* and blank verse, the chief English resorts, apart from prose, in translating the *Commedia*. Blank verse (as in Cary's Miltonic paragraphs) distorts the characteristic "thought-form" of Dante's unitary tercets; *terza rima*, in translation or close imitation of Dante, forces infertile English rhymers to "inevitable shifts and twists" (p. 129).[21] In such considerations Eliot interestingly does not mention meter or scansion at all, either of Italian hendecasyllables or of blank verse and English *terza rima*, except for what seems only a slip in distinguishing the two last as having "a different metre" (p. 129). He primarily wants a triadic line arrangement without tyrannous rhyme. For solution Eliot hit on "a simple alternation of unrhymed masculine and feminine terminations, as the nearest way of giving the light effect of the rhyme in Italian" (p. 128).[22] He might have added that, despite career-long chariness of Shakespearean and Miltonic blank verse, he molded most lines to iambic pentameter, having sensed, I suppose, some wraith of the great English line in Dante's accentual verse: Nel mézzo dél cammín di nóstra víta.

Eliot's imitation begins:

> In the uncertain hour before the morning
>   Near the ending of interminable night
>   At the recurrent end of the unending
> After the dark dove with the flickering tongue
>   Had passed below the horizon of his homing
>   While the dead leaves still rattled on like tin . . . [23]

On the whole, Eliot uses this instrument with most impressive deliberateness. Rarely does a line puzzle:

> Both intimate and unidentifiable,

must, in succession feminine, be taken as an awkwardly isolated *sdrucciolo* (fi'a·ble).

Eliot's second problem in imitation was stylistic. For its exploration two sets of Eliot's critical remarks guide best but suggest so much about poetic style in general as to discourage any brief treatment whatever. In his talk, Eliot emphasized the *limitations* imposed on him in following Dantesque diction, imagery, simile, figure of speech—all that "very bare and austere style" (p. 129). In the "Dante" essay, he compared Dante's translatability with Shakespeare's, stressing that simplicity which has made the former relatively accessible to European neighbors and descendants, and "that combination of intelligibility and remoteness" in Shakespeare so likely to defeat translators (p. 202–03). Though properly guarded in dwelling on Dante's "simplicity," Eliot does strongly imply that English poetic style since the Renaissance, but especially since Shakespeare, favors densest local texture, an intensity of wordplay and metaphor, that may diminish our response to foreign literary art. And Eliot probably felt that English styles might have benefited from strong correctives of clarity and precision.

Perhaps that is why, as it seems to me, Eliot in the tercets of *Little Gidding* appears to exhibit, beyond due mimetic severity, an exemplary stylistic abnegation. How few similes, for example, without one extended, developed in Dante's fashion. Once at least, however, he vividly displays Dantesque audacity and complexity. At the end of his passage, Eliot's magisterial "compound ghost" leaves the disciple:

> In the disfigured street
> He left me, with a kind of valediction,
> And faded on the blowing of the horn.

The street, disfigured by rubble and shrapnel, rattling with "dead leaves," fit meeting place for a "dead master," scene of a "dead patrol" (one searches *Little Gidding* for threes), has yielded up its *figura*, phantom, ghost. And *disfigured* forms part of a triad in the entire quartet: *figured* (part 1), *disfigured*, *transfigured* (part 3)—paradigm, I take it, for Christ incarnate, crucified, transfigured.

II

In his *Life of Shelley* (1847), Thomas Medwin published two translations from the *Commedia*. One, of *Purgatorio* 28.1–51, Shelley permitted Medwin to copy from "his papers"; the other, of *Inferno* 33.22–75, Medwin himself did "at Shelley's request, and with his assistance."[24] The former, which has been entitled "Matilda Gathering Flowers," has an editorial history, and a holograph version of Shelley survives.[25] The latter, which gives the "Ugolino" episode, must apparently be accepted as Medwin printed it, with Shelley's "numerous corrections" in italics. Shelley's contribution amounts to about one-fourth of the sixty-four lines. Thus Shelley as translator of the *Commedia* was concerned directly or indirectly with a little over one hundred lines.

In presenting the two versions, Medwin ascribed to Shelley two

basic rules for verse translation: (1) to follow the original form—
here, of course, *terza rima*; (2) to provide "those who do not understand the original" with versions which "should be purely English."[26] Formally, the "Matilda" clearly attempts *terza rima*; the
Medwin-Shelley "Ugolino" is notably eccentric and in fact, though
beginning deceptively with rhymes *a b a, b,* never conforms to
Dante's scheme at all. Actually, ten consecutive stanzas (lines 7–36)
suggest the creation of an entirely new form, which makes every
two stanzas a unit rhyming *a b a, b a b*; and Shelley's portion of
these stanzas (9 of 30 rhymes) shows him trying to pursue Medwin's apparent intention. Otherwise, the "Ugolino" rhyming seems
to aim chiefly at this curious pattern: *a b a, c a c, d c d* (which looks
like *terza rima* done backward); and again Shelley's rhymes, though
only a handful, conspire with Medwin's.

Viewing Shelley as Medwin's reviser, accommodating himself not
only to another's rhymes but to experimental schemes (which to be
sure may spring from Shelley's own inventive "assistance"), we
expect little of him, in fewer than twenty lines, as translator of
Dante. The very beginning of the revision is suspiciously nonsensi-
cal: "a sleep" (Medwin) visits Ugolino "*in dream*" (Shelley). Ordinarily, Shelley tends to pad, though never so egregiously as Medwin. Most interesting, I believe, is an impression that both Medwin
and Shelley kept glancing, as it were, at Cary's blank verse. This
might be hard to show definitively, but see how Cary first, then
Shelley render Dante's simple "tu ne vestisti / Queste misere carni"
(62–63):

> thou gav'st
> These weeds of miserable flesh we wear;[27]

> *you . . . clad*
> *Our bodies in these weeds of wretchedness.*

Cary's "Ugolino," by the way, generally satisfies much more than
the Medwin-Shelley.

Shelley's "Matilda," especially if read in the holograph transcript
by Jean de Palacio, attempts a relatively close translation done with
what seems to be deliberate disregard of Cary. This impressive
effort suffers in Medwin's presentation, even as repaired by Richard Garnett, who consulted the holograph.[28] The Medwin-Garnett
"Matilda," which is what most of us have known through Hutchinson's Oxford edition, has encouraged so estimable a scholar as Joseph Raben to suppose that Shelley tried to dress up Dante as an

Italian Milton.[29] Had Shelley sought an English stylistic model for Dante translation, probably he would have looked, with Arthur Symons, "to Wordsworth at his *best*" (Ezra Pound's emphasis).[30] In any case, Shelley's version of *Purgatorio* 28.10–18, preceded by Cary's, shows his great, unacclaimed advance toward a simple, modern idiom:

>   the sprays
> Obedient all, lean'd trembling to that part
> Where first the holy mountain casts his shade;
> Yet were not so disorder'd, but that still
> Upon their top the feather'd quiristers
> Applied their wonted art, and with full joy
> Welcom'd those hours of prime, and warbled shrill
> Amid the leaves, that to their jocund lays
> Kept tenor.[31]

>   the passive leaves tremblingly were
> All bent towards that part where earliest
> The sacred hill obscures the morning air.

> Yet were they not so shaken from their rest,
> But that the birds, perched on the utmost spray,
> Incessantly renewing their blithe quest,

> With perfect joy received the early day,
> Singing within their glancing leaves, whose sound
> Kept one low burthen to their roundelay.[32]

Shelley's choices as translator were likely to relate closely to his own work, as his Homeric *Hymn to Mercury*, for example, to *The Witch of Atlas,* or his elegiac fragments from Bion and Moschus to *Adonais.* His "Matilda," composition of which has been dated variously from 1819 to 1821, Raben associates particularly and persuasively with *The Triumph of Life.*[33] In *The Triumph,* beginning at line 335, the character Rousseau describes for the narrator his spiritual awakening in a scene of woods, shadows, water and light and music, and much here recalls Dante's entrance into the Earthly Paradise, along with, naturally, Shelley's own habitual philosophic themes of world harmony, with their systematic trains of images and symbols. (The woman, "Shape all light," that appears to Rousseau is not a Matilda but a semblance of the Beatrice of *Purgatorio* 30, wonderfully known, almost wholly lost, perhaps to be known again.) But the translation should not lead us to hunt for or insist on anything like close imitation of Dante's poetic texture in Shelley's great fragment.[34] That was not Shelley's way, certainly not his truest, and Keats's astonishing mimicry in *Hyperion* he never could or would have emulated. Shelley was rather gifted and inclined, I believe, to "imitate" comprehensive and subtle deployments of poetic energies, the *natura naturans* of imagination, not the *natura naturata*. And of this and of Dante's most deeply genuine inspiration in *The Trimph of Life* and others of Shelley's works we have yet to learn.

III

Eliot had quoted part of the ten-stanza Rousseau passage from *The Triumph of Life* even earlier than the Dante talk, in a chapter on "Shelley and Keats" in *The Use of Poetry and the Use of Criticism*.[35] There, notoriously, Eliot mounted his most sustained critical and personal attack on Shelley. Near its beginning he says that "an enthusiasm for Shelley seems to me . . . an affair of adolescence: for most of us, Shelley has marked an intense period before maturity, but for how many does Shelley remain the companion of age? I confess that I never open the volume of his poems simply because I want to read poetry, but only with some special reason for reference" (p. 89). And near the end: "I was intoxicated by Shelley's poetry at the age of fifteen, and now find it almost unreadable" (p. 96). The Rousseau quotation occurs in a relenting moment.

In [Shelley's] last, and to my mind greatest though unfinished poem, *The Triumph of Life*, there is evidence not only of better writing than in any previous long poem, but of greater wisdom:

> 'Then what I thought was an old root that grew
> To strange distortion out of the hillside,
> Was indeed one of those (*sic*) deluded crew
> And that the grass, which methought hung so wide
> And white, was but his thin discoloured hair
> And that the holes he vainly sought to hide
> Were or had been eyes . . .'

There is a precision of image and an economy here that is new to Shelley.[36]

(P. 90)

Shelley's seven lines may have lived long in Eliot's psyche, for Grover Smith notes their influence on "Sweeney Erect," published in *Ara Vos Prec* (1920): "The description of the epileptic in Eliot's fourth stanza evidently imitates [this] passage in . . . *The Triumph of Life*."[37] Eliot's description runs:

> This withered root of knots of hair
> Slitted below and gashed with eyes,
> This oval O cropped out with teeth . . .

But the Shelley associations of "Sweeney Erect" may extend further.
Two lines immediately preceding the above read:

> Gesture of orang-outang
> Rises from the sheets in steam.

Very curiously, in "Shelley and Keats," two pages before the Rousseau quotation, Eliot recalls a note to the "almost unreadable"
poet's *Queen Mab:* "from a poet who tells us, in a note on vegetari-
anism, that 'the orang-outang perfectly resembles man both in the
order and the number of his teeth,' we shall not know what to
expect" (p. 88).[38] Or, perhaps, not know what to expect at Shelley's
naturalistic *start* with the orang-outang, but certainly know, in the
face of Rousseau and the "greater wisdom" of Shelley's *finale,* what
might have been expected.

Neither Shelley nor Eliot, from start to end, lack ghosts. While
having no least wish to smirch Eliot's noble accolade to Shelley's
achievement and promise in *The Triumph of Life,* I do wish to note
that, generally speaking, his critical understanding of Shelley's poetry was very limited and that his interest in it seems indeed to have
been mainly "for reference." And the reference often enough is to
ghosts, as with Reilly's mysterious recollection in *The Cocktail Party*
(act 3) of the magus Zoroaster's apparition in Shelley's *Prometheus
Unbound* (act 1). In the Dante talk itself, Eliot cannot even quote *Ode
to the West Wind,* "like ghosts from an enchanter fleeing," without
significantly altering the wording to "stricken ghosts." (p. 130).
Rousseau's "stricken ghost" may have begun to haunt him when
fifteen and intoxicated with Shelley. And one wants to ponder a
passage Eliot published his next year:

> nobody can doubt
> Who knows the well known fact, as you do surely—
> That ghosts are fellows whom you *can't* keep out.[39]

NOTES

1. "What Dante Means to Me," in *To Criticize the Critic and Other Writings* (New
York: Farrar, Straus & Giroux, 1965), p. 125. Hereafter cited in the text.

2. *The Triumph of Life,* lines 176–205, was evidently quoted from *The Complete*

Poetical Works of Percy Bysshe Shelley, ed. Thomas Hutchinson (London: Oxford University Press, 1905).

3. *Dante* (London: Faber and Faber, 1929), reprinted in *Selected Essays* (New York: Harcourt, Brace, 1950). The latter edition, referred to as D, will be cited in the text.

4. The *Temple Classics Inferno*, trans. J. A. Carlyle, rev. H. Oelsner (London: J. M. Dent) was first published in 1900; the *Purgatorio*, trans. Thomas Okey, in 1901; the *Paradiso*, trans. P. H. Wicksteed, in 1899; all have been often reprinted. I have noticed slight changes in reprints. Here I have used the one-volume edition, *The Divine Comedy of Dante Alighieri*, introduction by C. H. Grandgent, (New York: Modern Library, 1932), having checked this against the following *Temple Classics* reprints: *Inf.*, 1954; *Purg.*, 1956; *Par.*, 1954. Hereafter cited as TC.

Eliot's Italian quotations in both *Dante* and "Dante" follow the *Temple Classics* text rather lamely. Some misspellings: *aguzzevan* for *aguzzavan* (D 205), *coronno* for *corrono* (D 208), *giusa* for *guisa* (D 220), *regge* for *rege* (D 220), *volsemi* for *volsimi* (D 224), *diedi* for *diede* (D 226), *voluntade* for *volontate* (D 226), *stiman* for *stimin* (D 227), *alledetta* for *allodetta* (D 227), *primo* for *prima* (D 227). Here and there grave accents are wanting over final letters of words like *sì, così, là, però, seguitò*.

Four lines of the Italian (one on p. 206, three on p. 213) go untranslated.

5. Charles Eliot Norton, trans., *The Divine Comedy of Dante Alighieri*, rev. ed., 3 vols. (Boston: Houghton Mifflin, 1902). Eliot, I believe, probably also consulted with some regularity Longfellow's famous verse trans.; C. H. Grandgent's versions in his *Dante* (1916, rpt. New York: F. Ungar, 1966), which Eliot specially noted in the preface to *Dante* (p. 12), seem to have little direct influence on him.

6. TC 290–91; D 220–21.

7. TC 528; D 227 (*Par.* 20.73).

8. TC 39; D 206 (*Inf.* 5.48–49).

9. D 215 (emphasis added); TC 221: "him who, first plighting troth, had wedded me with his gem" (*Purg.* 5.135–36).

10. TC 144; D 211 (*Inf.* 26.139–42).

11. D 215, 222, 228.

12. TC 352.

13. D 217.

14. TC 349; D 217 (*Purg.* 26.14–15).

15. D 208; TC 62 (*Inf.* 10.35–36).

16. TC 323; D 216 (*Purg.* 21.131–32).

17. D 224.

18. Charles S. Singleton, trans., *Dante Alighieri, The Divine Comedy*, 3 double vols. (Princeton: Princeton University Press, 1970–74).

19. Singleton, I, part 1, *Inferno* (Text and Translation), 372.

20. Gilbert F. Cunningham, *The Divine Comedy in English, A Critical Bibliography, 1901–1966* (New York: Barnes and Noble, 1967).

21. I do not know what to make of the following, reported by Levy as taking place in January 1959, in William Turner Levy and Victor Scherle, *Affectionately, T. S. Eliot: The Story of a Friendship: 1947–1965* (Philadelphia: Lippincott, 1968), "I told him [Eliot] that I had always been partial to the Carlyle-Okey-Wicksteed translation. Tom said, I recommend the Binyon translation. Read it and see what you think" (p. 113). The Binyon trans. is in *terza rima*.

22. Eliot's choice in this may have been suggested by Longfellow; see, e.g., the latter's *Inf.* 26.112–17:

"O brothers, who amid a hundred thousand
Perils," I said, "have come unto the West,
To this so inconsiderable vigil
Which is remaining of your senses still
Be ye unwilling to deny the knowledge,
Following the sun, of the unpeopled world."

23. This and, unless otherwise noted, all following quotations of Eliot's verse are from *Collected Poems, 1909–1962* (New York; Harcourt, Brace and World, 1970).

24. Thomas Medwin, *The Life of Percy Bysshe Shelley*, 2 vols. (London: T. C. Newby, 1847), II, 16–18, 19–22.

25. The holograph is in the Bodleian Library; for a transcript and commentary, see Jean de Palacio, "Shelley traducteur de Dante: le chant XXVIII du *Purgatoire*," *Revue de littérature comparée*, 36 (1962), 571–79; see also Joseph Raben, "Shelley as Translator," in *Shelley: Modern Judgments*, ed. R. B. Woodings (London: Macmillan, 1968), pp. 196–212.

26. Medwin, II, 15, 18.

27. Henry F. Cary, trans., *The Vision; or Hell, Purgatory, and Paradise, of Dante Alighieri*, 3 vols., 2nd ed. (London: Taylor and Hessey, 1819), I, 289. (Palacio, p. 576, speaks of "discrètes, mais très probables réminiscences de la *Vision* de Cary" in the Medwin-Shelley.)

28. In *Relics of Shelley* (London: Edward Moxon, 1862); see Palacio, pp. 572 ff.

29. Raben, pp. 198–99, 201–10.

30. Pound, *The Spirit of Romance* (London: J. M. Dent, and New York: E. P. Dutton, 1910), p. 150; Symons, *The Romantic Movement in English Poetry* (1909, rpt. New York: Phaeton Press, 1969), p. 123.

31. Cary, II, 255.

32. This conflates the Oxford edition text and Palacio's transcript.

33. Raben, pp. 200, 211; Palacio, p. 571.

34. Cf. Eliot, *To Criticize the Critic*, p. 130.

35. (London: Faber and Faber, 1933). Hereafter cited in the text.

36. The first line of Shelley's passage is misquoted, and Eliot's "Then" hardly improves Shelley's syntax.

37. Grover Smith, Jr., *T. S. Eliot's Poetry and Plays* (Chicago: University of Chicago Press, 1956), p. 48.

38. For Shelley's note, see the Oxford edition (1956) of the poetry, p. 828; for Eliot's "the number," read "number."

39. "A Fable for Feasters," in *Poems Written in Early Youth* (New York: Farrar, Strauss & Giroux, 1967), p. 7 (Eliot's emphasis); for a note on first publication (Feb. 1905), see p. 33.

JAMES A. W. HEFFERNAN

Politics and Freedom: Refractions of Blake in Joyce Cary and Allen Ginsberg

Santayana says that he who does not know the past is condemned to relive it. On Commencement Day at Dartmouth College in 1968, when Vietnam was turning into quicksand for thousands of U.S. troops, the valedictorian shocked a good many of his hearers by saying: "Thank God we are losing the war." Whether he knew it or not, this brand new graduate was reliving the feelings with which Wordsworth, some hundred and seventy-five years earlier, had beheld the frustration of English efforts to suffocate the newborn republic in France. Dismayed when England declared war on the infant regime, he

> rejoiced,
> Yea, afterwards—truth most painful to record!—
> Exulted, in the triumph of my soul,
> When Englishmen by thousands were o'erthrown,
> Left without glory on the field, or driven,
> Brave hearts! to shameful flight.   (*Prelude* 10. 283–88)

Without attempting to construct a parallel between the French Revolution and the revolution in Vietnam (itself the rebellious child of an imperialized and colonizing French republic), we can see at least that in this instance, the feelings of a young contemporary and the feelings of a young Romantic poet strikingly converge. And this particular convergence is in fact just one of many. In the late sixties, when the battle cry for "relevance" struck the groves of academe, Romantic poetry became almost uncomfortably relevant, almost too conveniently apposite. Anyone who knows what happened at Kent State University in the spring of 1970 can readily understand the feelings with which Shelley learned what happened near Manchester, England, in August 1819, when saber-flaunting horsemen charged an unarmed crowd of workers and their families who were demonstrating for parliamentary reform; they killed six and wounded seventy. If we lack a Shelley of our own to write another *Masque of Anarchy* on the killings at Kent State, his taut allegory of bitterly

177

grotesque indignation modulating into fervent hope nonetheless assumes a new relevance for our time—and a new poignancy.

It is, then, in the politics of our time that we seem to find the most striking parallels with the Romantic period, but in the literary reactions to our politics, the Romantic poet who casts the longest shadow is clearly William Blake. Blake remains enduringly relevant not because he turned poetry into political propaganda but rather because he turned politics into myth, and thus created a paradigm for all poets who would write of politics without ceasing to be poets. Indeed, to speak of Blake as a political poet we must somehow italicize both the adjective *and* the noun, for each is a dynamic part of the whole that contains them both. When Blake hears the clinking of "mind forg'd manacles" in every human cry, he is not simply condemning the institution of slavery; he is turning an instrument of political repression into a metaphor for psychic repression, and thereby suggesting how we enslave ourselves. A prophet against conventional thought and conventional art as well as a prophet against empire, Blake was essentially a poet of freedom, and the freedom he espouses is—among other things—a freedom from categorical thinking.

One measure of this freedom from categories is that in our own time, two rather different writers have found a common source in Blake: the British novelist Joyce Cary, who sees him as the embodiment of *artistic* independence, and the American poet Allen Ginsberg, who sees him—or tends to use him—as the champion of *political* independence. While Cary's Blake is largely an apolitical "artist" who defies both literary and pictorical conventions, Ginsberg's Blake is a weapon to wield against those who make laws and those who make war. Yet the poet who wrote of both Albion and America touches the Briton and the American in comparable ways. Equally aware, I think, of the relation between political and artistic freedom, their responses to Blake differ not so much in substance as in emphasis. In examining those responses, we can not only learn something about Blake's conception of freedom; we can also learn something about the relation between literature and politics in our time.

Andrew Wright tells us that Cary's unpublished novel *Arabella*, written in the 1930s, has a Blake-quoting hero, but the most Blakean of his published works is unquestionably *The Horse's Mouth*, which first appeared in 1944.[1] This concluding volume of Cary's *First Trilogy* is narrated by the destitute, iconoclastic, and irrepressibly resilient artist Gulley Jimson. The first volume of the trilogy, *Herself Surprised*, is narrated by Sarah Monday, Gulley's onetime mistress and model; the second, *To Be a Pilgrim,* is narrated by the rich lawyer Tom Wilcher, for whom Sarah once worked as a "housekeeper." As Hazard Adams lucidly argues, the trilogy as a whole has a Blakean pattern: Sarah is the eternal female who as model excites the creative spirit in Gulley but as mistress tries to button it up "in her placket-hole"; Wilcher, who prates of Modern Artists, Good Citizens, and Suspicious Characters, and who thus inhabits "a spectrous world of abstractions," is Urizen; and Gulley himself, who implacably defies convention and who struggles to create his pictures against all odds, is Los.[2] The Blakean pattern is largely implicit in the first two books, but it becomes unmistakably explicit in *The Horse's Mouth,* which is studded with quotations from Blake's poems and prophecies, and especially from *The Mental Traveller.* The quotations begin on the very first page, which offers a good example of the way Cary uses Blake:

I was walking by the Thames. Half-past morning on an autumn day. Sun in a mist. Like an orange in a fried fish shop. All bright below. Low tide, dusty water and a crooked bar of straw, chicken-boxes, dirt and oil from mud to mud. Like a viper swimming in skim milk. The old serpent, symbol of nature and love.

> *Five windows light the caverned man: through one he*
> *breathes the air;*
> *Through one hears music of the spheres; through*
> *one can look*
> *And see small portions of the eternal world.*

Such as Thames mud turned into a bank of nine carat gold rough from the fire.

The lines italicized are quoted (roughly, as is typical of Cary) from the very beginning of *Europe* (1794), the prophecy in which Blake condemns the war that Wordsworth was happy to see the English losing—namely, the war against the French Revolution. But Blake's poem is far more than a piece of political propaganda. As its opening lines suggest, it treats a political event in mythic terms. It takes the British declaration of war against a newborn republic as one more demonstration that man has fallen, that he consistently suppresses his own instincts, which are naturally creative and hence revolutionary. Fallen man is "caverned" by his anxieties, inhibitions, prejudices; the windows of his five senses give him glimpses of the eternal world, but in most cases, he is unable or unwilling to see it. Gulley Jimson—along with Blake—is one of the few who can. When Gulley quotes these lines from *Europe,* he is not

thinking of the French Revolution, nor even of the political implications of his own situation—the stuff of which protest literature is
usually made. He is, after all, just out of prison, and he was sent
there solely for the crime of making threatening telephone calls to a
wealthy collector named Hickson, who had cheaply acquired a
number of Gulley's pictures when they were sold to pay his debts.
Struggling to survive as an artist, Gulley has merely been asking
decent recompense for his work. The stuff of political protest is here
with a vengeance, but one looks in vain for the predictable outcry
against the bureaucratic oppression of artists. Fresh out of prison,
Gulley is no longer "caverned" in body or in mind. Free of stock
responses to his plight, windows opened wide, he feasts his eyes
upon the world:

They say a chap just out of prison runs into the nearest cover; into some
dark little room, like a rabbit put up by a stoat. The sky feels too big for
him. But I liked it. I swam in it. I couldn't take my eyes off the clouds, the
water, the mud.   (P. 3)

Gulley is genuinely free. Instead of running for the nearest cover—
resentment of a society that ruthlessly persecutes its artists—he
swims in a vision of infinity.

    The leap to that vision is decisively Blakean. There is nothing of
Wordsworth's lyricism in Gulley's view of the Thames: no city
bright and glittering in the smokeless air, no river gliding at his
own sweet will. The sun is misted, and the river is polluted—like
the Thames of Eliot's *Waste Land*, sweating oil and tar. Its pastoral
purity fouled by human refuse, it is fittingly seen as a serpent,
which for Blake symbolized the fallen body of man, and the serpent
in turn leads us to *Europe*, whose title page is adorned by a serpent
with five loops in its tail—representing the five fallen senses.[3]
Gulley himself, however, takes the serpent a little differently from
Blake. Determined (as Blake was) to redeem the fallen senses, he is
already beginning to see it as a creature of prelapsarian splendor,
like the water snakes transfigured by moonlight in part four of
Coleridge's *Rime*. Below the misted sun, where "all is bright," the
serpent-river becomes a symbol of nature and love, and the mud in
this scene is transfigured by sunlight. There *is* urban pollution here,
but Gulley is ultimately as indifferent to that as he is to the politics
of his present position. Looking beyond politics and ecology both,
breaking the windows of his cavern, Gulley sees with the eyes of
Blake, who envisioned the rising sun not as "a round disc of fire
somewhat like a Guinea" but as "an Innumerable company of the

Heavenly Host crying, 'Holy, Holy, Holy is the Lord God Almighty.' " God-like himself, Gulley raises up out of the primeval mud "a bank of nine carat gold rough from the fire." He is at once a god and a "son of Los," as he later calls himself: the divine smithy, forging a vision of his own.[4]

Given the echoes of Genesis here, and the intimations of a new genesis, it is singularly apt that Gulley is also an artist who is attempting—throughout *The Horse's Mouth*—to raise up Adam and Eve in his epic painting of the Fall. His model for Eve is Sarah Monday: not the grey-haired, red-nosed crawfish she has now become (pp. 29, 77–78), but the alluring young woman she was some thirty years ago, when he painted her standing by her bath. Hazard Adams observes that "Sarah constantly hovers in Gulley's mind between canvas and nature."[5] To put it another way, she hovers between the eternality of the artist's vision and the mortality of fallen human nature. Gulley's picture of her in her youth gives her a kind of immunity from the rude wasting of old time, but descriptions of the picture only sharpen the contrast between what she was and what she is now, and the aging Sarah clings to the picture— more precisely, to a study of it that she keeps in a locked box—with the same possessiveness with which she once clung to Gulley. Gulley recalls this possessiveness in terms of *The Mental Traveller*, which for him becomes an allegory of the relation between the artist and society, between the artist and his mistress-model, and finally between the artist and his art. All three relations show the artist struggling to produce a new genesis—in this case, a new vision of the Fall—in a land of men and women whose eyes are clouded by the Fall itself.

Gulley begins to quote *The Mental Traveller* in private response to a trio of Protestant preachers who come to see the "Fall" in progress—and to ask him stupid questions. Quoting the lines, "I heard and saw such dreadful things / As cold earth wanderers never knew," he glosses them with characteristic impudence:

Which probably means only that when Billy had a good idea, a real tip, a babe, some blue nose came in asked him why he drew his females in nightgowns. (P. 47)

Gulley's interpretation is of course very much his own: a painter's reaction to a painter's poem. At this moment, beset by questioners who cannot see out of their caverns, he is solely preoccupied with the conflict between conventional taste and genuinely original art.

As the preachers prattle on, Gulley hears the lines of the third stanza, slightly amended:

> And if the babe is born a boy, that is to say, a real
> vision,
> He's given to a woman old,
> Who nails him down upon a rock,
> Catches his shrieks in cups of gold.

Which means that some woman of a blue nose nails your work of imagination to the rock of law, and why and what; and submits him to a logical analysis.   (P. 47)

Most commentators would read this stanza in religious or political terms, making it signify either the crucifixion of Christ ("the babe") by the old woman of earth he has come to renew, or, once again, the mother country's effort to crush the newborn republic of France. Gulley reads it in artistic terms, making it signify the persecution of imagination by reason, the analytical nailing down of a newly created work of art.

But *The Mental Traveller* means a good deal more than that, and Gulley goes on to make the most of its complexity. The "woman old" is not merely the personification of blue-nosed insensitivity to art; she is also the personification of the female will: fallen, possessive, carnal. When Gulley sees a young girl "clinging to a young man's arm," he thinks again of nails: "Nail him, girlie," he says to himself, "Nail him to the contract" (p. 51). He is speaking out of his own experience with Sarah, who was constantly threatening his creative impulse by stirring his sexual one. "And when I was mad to paint," he remembers, "she was for putting me to bed and getting in after me." However rosy it may have been, this was one more crucifixion of the artist, and Gulley sees it as such: "*She binds iron thorns around his head / She pierces both his hands and feet*" (p. 51). But Gulley did not stay in bondage. Like the persecuted babe who becomes a bleeding youth, he found a way to rend up his manacles and bind Sarah down for his delight. First he hit her—a comically self-assertive "punch on the neb." Then, seizing her form in a first sketch for the bath picture, he "suddenly got hold of the idea. Mastered it. Yes, I can remember the feeling; your brushes like carpenter's tools." With equipment like Joseph's and determination like Christ's, the crucified artist now redeems Sarah by reversing the incarnation: "The flesh was made word; every day." By means of art, Sarah becomes "a virgin bright," for the mistress turns into a model, and the model into a picture. Quoting the lines in which the bleeding youth rends up

his manacles and turns his former persecutor into a "garden fruitful seventy fold," Gulley comments:

As Billy would say, through generation into regeneration. Materiality, that
is, Sarah, the old female nature, having attempted to button up the prophetic spirit, that is to say, Gulley Jimson, in her placket-hole, got a bonk
on the conk, and was reduced to her proper status, spiritual fodder.

(P. 52)

The typical impudence of Gulley's language aptly expresses the
resilience of his character. But in *The Horse's Mouth* as in *The Mental
Traveller*, no victory of spirit over materiality is ever permanent. As
soon as Gulley started to paint her, Sarah became "a bit jealous of
the paint" (p. 52), and in this respect she is kin to what Gulley calls
"the old woman of the world. Old mother necessity" (p. 55). If the
artist has the power to regenerate himself and redeem the world
about him, the world has the power to seduce him with material
gain, easing him into a comfortable but desiccated old age. Finally,
therefore, Gulley uses *The Mental Traveller* to describe his relationship with his art, his struggle to regenerate a new vision every time
he felt the old one fading.

Throughout *The Horse's Mouth*, Gulley is seeking two different
things, and he periodically distracts himself from one by his
search for the other. On the one hand, he wants to complete his
painting of the Fall; on the other hand, he wants to cash in on the
pictures of his early period, such as Sarah at her bath. These two
impulses correspond to "the alternating rhythm of effort and rest"
that Northrop Frye discerns in the cycles of *The Mental Traveller*.
"There is," he says, "the struggle to create, and the loving contemplation of what has been created."[6] In Gulley's case, the contemplation of past works is not only loving but mercenary: he
would like Hickson to pay him what they are worth. Yet even as
he badgers Hickson with mock-threatening calls about his old pictures, he knows that he must get on with the new one, that preoccupation with the value of the old ones makes him nothing but an
aged shadow of what he once was. Shortly after phoning Hickson
again to no avail, and barely escaping another arrest, he thinks
again of *The Mental Traveller*:

I felt so old I wondered how my legs kept hanging on to my body. And I
couldn't even think of what to do with the blank canvas. My eyes were as
dead as cod's and my ears only heard noises.

> *An aged shadow, soon he fades*
> *Wandering round an earthly cot,*

> Full filled all with gems and gold
> Which he by industry had got.   (P. 58)

Eventually, Gulley wanders round to Hickson's flat in the company of the barmaid Coker, who, as Gulley's leading creditor, is determined that he should get some of the gems and gold that his artistic industry has earned him. But Gulley himself takes little part in the discussion of his pictures. While Hickson and Coker argue over their value, Gulley is thinking about freedom, self-renewal, and the struggle to create. Ruminating on Spinoza's belief in the joys of contemplation, Gulley says to himself:

Contemplation, in fact, is ON THE OUTSIDE. It's not on the spot. And the truth is that Spinoza was always on the outside. He didn't understand freedom, and so he didn't understand anything. . . .

Whereas Old Bill, that damned Englishman, didn't understand anything else but freedom, and so all his nonsense is full of truth; and even though he may be a bit of an outsider, HIS OUTSIDE IS ON THE INSIDE. . . .

. . . I took a turn down the room. It was a long room. I got away among a lot of little tables covered with gold and enamel snuff-boxes. Set with diamonds and rubies painted by Boucher, and so on. Knick-knacks.

But what you get on the inside, I said to myself, is the works—it's SOMETHING THAT GOES ON GOING ON. . . . It's the kick in the old horse. It's the creation. And that's where it's leading me. Right up to that blasted picture of mine.   (P. 113)

Not to the old picture, but to the new one. Not to the contemplation of *Sarah at Her Bath,* which—for all its brilliance—has now become yet another pretty surface in a glitteringly furnished room, but rather to the liberation of a newly discovered "inside," the releasing of a vision that is even now struggling to kick its way out of Gulley's head. So far from resting on his laurels, Gulley cannot even rest with the present state of his new painting. "The Fall is a frost," he says to himself. "It's iced all over. It's something contemplated from the outside. It doesn't get under your skin" (p. 113). What Gulley here reveals is that in his continuing fight to survive as an artist, his worst enemy is neither a repressive society nor a predatory woman: it is the ice of his own established conceptions, the treacherous congelation of molten energy into frozen surface. His struggle to create a picture of the Fall is thus a perpetual reenactment of the Fall itself. As love turned to lust in Eden, Gulley's creative vision turns repeatedly into images that he himself finds superficial. Earlier, reviewing his career in terms of *The Mental Traveller,* Gulley tells us that he painted in the profitable neoclassic style (which got him gems and gold) until he discovered Impressionism: the "female babe" of "solid fire." As he pursued it night and day, Impressionism regenerated him, beguiling him to a creative infancy; but by the time he caught her (after four years) she had become a "woman old," a lucrative "pure sensation without a thought. . . . Good for the drawing-room. Tea cakes" (pp. 63–64). Having decided that he would have no more to do with "icing" such confections—the pun is implicitly made—Gulley tries to express "a new world with a new formal character." But the problem, says Gulley, "is always to get hold of the form you need. And nothing is so coy" (pp. 65–66). Or, he might have added, so susceptible to aging (to icing over) when caught. Throughout the novel, therefore, Gulley's efforts to create a picture of the Fall—to go on going on—are a succession of kicks at the ice of his own conceptions, no sooner realized in line and pigment than frozen there, compelling him to break them up.

Essentially, Gulley's struggle to create a picture of the Fall is the struggle—at once doomed and triumphant—to re-create the state of innocence that preceded it. Though he knows that any attempt to escape from our fallen condition will sooner or later be frustrated, he is nevertheless driven by the quintessentially Blakean conviction that we cannot understand the Fall until we know what it is to be unfallen. Musing on freedom and creation in Hickson's flat, Gulley thinks of Blake's *Visions of the Daughters of Albion,* and particularly of its heroine Oothoon, who offers the "Marygold" of her virginity to Theotormon, who is raped by the hypocritically moralistic Bromion, but who yet remains—in Gulley's words—an "everlasting maiden" (p. 114). For Gulley, Oothoon embodies something as strange and rare as sexually experienced maidenhood, "the virginity of the soul which never allows experience to grow stale" (p. 115). This is the virginity that Gulley struggles to keep alive in himself, and which, in spite of all his setbacks, stays alive and kicking to the very end of the book.

In one sense, Gulley's attempt to realize his picture of the Fall is a catastrophic failure. With the help of Nosy Barbon and a dozen would-be Oothoons from the Polytechnic art class, Gulley decides to paint it on the wall of a decrepit old chapel; and just as the picture begins to take shape, complete with giraffes, a whale, and a roaring sea, the wrecking crew arrives to demolish the building. The stuff of political protest is here again, for now an insensitive bureaucracy is destroying a work of art in progress. And again the artist is threatened by an overprotective woman, for after Gulley is injured by a fall from his painter's swing, a nursing sister takes his wrists and tells him, "Please don't talk." But Gulley will not be muzzled; and that, in the end, is his triumph. With his still unfinished picture of the fall literally about to fall itself, the ice is breaking up again; the old horse keeps on kicking, and his mouth continues to work. In his last long speech, he babbles not of green fields but of English walls, giving thanks for their surfaces even as he mocks their perishability. In the very act of failing, Gulley succeeds. Free at last of anxieties about even the duration of his own art, he creates a "Fall" that will in fact collapse: not a petrified surface but a profoundly liberating and profoundly comic "happening." "How you don't enjoy life, mother," he says to the nun. "I should laugh all round my neck at this minute if my shirt wasn't on the tight side." "It would be better for you to pray." "Same thing, mother" (p. 345). *Ridere est orare*, says Gulley, and as Nietzsche said once, *ridere est vincere* too.

There is less laughter now. In the thirty years since *The Horse's Mouth* first appeared, the literature of protest has become a serious business, and for the artist, the oppressiveness of modern civilization is not so much something to laugh at as something to howl at. Like the Chinamen of Yeats's *Lapis Lazuli*, Gulley Jimson goes out a laughing old man; but in England he was shortly succeeded by a generation of angry young ones, and in America by the Beats. It is true that only some of England's so-called Angry Young Men were actually angry; the term suited John Osborne, who wrote *Look Back in Anger*, better than either the droll John Wain or the wry Kingsley Amis, who once declared at a Washington lecture, "I enrage very slowly." And it is also true that the late Jack Kerouac more often wrote in sorrow than in anger, and often too in joy: the holy rapture of illumination that may spring from a state of exhaustion, of being "beat"—which he called "the root and soul of beatific." But another major figure of the Beat Generation began his poetic career as an indisputably angry young man, and the prevailing mood of his poetry is clearly suggested by the very title of the poem that first established his reputation when he read it in San Francisco in 1955: *Howl*.

Howl is aggressively polemical, and as such, it tends to summon up the Blake who was a prophet against empire, the champion of an essentially *political* freedom. "The best minds of my generation," says the poet (and here the very word "generation" has a Blakean ring), "passed through universities with radiant cool eyes hallucinating Arkansas and Blake-light tragedies among the scholars of war."[7] I do not know how to connect Arkansas with "Blake-light tragedies," or even what those tragedies are, but it is clear at least that students of Blake are being contraposed to "scholars of war," that the maker of illuminated books is being called upon to light the way of protest against the makers of war. Thomas Vance calls this line "uncannily prophetic" because it seems to anticipate the confrontations between war protestors and university administrations which convulsed the sixties.[8] But if we now "nostalgically" remember the fifties as a decade of peace and complacency, we should not forget that they began with two years of war in Korea and were dominated by the jingoistic voice of Joseph McCarthy, who helped to create the mood that sent the United States into Vietnam. In any case, one of the most vivid passages in *Howl* represents young draftees appearing for their physical examinations, "who broke down crying in white gymnasiums naked and trembling before the machinery of other skeletons" (p. 11). With its faint reminiscense of the creature in Blake's "Infant Sorrow" ("Helpless, naked, piping loud"), the line depicts the crushingly humiliating process of induction: stripped of their bodies as well as of their clothes, men are turned into machinelike skeletons, into functioning parts of the all-consuming war machine. And as a Jewish poet writing just ten years after the end of World War II, Ginsberg may well be alluding also to those naked and trembling figures led to the "gymnasiums" and crematoria of Dachau and Auschwitz, bodies consumed by the juggernaut of Nazism.

Ginsberg's conception of the war machine as juggernaut becomes explicit in part two of *Howl,* and here the warmongering that Ginsberg finds in America is specifically linked with the Blakean figure of Moloch. According to Frye, Blake regarded Moloch (or "Molech" in Blake's spelling) as the presiding spirit of the brazen age, the second of the seven great periods of the Fall. In this period the Titans worshipped Urizen, "thundergod of moral law and tyrannical power . . . in a cult of death consisting largely of human sacrifices. Since then, the belief that somehow it is right to kill men has been the underlying cause of all wars." And Frye goes on to say: "This is the period of Druidism, when giants erected huge sacrifical temples like Stonehenge and indulged in hideously murderous orgies."[9] In Blake's *Milton,* Moloch is plainly the juggernaut of crematoria, pestilence, and war:

> loud his furnaces rage among the Wheels of Og, &
> pealing loud the cries of the Victims of Fire:
> And pale his Priestesses infolded in Veils of Pestilence,
>   border'd
> With War . . .   (37.21–24)[10]

It is this figure that Ginsberg specifically and repeatedly invokes in part two of *Howl*. For Ginsberg, Moloch becomes the specter of the military-industrial establishment, the embodiment of everything in modern American civilization that feeds on the sacrifice of human blood or human imagination:

> Moloch the incomprehensible prison! Moloch the crossbone soulless jailhouse and Congress of sorrows! Moloch whose buildings are judgement! Moloch the vast stone of war! Moloch the stunned governments!
> Moloch whose mind is pure machinery! Moloch whose blood is running money! Moloch whose fingers are ten armies! Moloch whose breast is a cannibal dynamo! Moloch whose ear is a smoking tomb!
> Moloch whose eyes are a thousand blind windows! Moloch whose skyscrapers stand in long streets like endless Jehovahs! Moloch whose factories dream and croak in the fog! Moloch whose smokestacks and antennae crown the cities!
> Moloch whose love is endless oil and stone! Moloch whose soul is electricity and banks! Moloch whose poverty is the specter of genius! Moloch whose fate is a cloud of sexless hydrogen! Moloch whose name is the Mind!   (P. 17)

Ginsberg's language is at once contemporary and Blakean. Amid smokestacks and television antennae, skyscrapers appear as the new Jehovan thundergods of tyrannical power, the new Druidical megaliths. Near the Congress of sorrows, he implies, stands the Pentagon, the new Stonehenge of war. The war machine whose fingers are ten armies (fingers here become cybernetically mechanized) recklessly consumes both blood and money, and Ginsberg's concentrated account of the way it wastes them both ("whose blood is running money") recalls the equally concentrated imagery of war in Blake's "London": "And the hapless Soldier's sigh / Runs in blood down Palace walls." Dreaming is left to factories—cruelest of ironies—because, as the first line of part two tells us, the brains and imagination of men have been eaten up by that "sphinx of cement and aluminum" named Moloch. Finally, then, Moloch is a Urizenic figure, the embodiment of a tyrannical pure reason that is pitiless alike to body, imagination, and soul: "Moloch whose mind is pure machinery! . . . Moloch whose name is the Mind!" Ginsberg himself has said that while part one of *Howl* is "a lament for the Lamb in America," part two "names the monster of mental consciousness that preys on the Lamb."[11]

To this extent, Ginsberg is implicitly using Blake as a prophet of psychological freedom—not merely of political freedom. Ginsberg's relation to Blake is in fact anything but categorically neat. In the first place, Blake is only one of the many influences on Ginsberg, who owes at least as much (if not more) to Whitman, to his Paterson mentor Williams, and to his contemporaries Kerouac, William Burroughs, and Neal Cassady. Secondly, Ginsberg has said that "the only poetic tradition is the voice out of the burning bush."[12] Yet it is precisely his conception of the poet as prophet that prompts Ginsberg to admire the resoundingly prophetic Blake, just as Blake's own obsession with the Bible led him to admire the author of *Paradise Lost*. Moloch, after all, was both a Biblical and a Miltonic figure before he became a Blakean one, and his appearance in *Howl* perfectly demonstrates the continuity of what Ginsberg calls "the only poetic tradition." For Ginsberg, then, Blake is a good deal more than a prophet against political empire, and although he uses Blake in the cause of political freedom, he also knows that Blake is a prophet of ultimate freedom: the kind of freedom that comes from the individual imagination. Reflecting this side of Blake, Ginsberg's poetry seeks to liberate man not only from the machinery of war, government, and industry, but also from the machinery of a purely conceptualizing, abstracting, Urizenic mind. Four years after his reading of *Howl*, Ginsberg wrote:

A word on the Politicians: my poetry is Angelical Ravings & has nothing to do with dull materialistic vagaries about who should shoot who. The secrets of individual imagination—which are transconceptual and & non-verbal—I mean unconditioned Spirit—are not for sale to this consciousness, are of no use to this world, except to make it shut its trap & listen to the music of the Spheres. Who denies the music of the spheres denies poetry, denies man, & spits on Blake, Shelley, Christ & Buddha.   (N 417)

Inevitably, Blake takes his place in—or lends his voice to—a celestial harmony made by the other three: by Christ and Buddha, gods of love and meditation, and by Shelley, prophet of immortality, whose *Adonais* supplies the epigraph for Ginsberg's *Kaddish and Other Poems* (1961): "—Die, / If thou wouldst be with that which thou dost seek." Blake has been Ginsberg's muse. It is not a matter of verbal echoes; Ginsberg recently criticized his own "Western ballad" of 1948 (written to Neal Cassady) *because* it borrows the phrase "endless maze" from "The Voice of the Ancient Bard."[13] The Blakean voice that Ginsberg hears does not speak in handily traceable phrases any more than in handily transmittable (and politically useful) concepts. It speaks—if we can believe Ginsberg himself—the language of genuine inspiration. Blake's method of illuminating his poems is supposed to have been given to him in a trance by his dead brother Robert in 1787. Likewise, Ginsberg tells us that in the last section of *Howl,* part one, "I went on to what my imagination believed true to Eternity (for I'd had a beatific illumination years before during which I'd heard Blake's ancient voice & saw the universe unfold in my brain), & what my memory would reconstitute of the data of celestial experience" (N 415).

The concluding lines of part one transcend conventional patterns of literary influence just as much as they transcend politics. But one of these "lines" at once illustrates and expresses the object of Ginsberg's poetry:

> to recreate the syntax and measure of poor human prose and stand before you speechless and intelligent and shaking with shame, rejected yet confessing out the soul to conform to the rhythm of thought in his naked and endless head.   (P. 16)

To re-create the syntax and measure of poor human prose in a poetry that defies established conventions of verse form: this is Ginsberg's aim. More recently, in fact, calling to mind Wordsworth's desire to make poetry speak "the real language of men," Ginsberg has said that he and his contemporaries have been using in their poetry "the syntax of our actual speech, our actual thoughts in our actual speech."[14] But here he nonetheless differs from Wordsworth. Wordsworth wanted actual syntax only so far as it could be fitted "to metrical arrangement," and actual speech only after it had been purified "from all rational causes of dislike or disgust." Ginsberg's language is anything *but* purified and metrically arranged. It is the radically revolutionary language of a radically revolutionary imagination, and as such, it recalls the language of Blake. It is cloacal, of course, to a degree that Blake's is not, and we are still adjusting to the fact that what Blake calls a "marigold" Ginsberg calls a cunt. But the revolutionary quality of Ginsberg's language springs more from the shape of the words than from the words themselves. Like Blake, who delivered his intensely personal visions in a form that can only be called prophecy," and whose works were not even published in the normal way but rather printed "in the infernal method, by corrosives," Ginsberg seeks to individuate the form of his poetry just as sharply as he individuates its content.

In this aim, he is both like and unlike Blake. Blake's defiance of the categorical opposition between poetry and painting was expressed in books of illuminated prophecy, and while his curiously placed "periods" are often regarded as breath stops, his poetry remains for us primarily visual. Ginsberg's poetry is emphatically oral. *Howl* was delivered before it was published, and Ginsberg has said that he regards each of its lines (though they significantly elude the formal meaning of the term) as "a single breath unit" (N 416). It is poetry to be heard, poetry that reawakens the literal sense of the prophet's voice and of in*spir*ation, poetry that speaks not merely with the real language of men but with the poet's own breath.

Here Ginsberg owes less to Blake than to his contemporary Charles Olson, whose essay on "Projective Verse" (1950) stipulates that "the line comes (I swear it) from the breath, from the breathing of the man who writes, at that moment that he writes" (N 410). Yet the breath of Blake's own voice is something Ginsberg continues to hear. It inspires the celebratory Footnote to *Howl*, which is a furiously freehanded set of variations on the concluding line of *The Marriage:* "Everything that lives is Holy." It has prompted Ginsberg to sing some of the *Songs of Innocence and of Experience* at his poetry readings and to record his musical versions of them in 1970. And the voice of the ancient bard is audible even in Ginsberg's most recent collection of poems—a book suggestively entitled *The Fall of America* (1972). Here is yet another picture of the Fall—this time made for the ear as much as the eye. The country whose self-regenerating independence was once embodied in the indestructible virginity of Oothoon ("the soft soul of America," Blake calls her in *Visions*) has now been raped not by Bromion but by its own Urizenic conception of freedom: a system of freedom that would tolerate no other, that would go into war to defend an abstraction.

The new collection is subtitled *Poems of these States 1965–1971*, and through it writhes—inevitably—the serpent of Southeast Asia. Yet there is a good deal more than antiwar rhetoric here. If Ginsberg is more political than Joyce Cary, and uses Blake in a more aggressively political way, he nevertheless shares Cary's commitment to a freedom that transcends politics: to the freedom prophesied by Blake. In Ginsberg's words, it is the freedom of the mind "to deal with itself as it actually is and not impose on itself an arbitrarily preconceived pattern."[15] The new collection storms the Bastille of the mind in different ways. In "Kansas City to Saint Louis," Ginsberg juxtaposes the opening words of the Constitution, framed in innocence, with a phrase from yesterday's headlines, forged in experience: "We the People—shelling the Vietcong" (p. 29). And in "Autumn Gold: New England Fall," the words of poetry vie with the sounds of technology, the timeless voice of the ancient bard with the fleeting radio crackle of an airborne chief executive:

President Johnson in a plane toward Hawaii
Fighter Escort above & below
air roaring—
Radiostatic electric crackle from the
center of communications:
I broadcast thru Time,
He, with all his wires & wireless,
only an Instant—   (P. 51)

Here Ginsberg is again the prophet against empire, at once political and poetic, topical and enduring. Indeed, one of the most extraordinary poems in this collection is plainly political, for it was
prompted by the extensive U.S. bombing of North Vietnam and
Cambodia in 1970. Yet its spareness of reference and its stunning
simplicity of form make it much more than the crackle of a political
instant:

HUM BOM!

Whom bomb?
We bomb them!
Whom bomb?
We bomb them!
Whom bomb?
We bomb them!
Whom bomb?
We bomb them!

Whom bomb?
You bomb you!
Whom bomb?
You bomb you!
Whom bomb?
You bomb you!
Whom bomb?
You bomb you!

What do we do?
Who do we bomb?
What do we do?
Who do we bomb?
What do we do?
Who do we bomb?
What do we do!
Who do we bomb?

What do we do?
You bomb! You bomb them!

What do we do?
You bomb! You bomb them!
What do we do?
We bomb! We bomb them!
What do we do?
We bomb! We bomb them!

Whom bomb?
We bomb you!
Whom bomb?
We bomb you!
Whom bomb?
You bomb you!
Whom bomb?
You bomb you!   (Pp. 181–82)

Made with a vocabulary of just eight words, the poem looks numb-
ingly simple on the printed page. Its first appeal, in fact, is audi-
tory, and when Ginsberg reads the poem, when he makes it speak
with his very own breath, its relentlessly explosive *b*'s strike the ear
like the sounds of a bombardment. The simplicity is disarming.
Instead of Whitmanian exuberance, Ginsberg here gives us Blakean
concentration: the taut, terse, catechetical style of "The Tyger." Cut-
ting away all topical allusions, prophetically seizing the universal
meaning of a historical moment in the simplest possible terms, he
wages a Blakean war on the categorical thinking that makes all
military wars possible. Wars are predicated on the assumption that
"we" and "they" are neatly divisible: "Whom bomb? / We bomb
them!" But when "we" the people seek to bomb "them" the enemy
into submission, we end up by psychically devastating ourselves:
"Whom bomb? / You bomb you!" Just as the military opposition
between "we" and "they" disintegrates, so also does the grammatical opposition between subject and object. And what likewise disintegrates is the nationalistic "we." A war-making government now
appropriates this pronoun to itself—the imperial "we"—and becomes in the eyes of its own people an alien "you." "What do we
do?" asks the government. "You bomb! You bomb them!" answers
the people. The government responds by trying to justify its policy
again, ad nauseam, in terms of the already exploded categories:
"What do we do? / We bomb! We bomb them!" Finally it turns,
both figuratively and (at Kent State) literally, against its own
people: "Whom bomb? / We bomb you!" But since "we" and "you"
are categories also, they too must disintegrate, for no "we" that
bombs "them" or "you" can long ignore the damage that it does to

itself. The last line therefore epitomizes the self-destructiveness not only of this war, but of all war: "You bomb you!"

The blunt brutality of "Hum Bom!" sets it apart from the sunny impudence of *The Horse's Mouth*, and it is clear enough that as the light of Blake's influence enters the minds of Cary and Ginsberg, they bend it in different ways. But the light is each case is recognizably Blakean. The British novelist and the American poet share with Blake a redemptive purpose, a yearning to liberate man from the categories born of time. The myth of the Fall animates the work of all three. Blake sees it acted out by nations and individuals alike, by the tyranny of rulers over subjects and the tyranny of mind over imagination. Cary sees it acted out by the individual artist, who keeps his imagination alive not only by assaulting conventional attitudes toward art, but also by kicking away at the congenital rigidity of his own fallen mind. Finally, Ginsberg sees it acted out by a nation at war with itself, a fallen and divided people calling out to be freed from bondage to its own imperialism. In *The Fall of America* as in the very last words of Gulley Jimson, the voice of the ancient bard continues to resonate.

NOTES

1. A revised edition first appeared in 1957, and I quote from the Harper & Row Perennial Library edition (New York, 1965), which reprints this revised version. I wish to thank a former student, Cardie Texter, for alerting me to Cary's use of Blake.

2. "Blake and Gulley Jimson: English Symbolists," *Critique: Studies in Modern Fiction*, 3 (Spring-Fall 1959), p. 13.

3. See Northrop Frye, *Fearful Symmetry* (Princeton: Princeton University Press, 1947), p. 136, and Janet Warner, "Blake's Use of Gesture," in *Blake's Visionary Forms Dramatic*, ed. David Erdman and John Grant (Princeton: Princeton University Press, 1970), p. 194.

4. See *The Horse's Mouth*, p. 108, and Frye, p. 252.

5. "Blake and Gulley Jimson," p. 6.

6. P. 252.

7. I quote from *Howl and Other Poems* (San Francisco: City Lights, 1967), p. 9. *Howl* was first published in 1956.

8. "American Poetry of Protest, from World War II to the Present," in *Amerikanische Literatur im 20. Jahrhundert*, ed. Alfred Weber and Dietmar Haack (Göttingen: Vanderhoek & Ruprecht, 1971), p. 257.

9. P. 129.

10. I quote from *The Poetry and Prose of William Blake*, ed. David Erdman with commentary by Harold Bloom (New York: Doubleday, 1965).

11. "Notes for *Howl* and Other Poems" (1959), in *The New American Poetry*, ed. Donald M. Allen (New York: Grove Press, 1960). Hereafter cited as N.

12. Quoted in Richard Howard, *Alone with America: Essays on the Art of Poetry in the United States since 1950* (New York: Atheneum, 1969), p. 146.

13. "Early Poetic Community," *American Poetry Review,* 3 (May-June 1974), p. 56.

14. Ibid, p. 58.

15. Howard, p. 150.

"The Truer Measure": Setting in Emma, Middlemarch, and Howards End

Near the end of chapter five, book first of *Adam Bede*, George Eliot sketches a winning portrait of the Reverend Adolphus Irwine, as, accompanied by Arthur Donnithorne, he rides through the countryside to his parish of Hayslope:

But whatever you may think of Mr. Irwine now, if you had met him that June afternoon riding on his grey cob, with his dogs running beside him—portly, upright, manly, with a good-natured smile on his finely-turned lips as he talked to his dashing young companion on the bay mare, you must have felt that, however ill he harmonised with sound theories of the clerical office, he somehow harmonised extremely well with that peaceful landscape.[1]

This landscape, as we know, perpetuated a way of life whose values were dear to the author, and the rector's instinctual accommodation to it is not the least ingratiating aspect of his worldly and easygoing nature.

Many of the memorable figures in nineteenth-century fiction cannot be imagined apart from their environments, so close is the equivalence between salient traits of character and locality. One thinks of Heathcliff stormily ensconced at the Heights, or Joe Gargery reflected in the ruddy glow of his forge. For other characters, however, the harmony with one's surroundings so natural to Mr. Irwine is only to be attained through an arduous process of adaptation on which significant growth, if not survival, is dependent. In these cases setting, instead of seeming primarily a backdrop against which the narrative unfolds, is instrumental in forwarding the action. Related, though differing, versions of this functional use of setting occur in three novels published over almost exactly a century: *Emma* (1816), *Middlemarch* (1871–72), and *Howards End* (1910).[2]

Each of these works has as its protagonist a remarkable heroine, who possesses social rank and wealth, who is gifted with lively intelligence and magnetic charm, but whose lot has been cast in circumstances that allow insufficient opportunity for self-fulfilment through the exercise of these advantages. With reason Emma Woodhouse, Dorothea Brooke, and Margaret Schlegel feel themselves superior to their social milieus, which, in compensation, they seek to dominate, being equally strong-willed in the exertion of the authority that they enjoy. All, in addition, are "imaginists" (in the sense of the term that Jane Austen applies to Emma): they have in common a proneness to self-delusion which leads them to confuse real with supposititious purposes in the pursuit of their goals. The careers of all three, then, conform to a classic pattern of reversal. Through humiliating failure in the performance of her self-appointed role, each heroine discovers a truer sense of her relationship to the surrounding world. And for each the moment of recognition takes place in a scene which specifically evokes the agency of natural setting.

Emma Woodhouse's sway over the social life of Highbury is virtually absolute, unhesitatingly granted by her father, the Westons, Mrs. Bates and her daughter, even Mr. Knightley. Small as her circle is, she further constricts it through class-consciousness. She is not sure that she even knows Robert Martin by sight, although they have been near neighbors all their lives; and she has not met the Coles at the time she condescends to dine with them, although they "had been settled some years in Highbury, and were very good sort of people—friendly, liberal, and unpretending." Yet "on the other hand, they were of low origin, in trade, and only moderately genteel" (p. 159). John Knightley's comment with regard to Emma's new acquaintances is thus partly made with sardonic intent: "Your neighborhood is increasing, and you mix more with it" (pp. 242–43).

Given the limitations of her sphere of influence, Emma's problem is to find a sufficient vent for her overflowing vitality, a problem which she shares with Dorothea and Margaret Schlegel. In Jane Austen's world the choice for young women without means lay between matrimony and the kinds of vassalage that threaten Harriet Smith and Jane Fairfax; and for Emma, licensed, as she fancies, to arbitrate the fortunes of those less privileged than she, what more meritorious activity than matchmaking? That, as she practices it, this is also a form of michief-making she resolutely declines to acknowledge from an inability to distinguish between egoistic pleasure in holding the reins of power and genuine regard for the wellbeing of her associates. Her opposition to Robert Martin as a suitor for Harriet is motivated at least as much by the fact that he is Mr. Knightley's rather than her own candidate as by snobbery.

The scales begin to lift from Emma's eyes during the strawberry-picking party at Donwell Abbey. Mr. Knightley has conducted Harriet, with the others following, to a point of vantage, described as follows: "It was hot; and after walking some time over the gardens in a scattered, dispersed way, scarcely any three together, they insensibly followed one another to the delicious shade of a broad avenue of limes, which stretching beyond the garden at an equal distance from the river, seemed the finish of the pleasure grounds. —It led to nothing; nothing but a view at the end over a low stone wall with high pillars" (pp. 281–82). At this point Jane Austen breaks into a passage the tone of which is for her unusually fervid: "It was a sweet view—sweet to the eye and the mind. English verdure, English culture, English comfort, seen under a sun bright, without being oppressive" (p. 282).

The view overlooks Abbey-Mill Farm, the tenant of which is Robert Martin, and we realize that Mr. Knightley has brought the girl to this prospect with deliberate intent. He is not aware, as the author means the reader to be, that he is at the same time displaying to Emma the setting of her future life. There is double-distilled irony in the complacency with which Emma surveys the scene, confident that Harriet has outgrown Robert Martin's pretensions: "There had been a time also when Emma would have been sorry to see Harriet in a spot so favourable for the Abbey-Mill Farm; but now she feared it not. It might be safely viewed with all its appendages of prosperity and beauty, its rich pastures, spreading flocks, orchard in blossom, and light column of smoke ascending" (p. 282). For just as Harriet belongs at Abbey-Mill Farm, so Emma's destination is Donwell Abbey. As yet, she is hardly aware of the significance for her of the new perspective that has opened up. Before she can be content to fit her life within its confines, further checks to her self-regard must intervene: remorse over her treatment of Miss Bates at Box Hill and the shock of learning that she has unwittingly created a rival in Harriet. It is, nonetheless, the landscape viewed from the terrace at Donwell Abbey that first reveals to Emma the horizons within which she will find happiness.

To show English society in a transitional phase, George Eliot placed *Middlemarch* in the period of the First Reform Bill, forty years prior to its publication. Indeed, the book's very title is a complex pun on this intent. Mr. Brooke, Sir James and Celia Chettam, and the Cadwalladers are survivors from Jane Austen's world; but the winds of change are blowing strongly enough to ruffle even the remote backwaters of Loamshire. They are to be sensed in Lydgate's medical theories, in the encroaching railway, and perhaps most of all in Caleb Garth's enlightened agricultural procedures. Although he, like Robert Martin, belongs to the yeoman class, Caleb represents a new type of estate manager employed by the gentry to oversee their land. Even Dorothea Brooke, among her other fugitive plans, entertains the ambition to become (with Caleb's assistance) an improving landlord.

The novel's subtitle, "A Study of Provincial Life," indicates the importance attached by George Eliot to the shaping power of environment on the lives of her characters. The unspoken assumptions, which to so large an extent determine conduct in the society portrayed by Jane Austen and which she expected her audience to share, have been replaced in *Middlemarch* by a probing into the hidden depths of individual behavior of such subtlety that the reader must accept authorial guidance. Thus, the prelude proposes an analogy between Saint Theresa and Dorothea Brooke to heighten the contrast between the latter's idealistic aspirations and the dearth of opportunity available within her native sphere.

The dawning awareness that marriage to Casaubon, far from opening up the new vistas of knowledge for which she yearns, has condemned her to grope through a labyrinthine maze of pedantry is conveyed by imagery which consistently draws on English pastoral landscape. The first intimation of her fatal mistake comes in the following terms as she muses by the statue of the Ariadne in Rome: "She did not really see the streak of sunlight on the floor more than she saw the statues: she was inwardly seeing the light of years to come in her own home and over the English fields and elms and hedge-bordered highroads; and feeling that the way in which they might be filled with joyful devotedness was not so clear to her as it had been" (pp. 150–51). Subsequently, the view from the window of Dorothea's boudoir at Lowick (which is framed like that at Donwell Abbey by an avenue of limes) becomes the index to her moods at the various stages in her progress to full self-knowledge. "She had been so used," writes George Eliot, "to struggle for and to find resolve in looking along the avenue towards the arch of western light that the vision itself had gained a communicating power" (p. 272).

The winter-bound scenery on which she looks out immediately on her return from Rome, "the still, white enclosure which made her visible world" (p. 202), is emblematic of her saddened sense that the marriage state has brought imprisonment rather than release. After Casaubon's death the prospect, viewed now in summer, seems to Dorothea in imaging her present state to admonish her against allowing initial frustration to discourage her from further straining after altruistic goals: "Every leaf was at rest in the sunshine, the familiar scene was changeless, and seemed to represent the prospect of her life, full of motiveless ease—motiveless, if her own energy could not seek out reasons for ardent action" (p. 394).

In her moment of deepest distress she is to derive from this landscape the message that will sustain her future life. The scene occurs in the eightieth chapter after Dorothea has surprised Will and Rosamond in a compromising tête-à-tête. The anguish of betrayed hope awakens her to full recognition of how deeply she loves Will. Back at Lowick, her effort to grapple with heartbreak provokes the following soliloquy:

And what sort of crisis might not this be in three lives whose contact with hers laid an obligation on her as if they had been suppliants bearing the sacred branch? The objects of her rescue were not to be sought out by her fancy: they were chosen for her. She yearned towards the perfect Right, that it might make a throne within her, and rule her errant will. "What should I do—how should I act now, this very day, if I could clutch my own pain, and compel it to silence, and think of those three?" (P. 577)

The answer for which she is seeking emerges from the landscape outside the window where she sits:

It had taken her long to come to that question, and there was light piercing into the room. She opened her curtains, and looked out towards the bit of road that lay in view, with fields beyond, outside the entrance-gates. On the road there was a man with a bundle on his back and a woman carrying her baby; in the field she could see figures moving—perhaps the shepherd with his dog. Far off in the bending sky was the pearly light; and she felt the largeness of the world and the manifold wakings of men to labour and endurance. She was part of that involuntary, palpitating life, and could neither look out on it from her luxurious shelter as a mere spectator, nor hide her eyes in selfish complaining. (P. 578)

This passage stands in striking contrast to the vignette of Emma Woodhouse when she surveys "for amusement" the main thoroughfare of Highbury from the draper's shop:

Much could not be hoped from the traffic of even the busiest part of Highbury;—Mr. Perry walking hastily by, Mr. William Cox letting himself in at the office door, Mr. Cole's carriage horses returning from exercise, or a stray letter-boy on an obstinate mule, were the liveliest objects she could presume to expect; and when her eyes fell only on the butcher with his

tray, a tidy old woman travelling homewards from shop with her full bas-
ket, two curs quarreling over a dirty bone, and a string of dawdling children round the baker's little bow-window eyeing the gingerbread, she
knew she had no reason to complain, and was amused enough; quite
enough still to stand at the door. A mind lively and at ease, can do with
seeing nothing, and can see nothing that does not answer.   (Pp. 179–80)

No detail of this scene escapes Emma's alert gaze; but her attitude
remains that of detached spectator on the lookout for momentary
diversion. To Dorothea the Millet-like landscape before her brings a
transfiguring recognition of fellowship with her kind. The cherished belief that she has been reserved for some extraordinary mis-
sion gives way to that all-embracing compassion for human weakness and suffering which George Eliot said that it was the principal
purpose of her writing to arouse.

No sooner has Emma learned of Harriet's expectations with regard to Mr. Knightley than, in Jane Austen's words: "It darted
through her, with the speed of an arrow, that Mr. Knightley must
marry no one but herself!" (p. 320). And her joy in the ensuing
proposal is not deeply clouded by concern for her charge. "She felt
for Harriet," we are told, "with pain and with contrition; but no
flight of generosity run mad, opposing all that could be probable or
reasonable, entered her brain" (p. 338). How different is Dorothea's
readiness to resign herself to losing Will: "If we had lost our own
chief good, other people's good would remain, and that is worth
trying for" (p. 593).

Emma's enlightened selfishness is equally apparent in her
thoughts about her future home. The earlier solicitude that John
Knightley's son should inherit Donwell Abbey drolly vanishes once
she has come to think of the place as her rightful domain: "It is
remarkable, that Emma, in the many, very many, points of view in
which she was now beginning to consider Donwell Abbey, was
never struck with any sense of injury to her nephew Henry, whose
rights as heir expectant had formerly been so tenaciously regarded"
(p. 353). By the same token Celia Brooke finds perfect content at
Freshitt with Sir James Chettam. But for Dorothea there can be no
ultimate fulfillment in a localized setting; witness with how little
regret she forsakes Lowick to follow Will's career, despite her plans
for the estate. Just as the view from her window expands indef-
initely to become lost in immensity, so her spirit will continue to
soar "after some illimitable satisfaction" (p. 3).

The spreading countryside of *Emma* and *Middlemarch* lingers on
as little more than a memory in *Howards End*. Like the goblins

which Helen Schlegel reads into Beethoven's Fifth Symphony, the suburbs of London have crept up over the horizon, engulfing the tumuli where Danish warriors lie buried. Of the ancestral property of the Howards, sprung from yeoman stock, only the house with its adjoining meadow remains, fallen into the hands of Henry Wilcox, imperialist financier, who has converted it into a weekend dwelling for his family. The symmetry of the house has been marred by the addition of a garage; a tennis court has usurped the lawn.

Margaret Schlegel would appear to be as alien to Howards End as its residents. She is a city-dweller, caught in the flux of a rootless society: "London was but a foretaste of this nomadic civilization which is altering human nature so profoundly, and throws upon personal relations a stress greater than they have ever borne before. Under cosmopolitanism, if it comes, we shall receive no help from the earth. Trees and meadows and mountains will only be a spectacle, and the binding force that they once exercised must be entrusted to Love alone" (p. 261). Over the little world of Wickham Place Margaret rules with as high a hand as Emma at Highbury, and with as little real gratification. Her patronage of Leonard Bast is another such instance of misdirected charity as Emma's treatment of Harriet. Like Dorothea, she yearns for some noble cause on which to expend her stores of idealism; and like Dorothea again, she invests this need in a disillusioning marriage with an older man.

Although Mrs. Wilcox and Miss Avery perceive that Margaret is the destined owner of Howards End, she comes reluctantly and by gradual stages to this awareness. The first intimation that the house stands for values attuned to her profoundest convictions flashes over Margaret on the spring day when, now Henry's wife, she returns to Howards End for a second visit with the purpose of reprimanding Miss Avery for unpacking her possessions. As she pauses briefly in the neighboring farm, all the properties of the scene cohere into a single ineffaceable impression:

Here had lived an elder race, to which we look back with disquietude. The country we visit at week-ends was really a home to it, and the graver sides of life, the deaths, the partings, the yearnings for love, have their deepest expression in the heart of the fields. All was not sadness. The sun was shining without. The thrush sang his two syllables on the budding guelder-rose. Some children were playing uproariously in heaps of golden straw. It was the presence of sadness at all that surprised Margaret, and ended by giving her a feeling of completeness. In these English farms, if anywhere, one might see life steadily and see it whole, group in one vision its transitoriness and its eternal youth, connect—connect without bitterness until all men are brothers.   (Pp. 268–69)

The vision thus vouchsafed is to be confirmed soon after when Margaret and Helen spend the night together in the old house, shadowed by its wych-elm. As if a result of the healing virtues ascribed to the tree, the spell of the place enters into the sisters, lulling them into full and lasting harmony:

And the triviality faded from their faces, though it left something behind—the knowledge that they never could be parted because their love was rooted in common things. Explanations and appeals had failed; they had tried for a common meeting-ground and had only made each other unhappy. And all the time their salvation was lying round them—the past sanctifying the present; the present, with wild heart-throb, declaring that there would after all be a future, with laughter and the voices of children.

(P. 299)

To complete Margaret's felicity it is only needful that the harmony be extended to unite the prose of Henry's nature with the poetry of Helen's; and this is achieved once more through the agency of setting. With those dearest to her under her roof, Margaret has nothing more to ask of life; and in consequence, her ardent nature undergoes a change, adapting itself insensibily to the tranquil domesticity of her surroundings.

The epigraph of *Howards End*, "Only connect," might appropriately be applied to the relationship between protagonist and setting as it has been explored in each of these novels. Chronologically considered, moreover, they may be seen as recording the passing of a traditional way of life, that of rural England, and the increasing imaginative effort called for in coming to terms with the vestiges of that way of life.

Emma Woodhouse is the fine flower of the established social order into which she is born. In order to find herself fully at home in Highbury, however, she has to learn that the privileges of her position are inseparable from its limitations. The glimpse of happiness which Donwell Abbey held out to her can only be realized when she embraces these scenes as the natural frame of her future life. For Dorothea, Lowick offers no such easy solution as her sister enjoys at Freshitt. She is impelled by her insatiably aspiring spirit to explore wider and mistier horizons in the quest for self-fulfilment. In *Emma* evidence supports the common sense of the community, of which Mr. Knightley is spokesman, in assessing the merits of outsiders, Frank Churchill or Mrs. Elton. In *Middlemarch* public opinion is an obscurantist force powerful enough to subvert the progressive theories of Lydgate and Will Ladislaw. Like those two interlopers, Dorothea will be unable to localize her dreams out of a diffused concern for the welfare of the human kind at large. In her moment of crisis she perceives from the window at Lowick not individuals but types of enduring humanity, not a specific land- scape, but a tonal background, vast and unparticularized, to "that involuntary, palpitating life" which draws her to it.

Both Emma and Dorothea would have subscribed to Margaret Schlegel's appeal to personal relations, but would have done so under sanctions no longer existent in Margaret's world at the dawn of the twentieth century. The communal sentiment which, for better or worse, unites the inhabitants of Highbury and Middlemarch has given way to a cynical disregard for others in the fragmented soci- ety epitomized by the Wilcoxes. Settling at Howards End, Margaret submits herself to powers older and more elemental than any which emanate from the atmosphere of Donwell Abbey or Lowick. The influence of the locality is magical, springing from man's primitive kinship with the earth. The sympathy that has grown between Henry Wilcox and Helen Schlegel is inconceivable in any other setting. There is even a kind of rightness in the fact that Helen's bastard son will one day inherit the house, thus vindicating his father's unconscious impulse to regain connection with his yeoman origins. Between Margaret and her home there is a reciprocal bond. Like the first Mrs. Wilcox, who seemed always to bear a talismanic wisp of hay, Margaret has merged into her setting, of which she now seems the tutelary genius, her role manifest in the abundant yield of the harvest.

NOTES

1. George Eliot, *Adam Bede*, introduction by Gordon S. Haight, (New York: Rine- hart, 1948), p. 68.

2. Citations in the text refer to the following editions: Jane Austen, *Emma*, intro- duction by Lionel Trilling (Boston: Houghton Mifflin, 1957); George Eliot, *Middle- march*, introduction by Gordon S. Haight (Boston: Houghton Mifflin, 1956); E. M. Forster, *Howards End* (New York: Vintage Books, 1955).

JOSEPH BLOTNER

Romantic Elements in Faulkner

A spot whereon the founders lived and died
Seemed once more dear than life; ancestral trees,
Or gardens rich in memory glorified
Marriages, alliances and families . . .

We were the last romantics—chose for theme
Traditional sanctity and loveliness;
Whatever's written in what poets name
The book of the people; whatever most can bless
The mind of man or elevate a rhyme;
But all is changed. . . . [1]

"Coole Park and Ballylee, 1931" was published three weeks after *Sanctuary*. The meditative poem and the violent novel would seem to have little in common, but one of the hallmarks of both writers was their extraordinary range and versatility. The author of "Leda and the Swan" and "Easter 1916" was no stranger to lust and violence, and the poet of *The Marble Faun* and *A Green Bough* cherished images of past loveliness. Yeats published "Coole Park, 1929" seven months after *Sartoris*. The affinities between these two works are immediately apparent. Yeats's meditation upon "an aged woman and her house," his appeal for the dedication of "A moment's memory to that laurelled head" when all the beauty that now surrounds it shall also be vanished, this tribute to Lady Gregory, sounds much like the many passages in Faulkner's novel praising Aunt Jenny Du Pre, and through her gallant women like Sallie Murry Falkner and Holland Falkner Wilkins, and a whole passing era which they represent.

The point of these juxtapositions is not to set up an elaborate correspondence between the poet in his middle sixties and the novelist in his middle thirties, though Faulkner knew Yeats's work and liked it enough to recite from memory "An Irish Airman Foresees His Death." He liked other Irish writers too. He would also recite Joyce's "Watching the Needle Boats at San Sabba" and he would repeatedly paraphrase lines from Synge's *The Playboy of the Western*

World. But he shared with Yeats some of the impulses that caused the latter to call himself, if prematurely, one of the last romantics. This is also to accept the fact that romanticism is not a literary movement circumscribed in time like a political administration but rather a constellation of intellectual and emotional attitudes and certain embodiments of them given expression in literature. What I propose to do is first to mention some of these elements, these romanticisms, to use the broadest framework, and to explore Faulkner's affinities with some of them. Then, after a glance at some of the accumulating critical comments on these aspects of Faulkner's work, I want to look at the crucial novel *Sartoris* as perhaps the principal embodiment of them among the Yoknapatawpha novels.

If we like, we can use a definition of romanticism as broad as René Wellek's "imagination for the view of poetry, nature for the view of the world, and symbol and myth for poetic style."[2] And his use of the word poetry suggests a quality of Faulkner's work which is well known and should be mentioned early in this discussion: Faulkner began his serious writing as a poet, often in later years called himself a failed poet, and derived some of his most brilliant effects, indeed, one of the most pervasive characteristics of his art, from the employment of the methods and devices of poetry in his fiction. We can employ Morse Peckham's early formulation that Romanticism is "the revolution in the European mind against thinking in terms of static mechanism and the redirection of the mind to thinking in terms of dynamic organicism. Its values are change, imperfection, growth, diversity, the creative imagination, the unconscious."[3] Or we can think more inclusively yet in terms of Hugh Holman's listing of elements conspicuous in the Romantic movement: freedom from classical rules together with individualism sometimes extending to revolutionary politics, the revival of medievalism, the addition of strangeness to beauty, aspiration arising out of wonder and mystery, and the predominance of imagination over reason. Holman goes on to the elements of sensibility, primitivism, love of nature, sympathetic interest in the past, fresh language rather than poetic diction, the idealization of rural life, sympathy with animal life, and enthusiasm for the grotesque. Finally, there is the placing of the individual at the center of life and experience, the emphasis upon portrayal in psychological depth of that experience, the view of nature as a revelation of truth, and the view of art as "a formulation of intuitive imaginative perceptions that tend to speak a nobler truth than that of fact, logic, or the here and now."[4] One might respond that this is a net flung wide enough to catch almost anyone, and conversely, that Faulkner was so eclectic and his work so varied that many more elements than those associated with Romanticism are to be found there. In spite of these reasonable reservations, however, there are characteristics which one immediately associates with Faulkner's art: the strength of the past, the use of nature and the emphasis of its relation to human life, the employment of imagination to portray human experience, and a kind of intensity of experience often explored through characters whoe extraordinary traits and destinies remind us of great figures in Romantic literature.

William Faulkner's early life disposed him toward some of these elements. From the time he was old enough to remember, there was family around him, a clan of people unusual even for north Mississippi: able, artistic, gregarious, cantankerous, not only raconteurs in the Southern oral tradition but custodians of a rich family history. There were tales of gallantry and doom, of highland ancestors who brought their claymores with them to the New World when they left the Old after Culloden. Nor was it all tales. There was the old sword and a family kilt, and from later times souvenirs of wars and a great family Bible where the generations were recorded. The general outlines of the life of his great-grandfather, Colonel William C. Falkner, are well known: his manifold careers as lawyer, planter, soldier, writer, and railroad builder which made him the prototype of Colonel John Sartoris in the Yoknapatawpha saga. Though he was murdered before William Faulkner was born, he was still virtually a living presence not only in Ripley, where he lived and died, but in the family's lore and in the imagination of his great-grandson, whose schoolboy aim was to be "a writer like my great-granddaddy." The colonel's son, John Wesley Thompson Falkner, dominated the clan in his time, and often of a summer twilight he would sit on his front gallery, his grandsons about him, and tell of the days when his father was off fighting the Yankees in Virginia while he and his mother and the slaves still on the place did their best to keep it running while the Southern economy was slowly strangled and the Yankee marauders might appear any day. All this he absorbed, together with tales told by men who had fought with Lee and Jackson in Virginia or with Forrest and Van Dorn in Mississippi. Best of all must have been the stories of Colonel Falkner's veterans, old men now who had fired muskets and won glory with him in the infantry regiment at Manassas or ridden whatever mounts they could find in the skirmishes of the Partisan Rangers in the swamps and brakes of north Mississippi and south Tennessee. Raised in town but loving the country, Billy Falkner liked country people, and he heard country stories as well as family lore. He could read tales of glory as well as hear them, and his absorption was such that fifty years later he could walk a Virginia battlefield and know not just whose armies had fought there, but where the corps, massed brigades, and batteries went into action. In his teens he read the exploits of the "knights of the sky" who were fighting their duels in Camels and Fokkers. This was a complex of experience so intensely imaged that, reinforced with training for such warfare, it would last him throughout his life and provide vivid material for his fiction.

His reading was wide and varied, not just the prescribed school fare but also the books his mother read, Shakespeare and Conrad, the Dumas that his grandfather favored, and the Balzac that he and his friend, Phil Stone, would read with admiration and delight. Later he would write of his reading at sixteen, his oft-quoted lines about Swinburne, "springing from some tortured undergrowth of my adolescence, like a highwayman, making me his slave." He had only dipped into Keats and Shelley. He went on to Robinson, Frost, Aldington, and Aiken. Then he discovered Housman, who showed him "reason for being born into a fantastic world: discovering the splendor of fortitude, the beauty of being of the soil like a tree about which fools might howl and which winds of disillusion and death and despair might strip, leaving it bleak without bitterness; beautiful in sadness."[5] From him he went to the Elizabethans, he recalled, and then to Shelley and Keats, now ready to find in them strength, awareness, beauty, and sustenance. Later, as a special student at the University of Mississippi, he would enroll in courses in French, Spanish, and English, the latter principally Shakespeare. He would earn an A and a B in the first two and a D in the last, which he would drop. He did not care for grades, he told his father, but for what he kept in his head. With this course work perhaps, with his own reading certainly, he knew of the Romantic period as a literary phenomenon just as he knew intensively some of the work of its major figures. An eclectic student, he would take what he needed. It has been argued that he read and profited from the essays of T. S. Eliot.[6] He read his borrowed copy of Ludwig Lewisohn's anthology, *A Book of Modern Criticism*, and annotated it with pithy and profane comments generally hostile to German criticism and friendly to French. Late in his life, when he would speak impromptu about writing, he would generalize about the writer's sources: imagination, observation, and experience. Of his techniques, he might instance the use of theme and counterpoint or vaguely say that the writer moved things about until he found the most effective way of displaying them, as a window dresser would shift his dummies and garments. The comments were often acute and almost always suggestive, but it was a homemade poetics. He would speak of his own uncorrelated reading, despite his friend Phil Stone's tutelage and proffering of books which brought to Faulkner's attention much of the best writing of the 1920s. He was his own man and there was little of the avowed literary theorist about him; he was no Coleridge writing his poems and constructing a theoretical scheme that would encompass them. An omnivorous reader as a young man, he imitated the poets and novelists who pleased him, ultimately finding his own voice when he moved from poetry to prose and forging his own style when he found his fictional metier. But wherever his favorites would serve his purposes he would use them, through his maturity and until the end of his life. A large number of them fell within the Romantic tradition, and numerous scholars have commented in greater and lesser degrees on the influences and the borrowings.

The most compendious treatment is "William Faulkner's Romantic Heritage: Beyond America." Here Charles W. Dean, Jr., compares Faulkner's work principally with that of Balzac, Wordsworth, Byron, Shelley, and Keats. He sums up: "Vautrin-Sutpen, Luke-Ike, Cain-Christmas, Endymion-Quentin: the affinities between Faulkner and leading figures of the Romantic period are manifest throughout his saga of Yoknapatawpha County. Faulkner sees the world of men with the visionary inner eye of a romantic sensibility."[7] Amalgamating earlier criticism with his own work, Dean deals with Faulkner's use of nature, with his Faustian figures and Byronic protagonists, with their incestuous relationships and Satanic compulsions. Throughout Faulkner's career, however, while various reviewers and critics were calling him a disciple of Joyce or a Southern Decadent, a sadist or sensationalist, others were remarking that beneath the realistic or what they chose to call the grotesque, was a romantic poet, or at least a poet manqué. It may be useful to explore some of these comments on individual works before proceeding to a longer look at *Sartoris*.

The Marble Faun in 1924 and *A Green Bough* in 1933 were received with essentially the same verdict: the poems were interesting and showed talent, but they were essentially derivative and the author's major talent lay in another genre. One harsh verdict called the effect "one of immature romanticism."[8] In a kinder and fairer judgment George Garrett called the effect rather "one of strenuous effort to create a poetry which, had it been continued, might have been a sophisticated lyric strain in contemporary verse."[9] Ten years later Cleanth Brooks would declare, "One can hardly overstate the fact that Faulkner's verse is late romantic verse. Indeed, one might fairly call it decadent verse." Tracing the influence of Swinburne and Housman, noting resemblances to Keats and Eliot, he concluded that Faulkner was a born poet, that when he "gave up his Swinburnian model and came to see that even Housman's was a dangerous one . . . when, in short, Faulkner did call his muse home, it meant that she had to become homebred, in her rhythms, her language patterns, and everything else that went with a Yoknapatawpha girl."[10]

When *Soldiers' Pay* appeared in 1926 to be followed a year later by *Mosquitoes*, most reviewers emphasized the Modernist elements: the postwar waste land treated by Eliot and Hemingway and the society of bohemians and dilettantes presented by Arlen and Huxley. With the appearance of *Sartoris* and the consolidation of Yoknapatawpha County in the great novels that followed each other closely over the next dozen years, the work tended often to be seen primarily as a presentation of unlovely aspects of contemporary Southern life against the background of a vanished past at once picturesque and sinister. Happily, Faulkner had begun receiving the attention of serious critics early, both in this country and abroad, and it was inevitable that as the corpus grew the criticism would proliferate with increasing emphasis on style and source. The question of romanticism in Faulkner's fiction was considered by Robert M. Slabey, who viewed his first three novels (especially *Sartoris*) as permeated with the kind of romanticism that Mark Twain deplored and blamed on Sir Walter Scott, a view "from a traditional, nostalgic, and romantic perspective, not unlike that of Thomas Nelson Page, glorifier and defender of the Old South." With a continuing view of the Romantic hero likely to be uncongenial to many, Slabey saw Quentin Compson as a familiar figure in "the Romantic sensibility: all of them are clinging to an impossible ideal in the face of hard facts; all are egocentric, even narcissistic, trying to live in a private inner world of their own, in a way committing intellectual incest."[11] But he concluded that in *The Sound and the Fury* Faulkner abandoned the romantic position, assumed a moral perspective, and successfully employed the mythic method in achieving universal significance. In a more recent essay Gloria R. Dussinger saw Ike McCaslin as a Romantic hero manqué, one whose identity and function are best defined in terms of "the basic Romantic fable—the quest." The hero leaves society for forest, sea, or jungle in order to find true values which elude him in contemporary society. Finding them, he completes his journey by returning to society to function within it. Reading Faulkner's verdict upon

Ike's life as one of failure, the author argued that Ike completed the first half of the hero's quest but not the second, that he "pronounced nature good and society evil, failing to grasp that both are amoral, that both gain value only through the dynamic power of personality."[12]

One essay, in some ways the best of these, united images, idea, and theme. In "Faulkner's Grecian Urn" Joan S. Korenman analyzed Faulkner's use of Keats's great ode as he quotes it in *Sartoris* and *Go Down, Moses,* suggests it in *Light in August* and *The Mansion,* and deals through character and symbol in *The Sound and the Fury* with a kind of timelessness or stasis for which Keats's urn is a compelling symbol. Arguing an ambivalence toward the transience in the human condition, the author concluded that Keats finally turns to the "warmth and vitality" of imperfect human experience in preference to the "permanence and stasis" of the urn's cold pastoral. She saw Faulkner's characters similarly ambivalent and their creator himself similarly torn and often "rationally at war with his emotional commitment to the past and to the notion of stopping time. As a man of the twentieth century, he appreciates the need for progress and change; as a Southerner, he understands the danger of paying too much heed to the ghosts of the past. . . . Time must pass, life must change; for Faulkner as for Keats, this is the sadness and the essence of the human condition."[13]

Over the years, within the particular contexts of essays and books, many writers had remarked romantic elements in the works. The strength and influence of the past were noted not just in *Sartoris* and *The Unvanquished,* but in the lives of characters from Gail Hightower and Ike McCaslin to Lucius Priest. And although Faulkner would declare that stasis meant death, that life was motion, his writing was often imbued with a nostalgia coupled with a pervasive anti-Modernism seen not only in the description but the very imagery of novels such as *Pylon.* The love of nature that permeated *The Marble Faun* and much of *A Green Bough* illuminated great scenes in *The Hamlet,* and Faulkner's feeling for country people made extraordinarily vivid such country characters as the Bundrens in *As I Lay Dying.* One of their qualities, absolutely central to short stories such as "The Tall Men" and "Shingles for the Lord," was individualism, a fierce valuation of independence and a deep distrust of forces in government and society militating against it. Though nature was a great looming and shaping force—as in *Go Down Moses,* in the "Old Man" segments of *The Wild Palms*—man was still at the center of his world, and in one after another, from Caddie Compson to Addie Bundren to Joe Christmas, Faulkner probed the hearts and minds of his driven characters. Sometimes they were grotesque: not just as Popeye is in *Sanctuary* or Ike Snopes is in *The Hamlet*, but often grotesque in Sherwood Anderson's sense, people whose lives have been warped by forces they could not control. Byronic and Faustian were his heroes, determined and doomed like Thomas Sutpen in *Absalom, Absalom!*. And Faulkner was virtually alone in literature in creating a comic Faust who triumphed over Lucifer: Flem Snopes in hell in *The Hamlet*. Characterizing the treatment in *The Town* of Flem's opponent, V. K. Ratliff, Brooks would call Faulkner "an incorrigible romantic."[14] Obsessed not just with the past, some suffered with complex loves tainted with incest: Quentin Compson especially, but also to some extent Horace Benbow and Henry Sutpen, besides lesser characters in works both published and unpublished. And through all of the work, from *Soldiers' Pay* in 1926 to *The Reivers* in 1962 there was the style: the unmatched luxuriance, the form that derived from the material rather than from arbitrary rules, coupled with dialogue consisting of the words spoken by real men and women: earthy, tangy, colloquial, and precise. And over all was the play of an intensely creative mind which valued imagination over reason, intuition over fact, and heart over head.

In late 1926 or early 1927 Faulkner put aside the manuscript he had been writing. As he was "speculating idly upon time and death," he would later recall, the thought occurred to him that the day would come when he would no longer "react to the simple bread-and-salt of the world" as he had done during his growing years, and so he began casting about. "All that I really desired was a touchstone simply; a simple word or gesture, but having been these 2 years previously under the curse of words, having known twice before the agony of ink, nothing served but that I try by main strength to recreate between the covers of a book the world as I was already preparing to lose and regret . . . and desiring, if not the capture of that world and the feeling of it as you'd preserve a kernel or a leaf to indicate the lost forest, at least to keep the evocative skeleton of the dessicated leaf."[15] And so, drawing upon people he knew and tales he had heard, he began not only to re-create the world he knew but another world that had shaped his forebears, the world of the Falkners that gave shape to the world of the Sartorises. He began with an excursion into the distant past. He drew upon his great-grandfather's souvenirs from the Mexican War and the Civil War, but enlisting imagination he pushed back further. The chest in which old Bayard Sartoris rummaged contained not only the massive family Bible and Mechlin lace but a Toledo blade brought to Virginia in the time of Charles I by a Sartoris who had brought with him "little else save the romantic fatality of his name and the jeweled poniard which Aylmer Sartoris . . . had slung about the young hips of that first Bayard Sartoris who carried it to Agincourt."[16] Faulkner reinforced this reference to the late Middle Ages, to medieval chivalry, with the name Bayard, borne not just by the old man who opened the novel but by the protagonist, his grandson, who possessed in a different measure some of the qualities of the first Bayard Sartoris. Faulkner and his friend Phil Stone would talk of Pierre du Terrail, seigneur de Bayard, *le chevalier sans peur et sans reproche*, whose death in 1524 ended his gallant career of warfare. For them he represented a type, one apotheosized for them in a foolhardy gallantry particularly Southern, conspicuous in Civil War exploits but still to be seen in other forms. And so Faulkner traced this line to concentrate on the working of Sartoris destinies in the years 1918–22 against the background of other Sartoris destinies during the years 1861–73. He completed *Flags in the Dust* in October of 1927, and in November his publisher rejected it. The author reacted with shock and outrage, and it was not until a year later, with the novel cut and retitled *Sartoris*, that it was accepted by another publisher. Faulkner resented the cuts, but he had been convinced that the manuscript contained the material not of one book but of several, and so, he would later say, "I realized for the first time that I had done better than I knew."[17] And so the germ of his Apocrypha, as he would call it, appeared on 31 January 1929, not only adumbrating the Yoknapatawpha saga, but embodying at least as clearly as any of the novels the elements in Faulkner that might be called romantic.

The criticism that has been devoted to this novel is extensive, and for present purposes it will be sufficient to glance at that part of it concerned with romantic elements. Those most often treated are the foolhardy daring and fatality of the Sartorises, the sick and alienated protagonist, the compex of urn imagery as it relates to attitudes to past and present, and the use of irony as a controlling device with respect to that past and the characters most affected by it.

Morse Peckham's idea of Negative Romanticism accommodates the image often presented of Bayard Sartoris: "The typical symbols of Negative Romanticism are individuals who are filled with guilt, despair, and cosmic and social alienation. They are often presented, for instance, as having committed some horrible and unmentionable and unmentioned crime in the past. They are often outcasts from men and God, and they are almost always wanderers over the face of the earth."[18] For Slabey, young Bayard Sartoris, psychically wounded in World War I, is cut off from the past, from society, and from home. Alienated from the present, he suffers from guilt and an obvious death wish.[19] For Walter R. McDonald he is a more positive figure belonging to a distinct and more modern type: "the dauntless hero in modern American fiction." For him, "*Sartoris* sets the style of such abandon, and in his other stories the dauntless hero appears again and again, though Faulkner sees naive courage as waste, clearly mindless and often destructive of others as well."[20] For Charles Dean, young Bayard is a rebellious Byronic hero, and his dead twin, Johnny, shares with Thomas Sutpen, "the Satanic compulsions of Byron's Conrad and Lara."[21] For Lawrance Thompson, "all the romantic characters in this novel are treated in an ambivalent manner by Faulkner, whose attitude toward them is at once sympathetic, critical, ironic." He argues that Faulkner's description of the way Aunt Jenny Du Pre gradually elaborates the Carolina Bayard's Civil War escapade is essentially sarcastic, emphasizing her "romantic" mythmaking. She deflates the Sartoris men's vainglory, but she is a Sartoris herself, and even though her fondness for ironies may permit her to speak at times for Faulkner, "she is not permitted to recognize her own capacities for romanticizing." And at the novel's end, the reference to Keatsian quietude and peace is probably "endowed with appropriately ironic significance."[22] For Joan S. Korenman the pervasive urn imagery, seen in connection with Horace Benbow, suggests "the author's ambivalence toward stasis and change." For him, Narcissa, like the vases Horace blows, represents "serenity and changelessness." But in the novel Faulkner separates "the obsession with the past from the desire for stasis."[23]

Probably the most obvious romantic element in *Sartoris* is the strength of the past and the preoccupation of many of the novel's characters with it. Faulkner would later say there is no such thing as *was*, the past *is*. In this novel the long-dead John Sartoris is a presence more real, more palpable almost, than that of old Bayard Sartoris and Will Falls as the two old men engage in shouted conversation in Bayard's office, or of old Isom talking to the colonel as he goes about his chores. The novel's recapitulations of bygone heroism and vainglory have been cited many times: Aunt Jenny's tales of the Carolina Bayard and Jeb Stuart raiding General Pope's headquarters; Will Falls recounting the exploits of old Bayard's father, Colonel John Sartoris, capturing Yankee detachments; Narcissa Benbow's recollection of the boyhood devilment of the Sartoris twins; young Bayard's retelling of the suicidal exploits against German aircraft of his twin John. The same kind of action takes place of course in present time through young Bayard's own suicidal use of automobile and airplane, and one of the reinforcements of the past motif is the antimodernism embodied most clearly in the use of the automobile. This is to suggest also that the past comes to us not just through the tales of the characters; much of this lore is supplied to us by the author, who, true to the creative intention he later re-counted, attempted to re-create a vanished world, or perhaps bet-ter, worlds. The past is gone and nothing will bring it back, but one can still lament elements, customs, and attitudes that have vanished with it.

An element in some ways even more pervasive is that of nature. Throughout the novel, as the year changes, there are passages of description which constitute hymns to the beauty of the land. In scene after scene Faulkner places his characters in flower gardens or sets them against backgrounds of field, wood, or night sky. They hear birdsong and they work with horses and cattle. Nature is a source not only of beauty but of healing. Even the self-destructive young Bayard responds to it: "For a time the earth held him in a hiatus that might have been called contentment. He was up at sun-rise, planting things in the ground and watching them grow and tending them . . . and went to bed with grateful muscles and with the sober rhythms of the earth in his body and so to sleep." For a time this regimen even diminishes the power he turns against him-self: "He had been so neatly tricked by earth, that ancient Delilah, that he was not aware that his locks were shorn."[24] Whether a scene is set in the July heat or introduced with a prose poem to Novem-ber, we are never far from an awareness of nature. Indeed, there is something very like the pathetic fallacy as Bayard, bearing the guilt now for his grandfather's death as well as his brother's, seeks sleep in vain: "In the sky no star showed, and the sky was the sagging corpse of itself" (p. 323). And after the MacCallums eulogize Johnny Sartoris, and the hounds have given tongue, "the sound floated up on the chill air, died into echoes that repeated the sound again until its source was lost and the very earth itself might have found voice, grave and sad, and wild with all regret" (p. 333). Those close to nature, like the MacCallum family, scorning town life and town ways, live by a deep and constant rhythm. The old man and his stalwart sons "sat without words and with very little movement, their grave, aquiline faces as though carved by the firelight out of the shadowy darkness, shaped by a single thought and smoothed and colored by the same hand" (p. 318). Some of these qualities are shared by Negro characters in the novel, and Faulkner's sympathy extends to the animals juxtaposed to the men: in his famous apostrophe to the mule, saviour of the South in Reconstruction days; to the old hound that accompanies old Bayard; and to the marvellous stallion, lyrically described, with which young Bayard nearly fulfills his death urge.

The fierce individualism of young Bayard, of his kinsmen and the MacCallums—seen in their untrammeled ways and insistence on freedom—is heightened in Bayard until his character assumes Byronic proportions. Even after his marriage, when he lies at night in the arms of his loving wife, it is only "the temporary abeyance of his despair and the isolation of that doom he could not escape" (p. 289). All the men in his line have shown courage, some have shown fatal foolhardiness, but Bayard combines these qualities with a sense of guilt none of his forebears feels, even though his great-grandfather acknowledges that he has killed too many men. There are counterparts, even parodies, in other characters. Old Simon has a taste for the theatrical, and his son Caspey's tales of his war service are inflated parodies of the fatal heroics attempted by Johnny Sartoris. And as Horace Benbow's love for Narcissa is played off against Bayard's fierce courtship of her, so Horace embodies that sometime attribute of the Byronic hero: incestuous longings, which the changes from *Flags in the Dust* to *Sartoris* tended to lessen rather than increase.

Some of the obvious romantic elements in the novel do not require treatment here: the glass vases that Horace blows and names after his sister; the letter in which he calls her "thou still unravished bride of quietness" (p. 352); the perception of twilight, ever Faulkner's favorite time, in the repeated epithet, "foster dam of quietude and peace" (pp. 254, 380). Played off against the Keatsian urn imagery is another kind. Johnny's first wife, Caroline, is recalled as "a girl with a bronze swirling of hair and a small supple body in a constant epicene unrepose, a dynamic fixation like that of carven sexless figures caught in moments of action, striving, a mechanism all of whose members must move in performing the most trivial action." (pp. 55–56). The dangerous stallion is similarly described, as he stands "like a motionless bronze flame" (p. 130), soars "like a bronze explosion" (p. 132), or bursts "like bronze unfolding wings" (p. 133). Other references abound. Aunt Jenny prefers "lively romance to the most impeccable of dun fact" (p. 40), and old Bayard, her nephew, ends his day in bed "beneath the reading lamp with his Dumas" (p. 85), a volume drawn from the shelves in his office which hold "a miscellany of fiction of the historical-romantic school" (p. 34). When Horace writes of the spring, he tells his sister, "I'd be sad that I couldn't be everywhere at once, or that all the spring couldn't be one spring, like Byron's ladies' mouths" (p. 351). The woman he chooses, when Narcissa will not remain with him in their old relationship, is Belle Mitchell, a *belle dame sans merci* for both her former husband and for Horace, a voluptuously seductive femme fatale whose heavy perfume prompts Narcissa to exclaim "Oh, Horry, she's dirty!" and her brother to agree, "I know" (p. 199).

Though the probing into human motive and action which distinguishes the later novels is here, little of it is employed upon characters who suggest the grotesque. There is just one, ironically named Byron Snopes, whose love and longing for Narcissa are expressed in loathsome anonymous letters, a parody of the letters Horace writes her. Similarly, Byron's stealth is a parody of Bayard's brutal directness, and Byron's appearance contrasts with the traditional image of the bold lover. (Once when I described a handsome colleague William Faulkner had not met but had seen, he said, "Oh, yes, the young man with the dark Byronic look.") A plump, odious man who sweats profusely and whose arms are covered with reddish hair to the second joints of his fingers, Byron is a peeping tom who expresses his lust in smothered animal whimperings. Unlike his kinsman Mink Snopes, he does not suggest something deadly but rather something foul, something wholly antithetical to love.

The preoccupation with death in this novel is centered mainly in the consciousness and actions of young Bayard, but it runs in the family, as in the oft-quoted passage near the novel's end about the family's disasters and its name: "there is death in the sound of it, and a glamorous fatality, like silver pennons downrushing at sunset, or a dying fall or horns along the road to Roncevaux" (p. 380). It has been argued that this meditation is not that of the author or his third-person narrator persona, but of Aunt Jenny. But the tone and diction of the passage make this unlikely. It seems instead a sentiment, a construction of the name and family—drawn from his own— which absorbed Faulkner, which he contemplated under the ambivalent stasis-kinesis aspect, and of which he might have felt as did the speaker in Wallace Stevens' "Sunday Morning," the speaker who said, "Death is the mother of beauty. . . . "

There are many other elements in Faulkner's writing which suggest his affinities with Romantic attitudes and works. To name just one such possible affinity: Sir Walter Scott. Yet I would not pigeonhole him as a romantic, for he was widely read, greatly creative, and freely eclectic. But he is the man who said the artist "is completely amoral in that he will rob, borrow, beg, or steal from anybody and everybody to get the work done." And he is also the man who said, "the *Ode on a Grecian Urn* is worth any number of old ladies."[25] Admiring some if not all of the Romantics, feeling some if not all of the same impulses they did, why would he not borrow from them, as he expected others to borrow from him?

NOTES

1. William Butler Yeats, "Coole Park and Ballylee, 1931," *The Variorum Edition of the Poems of W. B. Yeats,* ed. Peter Allt and Russell K. Alspach (New York: Macmillan, 1957), pp. 490–92.

2. "The Concept of Romanticism in Literary History," *Comparative Literature,* 1 (1949), 161.

3. "Toward a Theory of Romanticism," *PMLA,* 66 (1951); rpt. in *The Triumph of Romanticism* (Columbia, S.C.: University of South Carolina Press, 1970), p. 14.

4. *A Handbook to Literature* (Indianapolis: The Odyssey Press, 1972), pp. 466–68.

5. *Willaim Faulkner: Early Prose and Poetry,* ed. Carvel Collins (Boston: Little, Brown, 1962), p. 117.

6. Richard P. Adams, "The Apprenticeship of William Faulkner," *Tulane Studies in English,* 12 (1962), 155.

7. "William Faulkner's Romantic Heritage: Beyond America," (Ph.D. diss., University of Massachusetts, 1974), p. 288.

8. Harry Runyan, "Faulkner's Poetry," *Faulkner Studies,* 3 (Summer-Autumn 1954), 23.

9. "An Examination of the Poetry of William Faulkner," *Princeton University Library Quarterly,* 18 (Spring 1957), 134.

10. "Faulkner as Poet," *Southern Literary Journal,* 1 (Dec. 1968), 5, 19.

11. "The 'Romanticism' of *The Sound and the Fury,*" *Mississippi Quarterly,* 16 (Winter 1962–63), 147, 153.

12. "Faulkner's Isaac McCaslin as Romantic Hero *Manqué,*" *South Atlantic Quarterly,* 68 (Summer 1969), 377, 385.

13. "Faulkner's Grecian Urn," *Southern Literary Journal,* 7 (Fall 1974), 22–23.

14. *William Faulkner: The Yoknapatawpha Country* (New Haven; Yale University Press, 1963), p. 28.

15. As quoted in Joseph Blotner, "William Faulkner's Essay on the Composition of *Sartoris,*" *Yale University Library Gazette,* 47 (Jan. 1973), 122–23.

16. As quoted in Joseph Blotner, *Faulkner: A Biography* (New York; Random House, 1974), p. 532.

17. "William Faulkner's Essay," p. 124. In this essay I use *Sartoris* as more accessible to most readers than the recently published *Flags in the Dust,* but my comments are equally applicable, I think, to both.

18. "Toward a Theory of Romanticism," p. 22.

19. "The 'Romanticism' of *The Sound and the Fury,*" pp. 149–50.

20. "Sartoris: The Dauntless Hero in Modern American Fiction," *Proceedings of the Comparative Literature Symposium,* 5 (Lubbock, Texas, 1972), 108.

21. "William Faulkner's Romantic Heritage," pp. 121, 136.

22. "Afterword," *Sartoris* (New York: New American Library, 1964), pp. 304, 309–10, 315.

23. "Faulkner's Grecian Urn," pp. 6, 7, 9.

24. *Sartoris* (New York: Random House, 1956), pp. 203–04. Hereafter cited in the text.

25. *Lion in the Garden,* ed. James B. Meriwether and Michael Millgate (New York: Random House, 1968), p. 239.

JOHN D. MARGOLIS

Joseph Wood Krutch:
A Writer's Passage
Beyond The Modern Temper

By the time the first of his essays on "The Modern Temper" appeared in the February, 1927, *Atlantic Monthly*, Joseph Wood Krutch was already well on the way to establishing his reputation as one of the foremost men of letters of his generation. His widely noticed, psychoanalytic biography of Poe had been published the previous year, and his thoughtful reviews of books and plays were found regularly in some of America's most distinguished periodicals—and in the *Nation*, weekly. But the appreciative interest generated by his *Atlantic* series on contemporary thought seemed fairly to suggest the consolidation of his position, and when those essays were collected and published as a book in 1929 it appeared his success was complete. There was hardly a dissenting note in the lively chorus of critical praise. Granville Hicks predicted that Krutch's book was "likely to become one of the crucial documents of his generation," and Van Wyck Brooks described it as "one of the most comprehensive statements of the modern point of view that has appeared in recent years." *The Modern Temper*, he said, "will add greatly to Mr. Krutch's reputation as a thinker and as a writer."[1]

Initially, there was no reason to doubt such predictions. For those who found in Krutch's portrait of the temper of his day an eloquent summary of their own, still inchoate feelings—and even for the many discomfited by his diagnosis—*The Modern Temper* was an unquestionably important book, an eloquently incisive survey of the spiritual geography of the age. Krutch in prose had essayed to do rather what T. S. Eliot had several years earlier done in *The Waste Land*: to describe the frame of mind then defining itself as distinctively modern. A token of his success was Krutch's installation by many young intellectuals of his generation as a new tutelary hero of that Modernism.

However, the timing of his effort was singularly unpropitious. The well-wrought despair of *The Waste Land* had its attractions, must indeed have even seemed somehow quaint, amid the confident prosperity of the early twenties. But the depressing uncertainties of the thirties dawned all too shortly after the publication of

223

Krutch's book; the studied skepticism of his essays—so fashionable when they appeared serially—now offered cold comfort to men and women struggling with concrete problems rather more urgent than the philosophical issues that preoccupied Krutch. Intellectuals who only recently had earnestly discussed Krutch were now discussing Marx and his interpreters with even greater intensity; rendered prematurely obsolete by events, his exposition of Modernism soon became a relic of an earlier age. The book fell out of print until, more than twenty-five years later, it was reprinted as a paperback. Then once again *The Modern Temper* was read and discussed widely, but less perhaps as the articulation of a lively current of popular feeling than as a classic statement of the spirit of a generation now part of history.

Ironically, however, by the time Krutch reemerged in the fifties as an expositor of the modern temper, he had himself passed well beyond that frame of mind. After more than two decades of relative obscurity he was then enjoying a new popular appreciation not only as a vigorous critic of the intellectual legacy of Modernism but also as a sensitive interpreter of nature. His passage from Modernism to a sort of romanticism corresponded to his domestic removal from Greenwich Village to Tucson, Arizona; by the time *The Modern Temper* reappeared he had found for himself a new life, a new philosophy, and a new literary career. The desert which earlier had served him as an image for the spiritual desolation of his generation was now to his new vision a source of beauty, insight, and joy; the Modernist's waste land had become richly fruitful. In two decades of earnest quest he had discovered, and in his writing he now endeavored to depict, the possibility of a passage beyond the modern hopelessness he had once so eloquently described.

I

For the 1956 reprint of *The Modern Temper* Krutch added a preface designed primarily to indicate the intellectual distance he had traveled since the book first appeared. So doing, however, he also offered a concise summary of its argument:

The universe revealed by science, especially the sciences of biology and psychology, is one in which the human spirit cannot find a comfortable home. That spirit breathes freely only in a universe where what philosophers call Value Judgments are of supreme importance. It needs to believe, for instance, that right and wrong are real, that Love is more than a biological function, that the human mind is capable of reason rather than merely of rationalization, and that it has the power to will and to choose instead of being compelled merely to react in the fashion predetermined by its conditioning. Since science has proved that none of these beliefs is more than a delusion, mankind will be compelled either to surrender what we call its humanity by adjusting to the real world or to live some kind of tragic existence in a universe alien to the deepest needs of its nature.[2]

The book had been obviously only a partial analysis of that vast movement we today recognize as Modernism; though Krutch's sense of his age was significantly shaped by the books and plays he was then reviewing, he said little, for example, of literary Modernism. Instead, he sought to suggest the spirit of his generation by selectively examining the origins and consequences of several attitudes and beliefs which then seemed representative.

What above all characterized Modernism, Krutch felt, was man's sense of emotional impoverishment in a world dominated by the debilitating, corrosive reason of science—a world where the cold assertions of the intellect were pitted against the moral demands of feeling and where there was no necessary correspondence between man's spiritual aspirations and the universe revealed by science. Science was the great enemy of the human spirit; in offering the sterile knowledge of nature, it robbed man of the warm human comforts of poetry, mythology, and religion. Living amid the modern temper, Krutch said, man was doomed to be "haunted by ghosts from a dead world," the world of traditional humanistic values, and "not yet at home in [his] own," the natural world revealed by value-blind science (p. 18).

If man were to have a sense of dignity, Krutch believed, it must be founded upon "those qualities, characteristics, and powers which distinguish the human being from the rest of animate nature and which . . . justify us in making a distinction between Man and Nature" (p. 20). But science seemed to suggest that such humanistic values as individualism, skepticism, irony, and the power of dispassionate analysis were squarely opposed to "those natural impulses which have made the human animal possible" (p. 29). Though mankind might fancy that the artist and philosopher are among its greatest achievements, to nature's eyes they are parasitic, "not, in the most fundamental or necessary sense, useful or productive" (p. 28). Man's spiritual discomfort was partly caused by science's insistence that his vaunted humanism had no place in nature's scheme; those very qualities that defined man's humanity seemed also to imperil his survivor. Though helpless to refute the contention that the humanist's art and philosophy were biologically inexpedient, Krutch was equally unable to surrender himself wholly

to the science which occasioned such doubts or to the standard of
"nature" by which that science judged. Nature and science both
seemed void of any positive human significance. "Science," he
said, "has always promised two things not necessarily related—an
increase first in our powers, second in our happiness or wisdom,
and we have come to realize that it is the first and less important of
the two promises which it has kept most abundantly" (p. 43). "In
the laboratory," he insisted, "there can be found no trace of the
soul . . . , no sign of the will . . . , and no evidence of the existence
of any such thing as morality except customs" (p. 46). The vigor of
the human spirit depended upon just such beliefs as science was
helpless to nurture and seemed destined to destroy. To partake of
the modern temper, then, was to be torn between, on the one hand,
such stubborn emotional convictions as that "the belief in God,
however ill founded, has been more important in the life of man
than the germ theory of decay, however true the latter may be" (p.
49) and, on the other hand, the intellectual appreciation that "the
universe with which science deals is the real universe" (p. 50).

It was not a situation Krutch could accept with equanimity; the
man for whom such cherished values as love and tragedy had lost
much of their traditional meaning was, he felt, a much diminished
creature. Love, he said, had once been "not merely one of the
things which make life worth while, but *the* thing which justifies
or makes it meaningful" (p. 63). Now, however, "illuminated" by
the rude investigations of the social as well as biological sciences,
love was "stripped of the mystical penumbra in whose shadow its
transcendental value seemed real, though hid" (p. 73). "If love has
come to be less often a sin," he said, "it has come also to be less
often a supreme privilege" (p. 67). With the demystification of
love, "a color has faded from our palette, a whole range of effects
dropped out of our symphony" (p. 77). As with love, so too with
tragedy. Tragedy, Krutch recalled, had flourished among people
"fully aware of the calamities of life [but] nevertheless serenely
confident in the greatness of man, whose mighty passions and
supreme fortitude are revealed when one of those calamities over-
takes him" (p. 84). In its grim positivism, however, modern society was incapable of the vigorous faith of a Sophocles or a Shakespeare. "Distrusting its thought, despising its passions, realizing
its impotent unimportance in the universe, it can tell itself no
stories except those which make it still more acutely aware of its
trivial miseries," he said (p. 88). The tragic spirit was now merely
the tragic fallacy. "The death of tragedy is, like the death of love,
one of those emotional fatalities as the result of which the human

as distinguished from the natural world grows more and more a desert" (p. 97).

It was hardly remarkable that, only a few years after Eliot redefined the term "waste land," Krutch should have thus portrayed the contemporary spiritual landscape. But the metaphor is not without irony in light of Krutch's later discovery that the desert of the Southwest could provide a refuge from precisely that spiritual drought he was describing. In *The Modern Temper*, however, nature seemed only to deepen man's sense of alienation from his universe. "To those who study her," he said, "Nature reveals herself as extraordinarily fertile and ingenious in devising *means*, but she has no *ends* which the human mind has been able to discover or comprehend" (p. 27). Understood in the modern, scientific fashion, "Nature's purpose, if purpose she can be said to have, is no purpose of [man's] and is not understandable in his terms" (p. 6).

To contemplate nature was for Krutch then to exacerbate rather than resolve the dilemma of the modern temper. Nor, any more than nature, did aestheticism, metaphysics, or communism seem to offer any satisfactory solution; the situation, he argued at length, was insoluble. Art furnishes "a means by which life may be contemplated," he said, "but not a means by which it may be lived" (p. 124). The artist's imaginative control over his created universe has no counterpart in the real world where man lives contingently on terms set largely by others than himself. Metaphysics was equally unpromising in its insistence that "certain 'human' truths may exist quite independent of the scientific truths which cannot contradict them because the two occupy completely separate realms" (p. 138). Permitting no external test of the adequacy of its theories, metaphysical religion, Krutch said, sought to "re-establish a liberty to believe whatever one happens to want to believe" (p. 143). But the conscientious modern, mindful of the findings of post-Renaissance science, could not help believing that "metaphysics may be, after all, only the art of being sure of something that is not so and logic only the art of going wrong with confidence" (p. 154). Of communism Krutch could write with the authority of a recent visitor to the Soviet Union. He had been impressed to find there a people philosophically untroubled, free from the decadent speculations of Western intellectuals like himself, absorbed wholly and gladly in the "processes of life for their own sake" (p. 161), and possessed of "a fundamental optimism unknown anywhere else in the world" (p. 166). Innocent of "any problem more subtle than those involved in the production and distribution of wealth," the Russian could energetically devote himself to the immediate practicalities of life with complete faith in their ultimate importance. But, like aestheticism and metaphysics, the primitivism of the Russian offered no adequate guide to conduct for the thoughtful Western man. "Skepticism has entered too deeply into our souls ever to be replaced by faith," Krutch said (p. 167). The conscientious modern seemed doomed to live in a world "in which an unresolvable discord is the fundamental fact. . . . For us wisdom must consist not in searching for a means of escape which does not exist but in making such peace with it as we may" (pp. 167–68). "Ours is a lost cause," he concluded not a little melodramatically, "and there is no place for us in the natural universe" (p. 169).

Intellectually appraised, *The Modern Temper* is hardly unexceptionable; but it remains a historically valuable and rhetorically compelling summary of many of the beliefs of Krutch's contemporaries. In his agony over the crisis of human values in the face of science, his studied philosophical pessimism, his indifference to nature, his feeling of historical impasse, and his conviction that man's reason is in hopeless conflict with his vital powers—in all this he was characteristically modern. Not least of all was he so in his defeatism and his almost gleeful acceptance of the insolubility of his situation. In placing Krutch's performance in the modern intellectual tradition, Irving Howe's remarks are helpful:

A modernist culture is committed to the view that the human lot is inescapably problematic. . . . In a modernist culture the problematic as a style of existence and inquiry becomes imperious: men learn to find comfort in their wounds. . . . Sincerity becomes the last-ditch defense for men without belief. . . . But a special kind of sincerity: where for the romantics it was often taken to be a rapid motion into truth, breaking past the cumbersomeness of intellect, now for the modernists it becomes a virtue in itself, regardless of whether it can lead to truth or whether truth can be found.[3]

Beyond the insistent Modernism of the book, however, it was clear that Krutch was not wholly free from the transcendental cravings of the romantic. "Intellectually," he remarked at one point, "we may find romantic people and romantic literature only ridiculous" (p. 77). But the qualifying adverb is telling. Emotionally, Romantic values and attitudes attracted him. Like the earlier Romantics in their rebellion against the rationalism of the Enlightenment, he was restless with a modern scientific rationalism that had estranged men like himself from effective belief in any spiritual universe which admitted of value as well as fact. Unable passively to accept the spiritual dispossession he described in *The Modern*

Temper, Krutch yearned to be able to see man in the context of some divine or transcendental continuum and as part of—rather than apart from—nature. Behind the book's tone of urgency lay his nostalgia for a world apparently lost. To move beyond the despair he described he would need to discover a means of reuniting man and a universe of value that modern positivism had separated and to discover a way of revivifying the natural world that science seemed to have robbed of its concreteness, its vitality, and above all its human significance. If only by implication, the essays pointed the way beyond the spiritual paralysis of Modernism.

II

To be sure, *The Modern Temper* had been written less for therapy than for reputation; exploiting some of the fashionable ideas of the day, Krutch had presented himself as the sympathetic expositor of a frame of mind with which he was, in fact, distinctly uncomfortable. But the fideism of the thirties then beginning would prove even less congenial to Krutch than had been the skepticism of the twenties just concluded. Hoping to capitalize on the attention he had gained with his "Modern Temper" essays, he presently published two further books—one a critical appreciation of five masters of the novel, the other a study in aesthetics.[4] However neither was much noticed, for Krutch was not addressing the political and economic preoccupations of the time. To continue writing in the thirties meant almost inevitably to direct one's attention thus; and when Krutch did so, reluctantly, it was to pursue a lonely critique of the enthusiasm for communism then sweeping the intellectual world. As drama editor of the *Nation* he could hardly avoid reviewing— and thus publicly assessing—products of the new, "revolutionary" American theater with which he was fundamentally out of sympathy. To the dismay of leftists who recognized the popular respect he enjoyed, Krutch continued to judge plays for their dramatic rather than ideological merit; the fashionable assumption that "art is a weapon" was for Krutch no excuse for artlessness. Even at the *Nation* itself, where he now directed the entire "Books and Arts" section and was a member of the controlling board of editors, he found himself part of a dissenting minority, intellectually and personally estranged from friends and colleagues with whom he had long worked closely but whose progress leftward was rather more pronounced than was his. Though Edmund Wilson accused him of "politicophobia" and the *New Masses* of still worse, Krutch devoted much of his literary energy during the thirties to essays criticizing the communist movement from his own insistently liberal perspective. Rather than on "The Modern Temper," Krutch was now writing groups of essays on such topics as "How Dead is Liberalism?" and "Was Europe a Success?"

Though written with a grace uncommon in such polemics, Krutch's political essays became fully as predictable as those of his opponents; judged by his literary achievement, the thirties was a barren decade. But in ways less immediately obvious it proved richly instructive. Curiously, perhaps, he mellowed amid the strident controversy as he recognized that many of the intellectual qualities he was criticizing in the leftists of the thirties had antecedents among the Modernist thinkers of the twenties. The new age of faith was in some respects merely the converse of the previous age of studied doubt. The doubters and believers were alike, he felt, in their mode of thinking: both tended to argue backwards from dogmatic conclusions to convenient premises. As they doggedly pursued their analyses, the advanced thinkers of both decades seemed to Krutch to have lost perspective; to have satisfied themselves with sophistry rather than reason; to have glibly disregarded history, tradition, and above all the evidence of experience; and to have succumbed in short to the vice of intellectual arrogance. The Marxist assumption about the perfectibility of man now seemed to Krutch no more tenable than the Modernist assumption that the absence of any *single* value in life implied the loss of *all* value; both, he felt, were based on a speciously narrow "pure" reason detached from the wisdom of common sense.

By the end of the thirties Krutch had resigned all but his drama editorship on the *Nation*, and, discouraged by the prospects of supporting himself solely by his pen, he had accepted a professorship at Columbia University. Partly to justify his new academic eminence, he turned in the early forties to preparing a biography of Samuel Johnson. But his choice of subject was hardly fortuitous. Like Johnson, Krutch had resisted contemporary revolutionary enthusiasms in his belief that "the cure for the greatest part of human miseries is not radical, but palliative." Like Johnson, Krutch had felt that "human life is everywhere a state in which much is to be endured, and little to be enjoyed."[5] But, what was more, Johnson—as Krutch wrote in the first sentence of his biography—"was a pessimist with an enormous zest for living." His ability to combine the latter with the former made Johnson, for Krutch, a useful guide beyond the despair of the modern temper. The common sense with which Johnson was so richly endowed suggested to Krutch a bracing alternative to the narrowly rationalistic monomanias of both Modernism and Marxism. Common sense, Krutch said, was "the acceptance of certain current assumptions, traditions, and standards of value which are never called into question because so to question any of them might be to necessitate a revision of government, society, and public conduct more thoroughgoing than anyone liked to contemplate."[6] In fact it had been something very much like such common sense which had stood between Krutch and any wholesale commitment to the intellectual fashions of both the twenties and thirties. Johnson confirmed Krutch's growing belief that common sense might be not only a check upon such excesses of doubt or faith but also a value in itself; that it might be at least as helpful a guide to philosophy and life as the denials of the Modernists or the arcane speculations of Marxist theoreticians; and that the evidence of feeling could be in its way no less compelling than that of reason. The great Neoclassicist of the eighteenth century helped Krutch take an important step beyond the dreary defeatism of the twentieth.

But in fact it was toward a kind of romanticism that he was moving, and the next major project to which Krutch turned—a biography of Henry David Thoreau published in 1948—advanced him still further in that direction. He had first read *Walden* shortly after the publication of *The Modern Temper* while returning by train from a cross-country lecture tour. In those early days of the Depression, Thoreau's social critique had an obvious relevance. But Krutch was moved even more by Thoreau's demonstration in his book that "there can be no very black melancholy to him who lives in the midst of Nature and has his senses still."[7] Reading the testament of Thoreau's spiritual healing, Krutch found it an instrument of his own.

Even as he had been composing his essays on the modern temper Krutch had begun regularly to pass weekends and summers in rural Connecticut and was surprised to begin experiencing there a wholly new appreciation of the natural world he was even then describing as alien and humanly meaningless. During the thirties and forties, as the attractions of New York became fewer for him, Krutch spent more and more time in the country and eventually made his primary home there, commuting to a Manhattan *pied à terre* a few days each week for his teaching and professional theatergoing. As nothing else had before, not even the theater, the natural world captured his interest, and he enthusiastically became a self-appointed inspector not only of the snow storms but also of the plants and animals of New England. Armed on his walks with field guides and informed by his growing collection of books about nature, Krutch discovered that science, at least of a certain type, was not necessarily so spiritually destructive as he had recently suggested. What was more, he began to feel that man's significance might lie within, rather than apart from, nature—that those human attributes which had rendered man so proud of his uniqueness might after all be less important than the many attributes he shared with a world of plants and animals he had not made.

Preparing his biography of Thoreau, Krutch had an opportunity to pursue such reflections on man and nature. Even before reading *Walden*, he had cited in *The Modern Temper* Thoreau's famous remark that "the mass of men lead lives of quiet desperation." However it was now not the social critic nor the metaphysician nor the "reluctant crusader" who most interested Krutch; rather it was the Thoreau who had discovered the human significance of nature through concrete experience and had preserved that discovery in his prose. Uneasy with Emerson's philosophy much as Krutch would be later with the abstractions of Modernism, Thoreau, Krutch wrote, moved "away from the transcendental assumption that the meaning of nature can be reached by intuition and toward what is the fundamentally scientific assumption—namely, that only through observation may one ultimately reach not merely dead facts but also those which understanding can make live."[8] For a modern like Krutch, Thoreau's experience was heartening evidence that science might contribute to rather than undermine man's appreciation of the human significance of the natural universe.

For Thoreau, however, *observation* was not like the work of the scientist whose activity was limited to collecting, dissecting, and classifying. On the contrary, Thoreau's primary purpose in his observation of nature "was what he himself would have been inclined to call, rather vaguely, 'poetic,'" Krutch said, "and it aimed at familiarity with, rather than knowledge about, living things" (p. 145). "What Thoreau had always sought in his intercourse with living things and even with the very hills and fields themselves was that warm and sympathetic sense of oneness, that escape from the self into the All, to which psychologists have given the chilly name 'empathy'" (p. 172). Thoreau's writings demonstrated that nature could be learned *from* as well as *about* and that the natural world could satisfy the emotions just as science had shown it could challenge the mind. Through nature, in fact, one could achieve something far more positive than the mere dissipation of the black melancholy; one could find gaiety, joy, and delight. "Joy," Krutch remarked tersely, "is a symptom by means of which right conduct may be recognized" (p. 85), and Thoreau's life was clearly abundant in both. "None of [Thoreau's] characteristics is more nearly unique," Krutch observed, "than his conviction that he, almost alone among men, had discovered how to live profitably and happily in nature."⁹ The conviction proved contagious.

But the example of Thoreau's writing was no less important to Krutch than that of his life. As he prepared his book, he considered the nature of Thoreau's literary achievement, and in so doing he began to sense that his own new interests might be related to his literary career. Shortly after completing the galley proofs for *Thoreau*, while reading a nature essay that pleased him greatly, Krutch first wondered if he might be able to do something of the sort. Within a few days he had written "The Day of the Peepers," an essay about the tiny tree toad *Hyla crucifer* whose spring song is one of the earth's oldest. Thoreau's having also written about the peeper in his *Journal* (21 March 1853) may have been mere coincidence, but his influence was clear in Krutch's discussing not so much the peeper itself as its significance to him. "*Hyla crucifer* is what the biologists call him," Krutch began, "but to most of us he is simply the Spring Peeper."¹⁰ At the outset Krutch was announcing that he would speak in the first person and from a perspective distinct from the mere scientist's. It was curious, he said, that the beginning of spring should conventionally be marked by Easter rather than by the peeper's proclamation that "life is resurgent," "the earth is alive again" (pp. 4, 7). Man's preference for Easter Day—a date determined by calculations understood by only a handful of theologians—rather than the Day of the Peepers was for Krutch another example of man's longstanding and unfortunate "tendency to prefer abstractions to phenomena" (p. 7). As man has developed, he said, "more and more he thinks in terms of abstractions, generalizations, and laws; less and less participates in the experience of living in a world of sights, and sounds, and natural urges" (p. 11). A consequence had been the anxiety of Modernism; an alternative, he now felt, was to renew one's sense of active membership in the natural world. No sentimentalist, Krutch recognized that the peeper, like all reptiles and amphibians, "has an aspect which is inscrutable and antediluvian. His thoughts, like his joy, must be inconceivably different from ours. But," Krutch insisted, "the fact is comforting rather than the reverse."

If we are nevertheless somehow united with him in that vast category of living things which is so sharply cut off from everything that does not live at all, then we realize how broad the base of the category is, how much besides ourself is, as it were, on our side. Over against the atoms and the stars are set both men and frogs.   (P. 10)

He concluded this first nature essay in what would soon be his characteristic tone in that genre, both personal and hortatory:

Surely one day a year might be set aside on which to celebrate our ancient loyalties and to remember our ancient origins. And I know of none more suitable for that purpose than the Day of the Peepers. "Spring is come!", I say when I hear them, and: "The most ancient of Christs has risen!" But I also add something which, for me at least, is even more important. "Don't forget," I whisper to the peepers; "we are all in this together."   (P. 13)

As he recalled some years later, the final sentence was particularly significant: "It stated for the first time a conviction and an attitude which had come to mean more to me than I realized and, indeed, summed up a kind of pantheism which was gradually coming to be an essential part of the faith—if you can call it that—which would form the basis of an escape from the pessimism of *The Modern Temper* upon which I had turned my back without ever having conquered it."[11]

Not only did "The Day of the Peepers" announce Krutch's new attitude toward nature; it also marked the beginning of a new—and for many of his readers the most important—phase of his literary career. Straight away he began a second essay, this one on the *Meloe*, a blister beetle whose life history seemed well to illustrate the contingency of existence in the natural universe. And in short order he had written twelve essays, each associated with events during one of the months of the New England year, which when collected in 1949 constituted his first nature book: *The Twelve Seasons: A Perpetual Calendar for the Country.*

In the forties, however, nature writing was a luxury Krutch could indulge only in hours not claimed by his teaching or reviewing. Happily, in 1950–51, he had a year's sabbatical from teaching; and he chose to spend it in the Southwest. Before the war he had motored extensively there, and he was eager now to enjoy not only the scenic beauties of the area but also a climate he hoped to find more healthful than that of New England. Not least, he hoped to determine whether he could find in the desert the same literary inspiration he had found so abundant in rural Connecticut. Not unlike Thoreau's to Walden Pond, Krutch's removal to Tucson was an experiment both human and literary; and he delighted to discover there not only that his health was markedly improved but also that, properly observed, the desert offered many subjects for a writer like himself. When he returned East in the fall of 1951 he brought with him the manuscript of a second nature book, *The Desert Year*, as well as the determination soon to return permanently to Tucson. There he would live in and write about a world largely unnoticed by previous nature writers—a world which, though a desert, was to one of his new vision hardly a waste land. By the following summer he had resigned his professorship, terminated his thirty-year connection with the *Nation* and the Broadway theater, and sold the farmhouse around which he had learned so much and also most of his library—keeping primarily books about the eighteenth century and, of course, nature.

III

The two projects to which Krutch first turned upon moving to Tucson were not, in fact, about nature; both, however, were important exercises in intellectual ground-clearing and in repudiating the Modernism with which many still identified him. The first was a series of lectures to be delivered at Cornell and later published as *"Modernism" in Modern Drama*. Reassessing the work of the major dramatists since Ibsen, he showed how far his sympathies now lay from the theater of which he had once been a leading, and generally sympathetic, interpreter. Announcing that he wrote "as a moralist, not as a critic," Krutch sought "to persuade [his] readers that much of what others have presented to them as the convictions necessary to anyone who wished to believe himself 'modern' is actually incompatible with any good life as the good life has been generally conceived of during many centuries before the nineteenth."[12] The "subtle disease" (p. 5) of Modernism, he said, lay behind the work of most of the period's leading playwrights; and the pathology of that disease could be seen conveniently summarized in the tenets of Darwinism, Marxism, and Freudianism. "All three are, or at least were popularly taken to be, hypotheses which tended to take man's fate out of his own hands, to assure him that he could not do the supremely important things for himself, and then to tell him also, by way of compensation, that he therefore could not be blamed for anything which happened to him" (p. 85). Behind post-Renaissance civilization, he said, lay the assumption that man is a creature capable of dignity; that life in *this* world—not some future world—is worth living; and that it is by a richly humane reason that man may most fruitfully live. "The modern drama," Krutch said sternly, "is . . . open to the same charge that may be made against modern literature as a whole. Its tendency has been to undermine the foundations of post-Renaissance civilization" (pp. 130–31). It has contributed, he said, to the creation of "an impossible mental environment" (p. 90). In many ways, of course, his demonstration of this thesis in his lectures on modern drama resembled his argument earlier in *The Modern Temper*. But where then he had felt helpless to venture beyond description of Modernism, he now wrote as an almost petulant critic.

The book to which he next turned was in fact explicitly conceived as a reconsideration, twenty-five years later, of the issues explored in *The Modern Temper*. His analysis of the causes and character of that temper was largely unchanged. The distinctly modern anxiety, he said, could be traced largely to "the contradictions inevitably incident to a life lived in two irreconcilable worlds—the world of intimate experience and that world of abstract convictions in which the validity of intimate experience is categorically denied."[13] As he had remarked in "The Day of the Peepers," the modern tends to neglect the former in his preoccupation with the latter—and especially with the sterile positivism and grimly mechanistic determinism that governed most contemporary thought. Since writing *The Modern Temper*, however, Krutch had himself come to value anew the world of intimate experience, particularly in nature. And building upon that experience he was now able to assert his renewed belief in the reality of some essential human attributes, in "the old-fashioned science of man," for which his earlier skepticism had allowed him at best to be merely nostalgic. In *The Measure of Man*, which was awarded the 1954 National Book Award for nonfiction, he went beyond his earlier critical attacks to argue constructively that belief in "Minimal Man" offered an alternative to the paralyzing anxiety which was the legacy of Modernism; the book was a romantic's brief, calmly and closely argued, against scientism and in support of the reality of consciousness and value. "What," he asked, "are the *minimal* powers and characteristics one would have to possess to be worthy of the designation man?" (p. 97).

Grant us only [he answered almost prayerfully] that what we call "reasoning" is not always rationalization; that consciousness can sometimes be more than merely an epiphenomenon accompanying behavior; that "value judgments," even if never more than "tastes" or "preferences," are nevertheless not absolutely and "nothing but" what we have been conditioned to accept—grant us this and those minimal concessions will free us from the dilemma in which the refusal to make them has placed us. They are levers with which, once more, we can move our world.   (P. 99)

Convinced that reasoning might include common sense, and reassured that, mechanistic theories notwithstanding, his consciousness "is the one thing that incontrovertibly *is*" (p. 165), man could be free again to make value judgments and to resume "that Moral Discourse which has gone on in Western civilization uninterruptedly for at least three thousand years" (p. 224). Much of Krutch's writing after moving to Tucson was devoted to that Discourse, to the examination of "eternal problems in their contemporary forms."[14] Condemning the debilitating Modernist assumptions in current thought and questioning the premises of many contemporary social enterprises, Krutch became an intellectual muckraker, and scores of his essays received broad circulation in such publications as the *Saturday Review*, the *New York Times Magazine*, and the *American Scholar* (where for fifteen years he wrote a column each issue, appropriately entitled "If You Don't Mind My Saying So"). Even if final Truth seemed no more accessible than it had twenty-five years before, he could at least accept many truths about man and nature which rendered life somewhat less a spiritual desert than once it had seemed.

Behind that recovery of faith, of course, lay several decades of eager observation of the world not made by man; seen with his empathy and curiosity, nature was everywhere a source of knowledge and inspiration. Having moved to Arizona, he wrote now of saguaros and roadrunners rather than "frost flowers" and squirrels, and his growing interest in science was more conspicuous in his desert essays than it had been in those about New England. But as in his earliest nature writing, he exploited the informality of the familiar essay and wrote as an unabashed amateur, a lover, who delighted in narrating his experiences in nature, in exhibiting his understanding of its ways, and in sharing the insight he earned in its presence. If such writing was only the latest of Krutch's varied enterprises as a man of letters, it was also the most deeply felt, the closest approximation for a professional writer to a labor of love. By his death in 1970 he had published seven books and dozens more uncollected essays on nature; together they were his celebration of nature as "the great reservoir of energy, of confidence, of endless hope, and of that joy not wholly subdued by the pale cast of thought."[15]

However pale such thought as that of the modern temper could become, his stubborn rationality never allowed Krutch to reject outright the value of thinking. The ecstatics of much Romantic nature poetry —what he disapprovingly called "that cult of the sublime"—was not his. Nature offered more than an opportunity for emotional indulgence; it was, he said, "not merely a soothing presence" but also "a challenge to thought."[16] "If nature is to be learned from, she must be known, and to be known she must be looked

at"—and that, in all of her particularity.[17] For Krutch one of nature's especial attractions was precisely its concreteness, its offering
a refuge from the abstractions of Modernism, Marxism, Freudianism, and other ideologies that had rendered a certain kind of thinking so sterile. Experience of the actual rather than contemplation of
the theoretical, he now believed, offered the best hope of satisfying
those spiritual cravings that had survived even the skepticism of
the modern temper. "The human mind," he said, "can appreciate
the One only by seeing it first as the Many." And science, earlier to
Krutch's mind so spiritually destructive, now seemed the surest
avenue to that appreciation. He often criticized scientists who
"spend too much time in laboratories . . . and too little observing
creatures who are not specimens but free citizens of their own
world."[18] But he depended increasingly upon the learned books
and articles which they produced and which enabled him to relish
nature with intelligence as well as feeling. "It is not ignorance but
knowledge which is the mother of wonder," he insisted.[19] As the
one grew for him, so did the other.

Nevertheless, he rarely sentimentalized the world he now so
loved. To imagine nature simply as a kind mother was to him no
more reasonable than to see it as red in tooth and claw. "She is
both, or neither, or something that includes and transcends the
two," he said.[20] The simplistically partial view of nature in *The
Modern Temper* was far behind him; but his acceptance of the necessity of predation and his recognition that winter's lovely blanket of
snow was often stained by the blood of one of nature's sacrifices
were far less lively to him than was the knowledge of the joy which
nature so abundantly manifested. Animals, even plants, seemed to
Krutch richly possessed of that very sense of purpose of which the
modern temper had apparently robbed man. His own observations
and reflections contradicted the grimly mechanistic Darwinian notion that evolution was wholly "the result of blind accident"; to
Krutch nature repeatedly demonstrated that "choice, consciousness,
awareness, and will have sometimes been able to intervene." And
to feel that was to be able to feel further that, "To call man 'an
animal' is to endow him with a heritage so rich that his potentialities seem hardly less than when he was called the son of God."[21]

Desert plants and animals offered especially rich examples of
those potentialities. Even amid severe heat and dryness they "have
shown courage and ingenuity in making the best of the world as
they found it," Krutch said. By no violent inference they also suggested how man might cope even in the uncongenial climate of
Modernism. "In the desert . . . the very fauna and flora proclaim

that one can have a great deal of certain things while having very little of others; that one kind of scarcity is compatible with, perhaps even a necessary condition of, another kind of plenty." If the spiritual certainties of an earlier era were irretrievable, there was still the possibility of profiting from the example of the desert which teaches, among so much else, "the great art of how-to-do-without"—indeed, how to thrive.[22] Even amid such austerity, desert life suggested a gladness which seemed to Krutch characteristic of nearly every body. "Joy," he said, "is the one thing of which indisputably the healthy animal, and even the healthy plant, gives us an example."[23] When all other values seemed doubtful, the very fact of life—and its concomitant, joy—became the foundation of a new kind of faith hardly less rich than that which had vanished. "Everything that lives is incommensurate with everything that does not," he affirmed. "It has characteristics no nonliving thing even hints at, and in that sense life is an absolute."[24]

To appreciate the significance of being a coinhabitant of Earth with so many other living bodies was considerably to mitigate the loss of those cherished values and ideas which man had once proudly thought were uniquely his. To see oneself as part of the life of nature rather than apart from it was to gain a sense of belonging to something greater—and more fundamental—than even the precious humanist tradition: "From Nature we learn what we are a part of and how we may participate in the whole; we gain a perspective on ourselves which serves, not to set us aside from, but to put us in relation with, a complex scheme."[25] The effect, though perhaps humbling, was hardly humiliating. Early on, in his first nature essay, Krutch had whispered to the peeper, "We are all in this together" and had thus uttered the initial words of his romantic credo. For more than two decades he elaborated his new convictions to a large and admiring readership. "Man," he said, "needs a context for his life larger than himself; he needs it so desperately that all modern despairs go back to the fact that he has rejected the only context which the loss of his traditional gods has left accessible."[26] Embracing nature as the context for his own life and thought, Krutch successfully transcended that variety of modern despair he himself had once so eloquently articulated. In the process of announcing that acceptance he was instrumental in achieving a new popularity for an old literary form, the nature essay, which itself had been one the casualties of Modernism.

NOTES

1. *Forum*, 82 (1929), x; *Outlook*, 151 (1929), 587–88.

2. *The Modern Temper: A Study and a Confession* (New York: Harcourt, Brace, and World, 1956), p. xi. Hereafter cited in the text.

3. *Literary Modernism* (New York: Fawcett Publications, 1967), pp. 18–19.

4. *Five Masters: A Study in the Mutation of the Novel* (1930); *Experience and Art: Some Aspects of the Esthetics of Literature* (1932).

5. *The Rambler*, no. 32 (7 July 1750); *Rasselas*, chapter 11.

6. *Samuel Johnson* (New York: Harcourt, Brace and Co., 1944), pp. 1, 363.

7. *Walden*, ed. Sherman Paul (Cambridge, Mass.: Houghton Mifflin, 1960), p. 90.

8. *Henry David Thoreau* (New York: William Sloane Associates, 1948), p. 175. Hereafter cited in the text.

9. *Great American Nature Writing*, ed. Joseph Wood Krutch (New York: William Sloane Associates, 1950), p. 75.

10. *The Twelve Seasons* (New York: William Sloane Associates, 1949), p. 3. Hereafter cited in the text.

11. See *More Lives than One* (New York: William Sloane Associates, 1962), pp. 294–95.

12. *"Modernism" in Modern Drama: A Definition and an Estimate* (Ithaca: Cornell University Press, 1953), p. viii. Hereafter cited in the text.

13. *The Measure of Man: On Freedom, Human Values, Survival, and The Modern Temper* (Indianapolis: Bobbs-Merrill, 1954), p. 194. Hereafter cited in the text.

14. *More Lives than One*, p. 367.

15. "Wilderness as More than a Tonic," *If You Don't Mind My Saying So: Essays On Man and Nature* (New York: William Sloane Associates, 1964), p. 369.

16. *Twelve Seasons*, p. 178.

17. *The Best of Two Worlds* (New York: William Sloane Associates, 1953), p. 121.

18. *The Desert Year* (New York: William Sloane Associates, 1952), pp. 268, 106.

19. *The Voice of the Desert: A Naturalist's Interpretation* (New York: William Sloane Associates, 1955), p. 149.

20. *Twelve Seasons*, p. 44.

21. *The Great Chain of Life* (Boston: Houghton Mifflin, 1956), pp. 201, 153–54.

22. *Desert Year*, pp. 28–29, 181–82, 56.

23. *Best of Two Worlds*, p. 16.

24. *Great Chain of Life*, p. 39.

25. *Twelve Seasons*, p. 125.

26. "Wilderness as More than a Tonic," p. 372.

Biographical Notes

Index

Biographical Notes

JOSEPH BLOTNER (University of Michigan) is the author of several books on American literature, including *Faulkner: A Biography*.

GEORGE BORNSTEIN (University of Michigan) is the author of several books on nineteenth- and twentieth-century literature and periodicals, including *Yeats and Shelley*.

WALTER H. EVERT (University of Pittsburgh) is the author of *Aesthetic and Myth in the Poetry of Keats*.

MICHAEL GOLDMAN (Princeton University) is the author of *The Actor's Freedom: Toward a Theory of Drama* and other works on theater.

RICHARD HAVEN (University of Massachusetts) is the author of *Patterns of Consciousness: An Essay on Coleridge*.

JAMES A. W. HEFFERNAN (Dartmouth College) is the author of *Wordworth's Theory of Poetry: The Transforming Imagination*.

E. D. H. JOHNSON (Princeton University) is the author and editor of several books on Victorian literature, including *The Alien Vision of Victorian Poetry*.

A. WALTON LITZ (Princeton University) is the author and editor of several books on nineteenth- and twentieth-century literature, including *Introspective Voyager: The Poetic Development of Wallace Stevens*.

JOHN D. MARGOLIS (Northwestern University) is the author of *T. S. Eliot's Intellectual Development: 1922–1939*.

GLENN O'MALLEY (Arizona State University) is the author of *Shelley and Synesthesia*.

HERBERT N. SCHNEIDAU (University of California at Santa Barbara) is the author of a book on Ezra Pound and the forthcoming *Sacred Discontent: The Bible and Western Tradition*.

STUART M. SPERRY (Indiana University) is the author of *Keats the Poet*.

HUGH WITEMEYER (University of New Mexico) is the author of *The Poetry of Ezra Pound: Forms and Renewal, 1908–1920*.

243

Index